ORDNANCE SURVEY MEMOIRS OF IRELAND

Volume One

PARISHES OF COUNTY ARMAGH 1835–8

Published 1990.
The Institute of Irish Studies,
The Queen's University of Belfast,
Belfast.
In association with
The Royal Irish Academy,
Dawson Street,
Dublin.

Grateful acknowledgement is made to the Economic and Social Research Council and the Department of Education for Northern Ireland for their financial assistance at different stages of this publication programme.

ISBN 0 85389 341 1

Printed by W. & G. Baird Ltd, Antrim.

Ordnance Survey Memoirs of Ireland

VOLUME ONE

Parishes of County Armagh
1835-8

Edited by Angélique Day and Patrick McWilliams

The Institute of Irish Studies
in association with
The Royal Irish Academy

CONTENTS

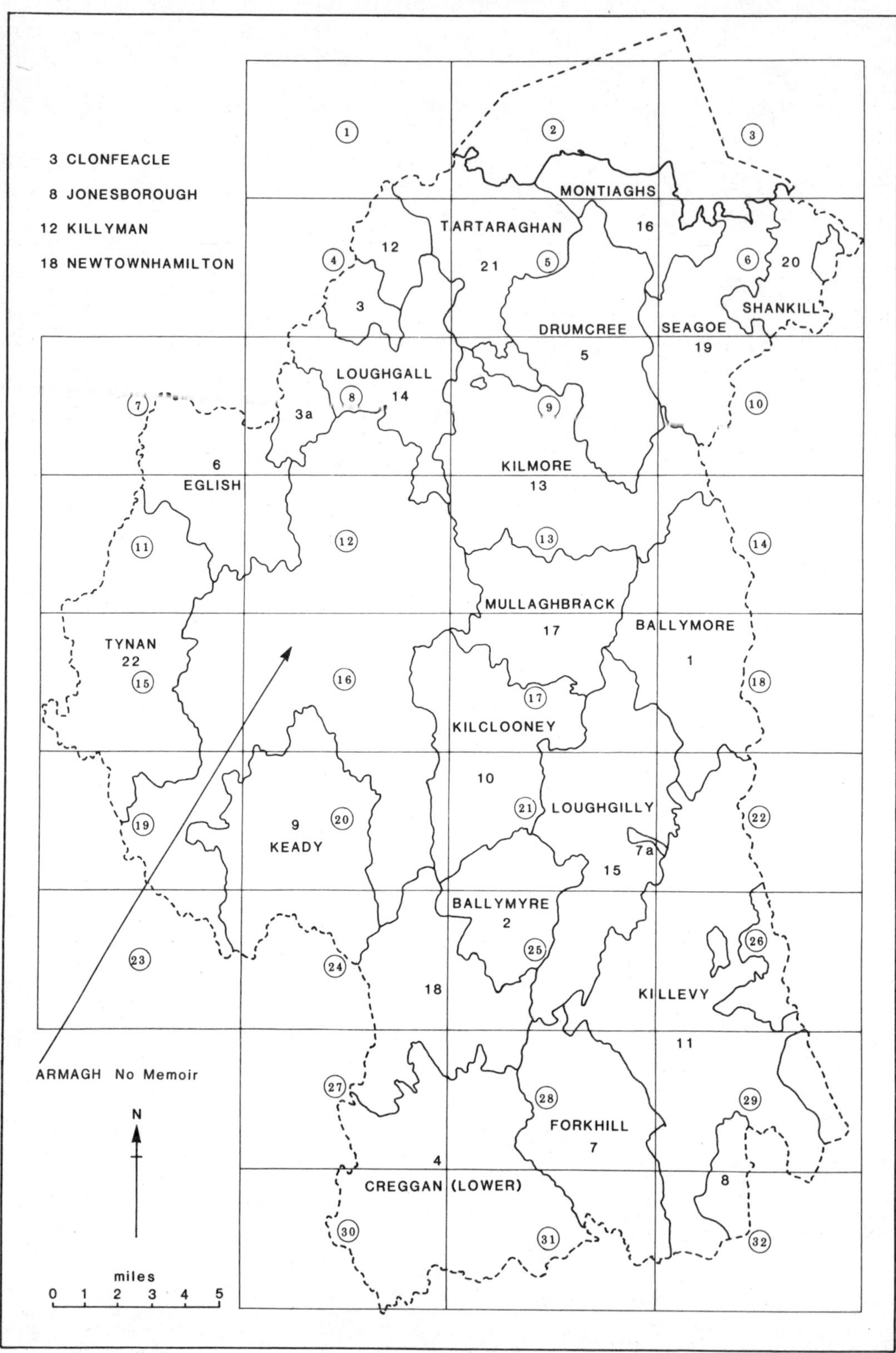
3 CLONFEACLE
8 JONESBOROUGH
12 KILLYMAN
18 NEWTOWNHAMILTON
MONTIAGHS
16
TARTARAGHAN
21
12
3
20
SHANKILL
DRUMCREE
5
SEAGOE
19
LOUGHGALL
14
3a
6
EGLISH
KILMORE
13
MULLAGHBRACK
17
BALLYMORE
1
TYNAN
22
KILCLOONEY
10
LOUGHGILLY
7a
15
9
KEADY
BALLYMYRE
2
18
KILLEVY
11
ARMAGH No Memoir
N
FORKHILL
7
4
CREGGAN (LOWER)
8
miles
0 1 2 3 4 5

ACKNOWLEDGEMENTS

During the course of the transcription and publication project many have advised and encouraged us in this gigantic task. Thanks must first be given to the Royal Irish Academy, and the library staff, particularly the librarian, Mrs Brigid Dolan, for making the original manuscripts available to us.

We should like to acknowledge the following individuals for their special contributions. Dr Brian Trainor led the way with his edition of the Antrim memoir and provided vital help on the steering committee. Dr Ann Hamlin also provided valuable support, especially during the most trying stages of the project. Professor R.H. Buchanan's unfailing encouragement has been instrumental in the development of the project to the present. Without Dr Kieran Devine the initial stages of the transcription and the computerising work would never have been completed successfully: the project owes a great deal to his constant help and advice. Dr Kay Muhr's continuing contribution to the work of the transcription project is deeply appreciated. Mr W.C. Kerr's interest, as well as his own work on the Memoirs, gave inspiration. The essential task of inputting the texts from audio tapes was done by Miss Eileen Kingan, Mrs Christine Robertson, Miss Eilis Smyth, Miss Lynn Murray, and, most importantly, Miss Maureen Carr, whose energy and interest outlasted the others.

We are grateful to the Linen Hall Library for lending us their copies of the first edition 6" Ordnance Survey Maps: also to Ms Maura Pringle of QUB Cartography Department for the index maps showing the parish boundaries. For providing financial assistance at crucial times for the maintenance of the project, we would like to take this opportunity of thanking the trustees of the Esme Mitchell trust and The Public Record Office of Northern Ireland.

Left:
Map of parishes of County Armagh. The square grids represent the 1830s 6" Ordnance Survey maps. The encircled numbers relate to the map numbers as presented in the bound volumes of maps for the county. The parishes have been numbered in all cases and named where possible, but where this has not been possible a key is provided.

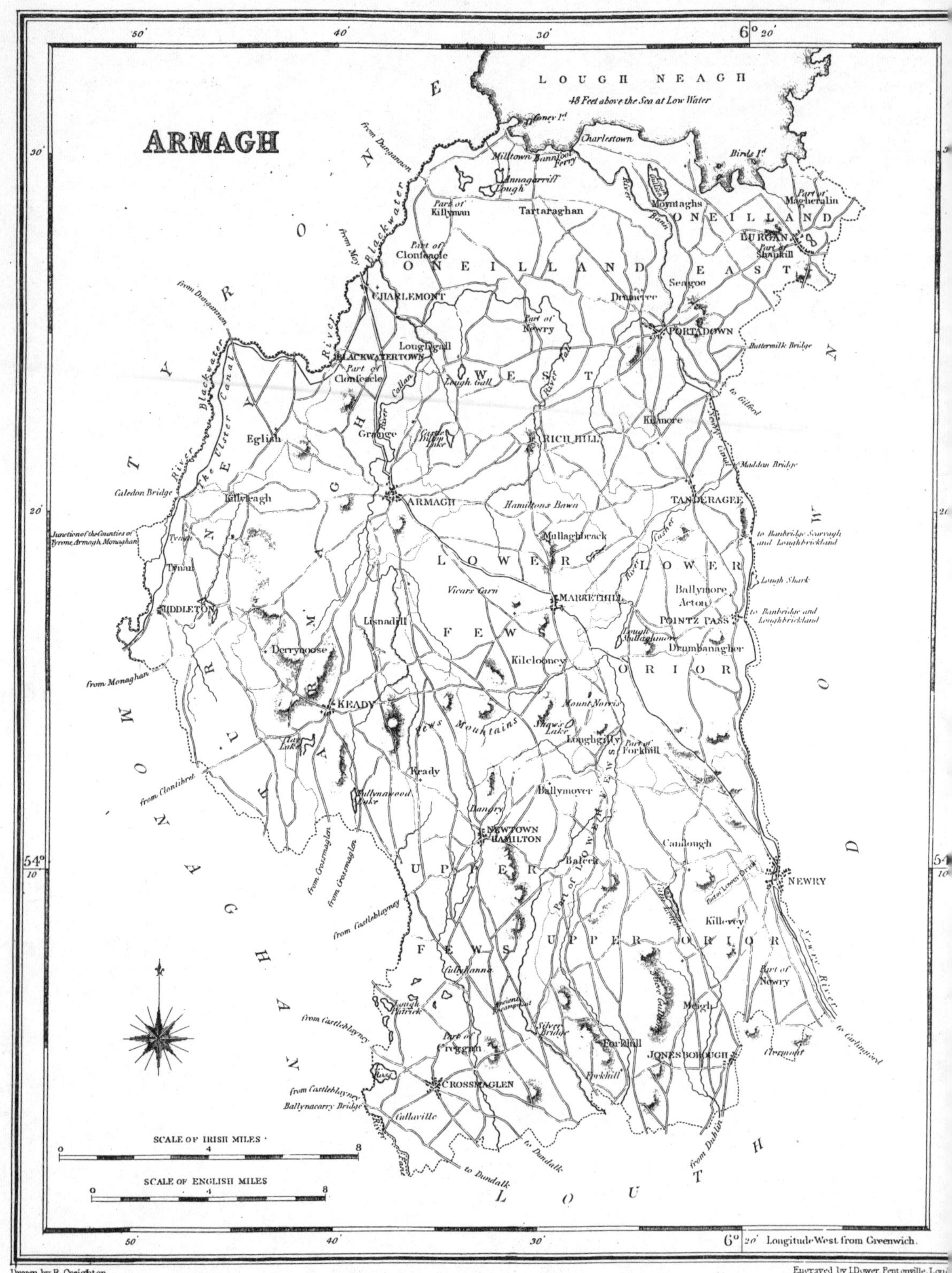

Map of County Armagh, 1837, from Samuel Lewis, *Atlas of the Counties of Ireland*, 1837

INTRODUCTION AND GUIDE TO THE PUBLICATION OF THE ORDNANCE SURVEY MEMOIRS

The following text of the Ordnance Survey Memoirs was first transcribed by a team working in the Institute of Irish Studies at The Queen's University of Belfast, on a computerised index of the material. For this publication programme the text has been further edited. Spellings have been modernised in all cases except for townland and other place-names, although where the original spelling was thought to be of any interest it has been retained and is indicated by angle brackets in the text. Punctuation has been modernised and is the responsibility of the editors. Editorial additions are indicated by square brackets. Original drawings are referred to, and some have been reproduced. Original page references have been omitted from this edition. Because of the huge variation in size of Memoirs for different counties, the following editorial policy has been adopted: where there are numerous duplicating and overlapping accounts, the most complete and finished account, normally the Memoir proper, has been presented, with additional unique information from other accounts like the Fair Sheets entered into a separate section, clearly titled and identified; where the Memoir material is less, nothing has been omitted. To achieve standard volume size, parishes have been associated on the basis of propinquity, although where there is less material, parishes of one county have been included in one volume. There are considerable differences in the volume of information recorded for different areas: counties Antrim and Londonderry are exceptionally well covered, while the other counties do not have the same detail. This series is the first systematic publication of the parish Memoirs, although individual parishes have been published by pioneering local history societies.

Brief history of the Irish Ordnance Survey in the nineteenth century and the writing of the Ordnance Survey Memoirs

In 1824 a House of Commons committee recommended a townland survey of Ireland with maps at the scale of 6", to facilitate a uniform valuation for local taxation. The Duke of Wellington, then prime minister, authorised this, the first Ordnance Survey of Ireland. The survey was directed by Colonel Thomas Colby, who commanded officers of the Royal Engineers and three companies of sappers and miners. In addition to this, civil assistants were recruited to help with sketching, drawing and engraving of maps, and eventually, in the 1830's, the writing of the Memoirs.

The Memoirs were written descriptions intended to accompany the maps, containing information which could not be fitted on to them. Colonel Colby always considered additional information to be necessary to clarify place-names and other distinctive features of each parish; this was to be written up in reports by the officers. Much information about parishes resulted from research into place-names and was used in the writing of the Memoirs. The term "Memoir" comes from the abbreviation of the word "Aide-Memoire". It was also used in the 18th century to describe topographical descriptions accompanying maps.

In 1833 Colby's assistant, Lieutenant Thomas Larcom, developed the scope of the officers' reports by stipulating the headings under which information was to be reported, and including topics of social as well as economic interest. By this time civil assistants were writing some of the Memoirs under the supervision of the officers, as well as collecting information in the Fair Sheets.

The first "Memoirs" are officers' reports covering Antrim in 1830, and work continued on the Antrim parishes right through the decade, with special activity in 1838 and 1839. Counties Down and Tyrone were written up from 1833 to 1837, with both officers and civil assistants working on Memoirs. In Londonderry and

Fermanagh research and writing started in 1834. Armagh was worked on in 1835, 1837 and 1838. Much labour was expended in the Londonderry parishes. The plans to publish the Memoirs commenced with the parish of Templemore, containing the city and liberties of Derry, which came out in 1837 after a great deal of expense and effort.

Between 1839 and 1840 the Memoir scheme collapsed. Peel's government could not countenance the expenditure of money and time on such an exercise; despite a parliamentary commission favouring the continuation of the writing of the Memoirs, the scheme was halted before the southern half of the country was covered. The manuscripts remained unpublished and most were removed to the Royal Irish Academy, Dublin.

The Memoirs are a uniquely detailed source for the history of the northern half of Ireland immediately before the Great Famine. They document the landscape and situation, buildings and antiquities, land-holdings and population, employment and livelihood of the parishes. They act as a nineteenth century Domesday book and are essential to the understanding of the cultural heritage of our communities.

Definition of descriptive terms.

Memoir (sometimes Statistical Memoir). An account of a parish written according to the prescribed form outlined in the instructions known as "Heads of Inquiry", and normally divided into 3 sections: Natural Features and History, Modern Topography and Ancient Topography, Social and Productive Economy.

Fair Sheets: "Information gathered for the Memoirs", an original title describing paragraphs of additional information following no particular order, often with marginal headings, signed and dated by the civil assistant responsible.

Statistical Remarks/Accounts: Both titles are employed by the Engineer officers in their descriptions of the parish with marginal headings, often similar in layout to the Memoir.

Office Copies: These are copies of early drafts, generally officers' accounts and must have been made for office purposes.

Ordnance Survey Memoirs for County Armagh

There is Memoir material for 22 parishes of Armagh: unfortunately, the parish of Armagh containing the historic city and ancient ecclesiastical capital was not written up. It is significant that the writing of Memoirs for this county took place at three periods: in 1835, during the latter part of 1837 and in 1838. This was a time when a great deal of effort was being concentrated on the Londonderry parishes, and in 1838 all the Ancient Topography sections for Antrim were reworked. Perhaps the research involved in the recording of Armagh city was not possible within the time allotted to the Ordnance surveyors. Despite this, there are important detailed analyses of townlands in four of the parishes, and other fascinating descriptions of localities in Armagh. There are no detailed drawings, merely ground plans for churches, which are referred to in the text, but not reproduced. The manuscript material is to be found in Box 18 of the Memoirs owned by the Royal Irish Academy, and section references are given beside each parish name below.

Box 18 Parishes of County Armagh

II	Ballymore	VI	Creggan
III	Ballymyre	VII	Drumcree
IV	Clonfeacle	VIII	Eglish

Box 18 Parishes of County Armagh

IX	Forkhill	XVII	Loughgilly
X	Jonesborough	XVIII	Montiaghs
XI	Keady	XIX	Mullaghbrack
XII	Kilclooney	XX	Newtownhamilton
XIII	Killevy	XXI	Seagoe
XIV	Killyman	XXII	Shankill
XV	Kilmore	XXIII	Tartaraghan
XVI	Loughgall	XXIV	Tynan

Parish of Ballymore, County Armagh

Draft Memoir and Notes by J. Hill Williams, January 1838

NATURAL STATE AND FEATURES

Locality

The parish of Ballymore is situated in the county of Armagh, on the eastern side in the barony of Lower Orior, bounded to the north and north west by the parish of Kilmore, to the south west by the parish of Loughgilly and to the south by the parish of Killevy and to the east by the county of Down, its extreme length from north to south being 9 miles and extreme breadth from east to west 4 and a half miles, its superficial content being 14,158 acres 3 roods 32 perches, of which 49 acres and 29 perches are water.

Lakes

The parish contains no lakes of any considerable magnitude. The following are contained in it: nearly the western half of Lough Shark, situated half a mile to the eastward of the village of Acton, its remaining or eastern portion being in the county of Down. It is elevated to the height of 80 feet above the level of the sea and its dimensions are as follows: extreme length from north north east to south south west half a mile, and extreme breadth from east south east to west north west a third of a mile. Also Lough Moss or Scarva lough, situated in the townland of Aughlish, 2 miles to the south east of Tanderagee at the height of 63 feet above the sea; extreme length from north to south 285 yards, extreme breadth from east to west 132 yards. McCourt's lough, situated 1 mile south west of the village of Poyntzpass <Pointzpass>, extreme length from north east to south west 374 yards, extreme breadth south east to north west 242 yards. Also a lake situated 2 miles west of the village of Acton, in the townlands of Corlust and Ballyargan and Crewbeg, elevated 258 feet above the level of the sea, extreme length from north to south 418 yards, extreme breadth from east to west 285 yards.

MODERN TOPOGRAPHY

Towns: Tanderagee

The towns contained in the parish are Tanderagee, Poyntzpass and Acton. The principal of these, Tanderagee, is situated in the diocese of Armagh, province of Ulster, county of Armagh, parish of Ballymore and north east circuit of assize, on the road between Portadown and Newry, at the distance of 5 and a quarter statute miles from the former and 12 and a quarter statute miles from the latter. Distance from Dublin 61 Irish miles, latitude north [blank], longitude west [blank]. The following are its distances from the neighbouring towns in English or statute miles: east of Armagh 10 miles, north by west from Newry 12 and a quarter miles, north east of Markethill 6 miles, east south east of Rich Hill 5 and a half miles, south by east of Portadown 5 and a quarter miles.

Streets: Tanderagee

The town consists of 3 streets, the continuation of one another: Church Street, running in a direction north north east 220 yards, Market Street, in a direction north west and south east 285 yards, Mill Street, in a direction south by east 310 yards, the total length of the town being 815 yards. The town is built in the townland of Ballymore on the slope of a hill called Tanderagee hill. The descent from the church, which is situated near the northern extremity of the town, to the mill dam at its lower extremity is very steep, the fall being 126 feet, i.e. from 238 feet to 112 feet above the level of the sea, the breadth varying from 100 to 20 feet.

Public Buildings: Tanderagee

The principal buildings contained in the town are the church, 2 Methodist meeting houses and 5 schoolhouses and Tanderagee Castle, 1 police station, 2 banks.

Houses: Tanderagee

The greater number of the houses in Tanderagee are in good order. The following is their number: 46 3-storey houses, 133 2-storey houses, 57 cabins and 1-storey, 236 total number of houses. They are, with the exception of 2 brick houses, built of unhewn stone and covered with plaster and roughcast. With the exception of Church Street the town presents a uniform appearance.

Tanderagee Church

The church of Tanderagee, situated near the northern extremity of the town off Church Street, is a plain rectangular building with a square tower and

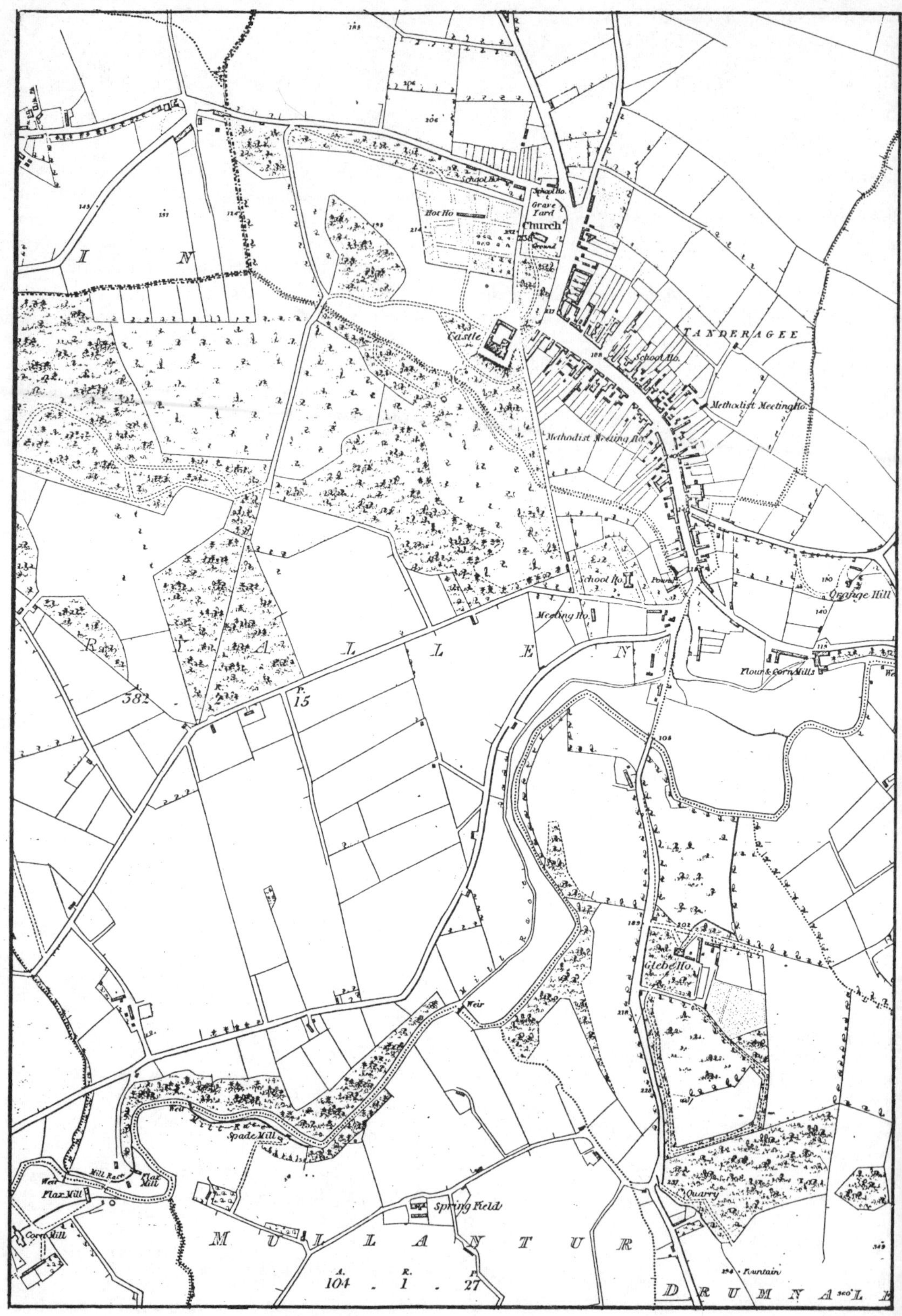

Map of Tanderagee from the first 6" O.S. maps, 1830s

belfry, the body of the church being 76 feet long and 38 feet broad. It was built in the year 1812 at an expense of 2,300 pounds, of which 700 pounds were given by Lady Mandeville, then Miss Sparrow, the remaining 1,600 pounds being furnished by the parish. It can accommodate 1,000 persons, the average number of persons attending being 600. It has a large gallery. It is neatly ornamented in the inside. On the baptismal font are the following inscriptions: "Built 1622, rebuilt 1812, T. Carter, rector, L. Creery, curate, T. Stratton, clerk, R. Greenaway, W. Loftie [the last 2 bracketed together with the initials C.W. church warden]." The church, being elevated and surrounded with trees, may be seen to great advantage from different parts of the surrounding country. Rector the Reverend Thomas Carter, Dean of Tuam, Tanderagee Glebe. Curates [bracketed together] Reverend James Wilson, Tanderagee, Edward Lindsay Elwood.

Wesleyan Methodist Chapel

The Wesleyan Methodist chapel of Tanderagee, situated on the eastern side of the street, is a plain neat rectangular building of stone, 76 feet long and 35 feet broad. Was commenced in the year 1835 and finished in 1837, cost nearly 800 pounds, procured by subscription. Could accommodate 800 persons, the average number in attendance being 100. The ministers always change.

Primitive Wesleyan Methodist Chapel

The Primitive Wesleyan Methodist chapel, Tanderagee, situated on the western side of the street, is a plain rectangular building of uncut stone, with a portico. Its length is 60 feet and breadth 38 feet. It was commenced in the year 1835 and finished in 1837. The cost of building was 600 pounds, raised by subscription. It accommodates 500 persons, the average number attending being 100. Its ministers are also changing.

Presbyterian Meeting House

The Presbyterian meeting house, situated 200 yards to the west of the lower end of Mill Street (Tanderagee), is a plain rectangular building in good order, standing nearly north and south, 60 feet long and 30 feet broad. It is connected with the Synod of Ulster. It was built in the year 1828 at a cost of about 700 pounds, raised by subscription. The average attendance is 250 persons and the house can accommodate 400. The congregation consists of 145 families, minister the Reverend James Bell, Tanderagee, income, stipend 50 pounds, Regium Donum 50 pounds (Irish).

Tanderagee Castle

Tanderagee Castle, the residence of Lord Viscount Mandeville and Lady Mandeville, is a fine large stone building of the Elizabethan style of architecture, enclosing a good court. It was commenced in 1830 and will probably be finished in 1838. It contains a large handsome chapel, wainscoted with richly carved oak and it will also have an organ and gallery. The house contains large and commodious apartments, also a very valuable collection of theological works consisting of the old English and French divines collected by Lord Mandeville. Lord Mandeville occasionally resides in it with his sons Lord Kimbolton, Lord Robert Montagu and Lord Frederick. It was formerly, with the adjoining estates, the property of Miss Sparrow (now Lady Mandeville), daughter of Colonel Sparrow and Lady Olivia Sparrow who resided in the castle. It is built on the site of the former one and in making the improvements about the house a quantity of human skulls and bones have, at different times, been found by the workmen. Attached to the house is a good garden and conservatories, also a fine demesne, well planted and tastefully laid out.

Tanderagee Flour and Corn Mills

The flour and corn mills, situated 150 yards from the end of Mill Street, consist of a large stone building the property of John Creery Esquire, situated in the townland of Tullyhugh. The diameter of water wheel is 25 feet, breadth of water wheel 8 feet, fall of water 16 feet. Was built in the year 1824, the machinery is metallic and 16 persons are employed.

Roads

The principal roads which traverse this parish are the northernmost road from Armagh to Banbridge and Loughbrickland which runs nearly through the middle of the parish in an easterly direction for the distance of 3 and three-quarter miles, its average breadth being [blank]. It is macadamised and kept in good repair.

The southernmost road from Armagh to Banbridge and Loughbrickland (through Markethill) traverses the parish in an east north easterly direction for the distance of 2 and a half miles, its average breadth being [blank] feet. It is macadamised and kept in repair.

The road from Portadown to Newry (through Tanderagee and Poyntzpass), entering the parish to the north west, three-quarters of a mile north west of Tanderagee, runs to Acton village 4 and a half miles in a south westerly direction, then 3 miles in a southerly direction, its average breadth being 20 feet. It is injudiciously laid out and very hilly, macadamised and kept in good repair at the expense of the county.

Social Economy

Local Government

The following is a list of the magistrates with their residences, which are all in the parish with the exception of Colonel Close: Viscount Mandeville, Tanderagee Castle, J.P. and Deputy Lieutenant of the county; Charles Hunt, seneschal, J.P., Manor House, Tanderagee; Robert Harden Esquire, J.P., Clare; Conway Richard Dobbs Esquire, J.P., Acton House, Acton; Lieutenant-Colonel Maxwell Close, J.P., Drumbanagher Castle in the parish of Killevy.

Constabulary

The constabulary station in Tanderagee consists of 1 sergeant and 3 men.

Civil Jurisdiction

The manor court, Tanderagee, is held on the first Friday of every month for the recovery of fines not exceeding 40s Irish currency. Lord of the manor Viscount Mandeville, J.P., Castle, seneschal Charles Hunt Esquire, J.P., Manor House. A court leet held on the first Friday in May, in which court money matters are not taken cognisance of, its business being confined to framing by-laws for the regulation of the estates and the appointment of its bailiffs.

Petty Sessions

Petty sessions are held every alternate Tuesday in Tanderagee, in a house hired for the purpose for 10 pounds paid by the county. There are generally 3 and sometimes 2 of the above named magistrates in attendance. The cases brought before the magistrates at these sessions are generally of a light nature, such as usually result from the quarrels of the peasantry. Sometimes these quarrels are caused by drunkenness which, however, has been diminishing some years, it is said, from the introduction of temperance societies. There are no illegal or other combinations existing among workmen to deprive others of working as they please.

Dispensaries

There are 3 dispensaries within the parish: the Tanderagee dispensary, [blank] Patton M.D. (surgeon), connected with the county, open every Tuesday and Friday from 10 a.m. to 1 p.m. Lord Mandeville's private dispensary for the relief of his tenants, held in the castle at Tanderagee, open every Thursday from noon to 6 p.m. [Insert footnote: also one in Pointzpass].

Schools

The improvement resulting from education is said to be remarkable and the education of the poorer class has become popular. On the property of Lord Mandeville it is attended to with the greatest liberality as to the number of the schools, the donation of the patrons and the strictness with which the regular attendance of the children and improvement is enquired into, Lord Mandeville receiving weekly reports of the numbers of children attending. In the town of Tanderagee and parish of Ballymore are 7 schools under his patronage or Lady Mandeville's: of these one is a male and female infant school in Tanderagee, held in a good new house attended by 141 children of an age varying from 2 to 7 years.

Poor

There are no funds or bequests for the relief of the poor in Tanderagee. They are supported by private subscription and also relieved by the following means: a fever hospital supported by private subscription and also by fines from the petty sessions. Four small houses are given rent free by Lady Mandeville for the habitation of 8 widows, 2 to reside in each house; 20 widows and other destitute persons receive a portion of meal weekly at the Castle, and in general the poor are very carefully supported by Lord and Lady Mandeville. There is also a clothing store at the Castle for supplying the tenants at cost price, the clothing being made in the schools.

Emigration

There is very little, either emigration or migration from the parish.

Social and Productive Economy

Fairs

There is in Tanderagee an annual fair, a quarterly fair and a monthly fair held on the first Wednesday on every month, all of which are very numerously attended for business and largely supplied with linen, flax, grain, cattle.

Markets

A market is held in Tanderagee every Wednesday and very numerously attended by traders from different towns around and the adjacent country. It is also abundantly supplied with linen, flax, corn, butter, potatoes, meal, cattle, pigs, meat, poultry, fruit, vegetables. Some of the commodities exposed for sale are bought for the immediate consumption of the inhabitants and a large quantity bought for the purpose of exportation from Belfast and Warrenpoint.

Trades and Occupations in Tanderagee

Surgeons 3, grocers 17, haberdashers 8, spirit dealers 36, painters and glaziers 1, bakers 3, tailors 2, shoemakers 6, watchmakers 2, hardware shops 2, earthenware shops 2, leather stores 2, saddlers 3, nailors 1, tinsmiths 1, smiths 1, reedmakers 1, pawnbroker 1.

Religious Libraries

There is a lending library in the Castle, Tanderagee, for the use of the gentry and shopkeepers, and one in each of the schools on Lord Mandeville's property for the use of the poor. The books of which they consist are all religious.

Banks

There are in the town of Tanderagee 2 branch banks, one of the Ulster Banking Company and one of the Belfast Banking Company, the offices of which are open every day from 10 a.m. to 4 p.m.

Amusements

No peculiar amusements can be described as belonging to the inhabitants of the parish and adjoining country, except one to which they resort in great numbers on the 13th July every year. It is called the Sham Fight of Scarva, from its taking place near that town. The battle, fought in imitation of the battle of the Boyne, is commenced at the eastern boundary of this parish on the western bank of the Newry Canal, which in the course of the battle is crossed in imitation of the crossing of the Boyne, and it continues on the eastern bank of the canal in the county of Down. The combatants being all Protestants divide themselves into opposite parties, and from there being no real opponents no accidents take place. In 1836 more than 5,000 persons assembled and were dispersed by the military collected there in great force with 6 pieces of artillery. In 1837 they met at 2 o'clock in the morning and the day passed very quietly.

MODERN TOPOGRAPHY

Clare (of Tanderagee) Presbyterian Meeting House

The Presbyterian meeting house of Clare, situated near the western boundary of the parish in the townland of Clare near the road from Armagh and Rich Hill to Banbridge at a distance of 5 and a half miles from Rich Hill, is a slated good house rebuilt in 1828, capable of accommodating nearly 1,000 persons; length 60 feet, breadth 44 feet. Minister the Reverend John Bell, Clare.

Clare Seceding Meeting House

The Seceding meeting house, situated near Clare in the townland of Clare on the road from Armagh and Rich Hill to Banbridge at the distance of 5 and a half miles from Rich Hill, is a plain slated rectangular building in good repair, built about 1825; length 50 feet, breadth 27 and a half feet. Minister the Reverend Robert Hawthorn, Tanderagee.

Corn Mills

The corn mill, situated at the north east of the Presbyterian meeting house of Clare, is an old 2-storey building in bad repair, the property of William Cleland, situated in the townland of Clare on the western bank of the River Cusher. [Nature of wheel, diameter of wheel, fall of water, wooden or metal machinery: no details].

Mr Harden [proprietor], corn mill near Clare in the townland of Drumin, is a slated 2-storey house in good repair, built 1817, water supplied by the Cusher river; nature of wheel breast, diameter 10 feet, breadth 3 feet, wooden and metallic machinery.

There are 2 corn mills situated a quarter of a mile to the westward of Poyntzpass on a by-road. They are both the property of Alexander Crothers, the first is in the townland of Tullmakross. Their dimensions are as follows: first mill, nature of wheel breast, diameter 15 feet, breadth 2 feet, fall of water 17 feet, works of wood, 1-storey, in good repair; second mill, in townland of Brannock, nature of wheel breast, diameter 15 feet, breadth 2 feet, fall of water 12 feet, works of wood, 1-storey and in good repair.

Ballyargan Roman Catholic Chapel

The Roman Catholic chapel of Ballyargan is situated at a distance of 2 miles to the south of Tanderagee, on the road between the latter place and Newry. It is a plain rectangular whitewashed building, 66 feet long and 24 feet broad, rebuilt in the year 1807 and is now (1837 July) undergoing repairs. It has a gallery round 2 sides and is capable of accommodating 900 persons. Over the altar there is a large oil painting of St Peter in good preservation. Priest [blank] Campbell, curate [blank] Daly.

Flax Mills

A flax mill, situated 2 miles to the south west of Tanderagee, is the property of George Hamilton, supplied with water from the River Cusher, can only work 2 months in the year, water failing. Nature of wheel breast, diameter 10 feet, breadth 5 and a half feet, fall of water 11 feet, [signed and dated 1838].

A flax mill, situated quarter of a mile nearly to the westward of the town of Poyntzpass near the above mentioned corn mills, is the property of Alexander Crothers. The following are its dimensions: nature of wheel breast, diameter 16 feet, breadth 3 and a half feet, fall of water 19 feet, water wheel and inner works of metal, consists of 1 storey in good repair, situated in the townland of Brannock.

Town of Poyntzpass

The town of Poyntzpass is situated on the road between Tanderagee and Newry, at the distance of 4 and a half miles to the south east of the former and 8 and three-quarters nearly north of the latter. On approaching the village from the Newry road its general appearance is good. It is situated in a hollow at the foot of several round hills on the banks of the canal. At the distance of a quarter of a mile to the northward is the residence of Mr Dobbs, J.P., a large square house of a plain and comfortable appearance. The town on a closer inspection presents a more unfavourable aspect: the houses are built of stone and generally whitewashed. The following is their number: 3-storey houses 2, 2-storey houses 86, 1-storey houses 5, mud cabins 22.

PRODUCTIVE ECONOMY

Poyntzpass: Trades and Occupations

Spirit dealers 9, grocers 2, haberdashers 2, apothecaries 3, bakers 1, reedmakers 1, shoemakers 3, nailmakers 1, hardware shop 1, painter and glazier 1, lodging house keepers 4, tailors 2, dispensary 1, smith 1.

MODERN TOPOGRAPHY

Poyntzpass Church

The church of Poyntzpass, situated in the town, is a plain rectangular whitewashed building with a square tower, and is altogether much out of repair. It was built in 1793 and rebuilt and slightly repaired in 1835; 54 feet long and 27 feet broad, accommodates 190 people. Dean the Reverend Carter of Tanderagee, vicar the Reverend Darby.

Poyntzpass Chapel

The Roman Catholic chapel of Poyntzpass, situated a little to the outside of the town, is a plain rectangular building of stone in good repair, built in 1790; length 62 feet,breadth 30 feet, accommodates1,000 people. Priest the Reverend Edward Campbell.

Poyntzpass Meeting House

The Presbyterian meeting house of Poyntzpass, now in progress at the west end of the village, is a plain rectangular building, raised by subscription; length 56 feet, breadth 36 feet. The congregation consists of 120 families.

Acton Village

The village of Acton is a poor collection of 55 houses, 4 of which are of 2-storeys, 50 cabins and 1 public house.

ANCIENT TOPOGRAPHY

Acton Old Church

Acton old church (in ruins) is situated near the village of the same name on the road to Markethill. Nothing now remains of the building but a part of the north wall, 19 feet long and 11 feet high, built of whinstones, partially squared and laid in courses.

Within the surrounding burying ground and used as a headstone to one of the graves stands the half of a stone formerly part of the building itself, with the following inscription [sketched out]: "This church was built at the sole expense of Sir Toby Poyntz, Knt, the son of Sir Charles Poyntz, Knt, of Acton, anno 1684, and dedicated to the Blessed and Undivided Trinity."

Social Economy

Education

[Table of schools contains the following headings: name, situation and description, when established, income and expenditure, physical, intellectual and moral instruction, number of pupils subdivided by age, sex and religion, name and religion of master or mistress, date on which visited].

Corlust male and female school, a thatched cabin in bad repair, situated in the townland of Corlust; income: under the Kildare Street Society; intellectual instruction: Scriptures and books, patronised by the Kildare Street Society, reading, writing and arithmetic; number of pupils: males, 11 over 15 years of age, a total of 80; females, 4 over 15 years of age, a total of 50; total number of pupils 130; the above is the number on the books; master Thomas Salmond, visited 19 August 1837.

Poyntzpass national male and female school, a small 2-storey house in good repair; income: National Board of Education; expenditure: salary paid by the board; intellectual instruction: visited only by the inspectors of the board, books of the National Board of Education; number of pupils: males, 3 above 15, total 118; females, 10 above 15, total 180; master Patrick Conroy.

Poyntzpass male and female school (Kildare Street), at the east end of the village; moral instruction: reading, writing, arithmetic and usual course of the Kildare Street Society; number of pupils: males, 14 under 10 years of age, 3 from 10 to 15, a total of 17; females, 4 under 10 years of age, 2 from 10 to 15, a total of 6; total number of pupils 23; master James Sexton.

Poyntzpass male and female infant school; income: under the Kildare Street Society; expenditure: from W.J. Close, Drumbanagher, 10 pounds per annum and small sums from children; moral instruction: visited by Mrs Close and by the Reverend Darby, Protestant curate; number of pupils: males, 20 under 10 years of age, a total of 20; females, 19 under 10 years of age, 7 over 15; total number of pupils 46; mistress Jane McCann; number of children on the books 90. NB The above 2 schools are both included in a square whitewashed house in good repair, built by Colonel Close of Drumbanagher House, [initialled] JHW.

Memoir by Lieut G.A. Bennett, June 1835

Natural State

Name and Derivation

Ballymore [2 short stresses and 1 long stress over syllables] or "the large town" is said to take its derivation from the town of Tanderagee, situated in the north end of the parish.

Locality and Extent

It is situated in the east side of the county and in the barony of Lower Orier and is bounded on the north by Kilmore, east by Tullylish, Aghaderg and Donoughmore, west by Kilmore, Mullaghbrack and Loughgilly and south by Killevy <Killeevy>. Its greatest length is 9 English miles from its extreme southern point in Cullentrough townland joining Killevy <Killeavy> parish, to its most northern point in Ballymore joining Kilmore parish. Its greatest breadth is 4 and a quarter miles from east to west. It contains [blank] acres and is divided into 48 townlands. Of these 65 and a half are water, 100 spent bog, 121 marsh and 403 of wood, besides about the half of Derryallen townland containing Lord Mandeville's demesne, and half of Skigatallagh containing part of Colonel Close's demesne, both of which are thickly wooded.

Natural Features

Hills

The surface of this parish is broken up into a large number of hills which do not exceed in height above the sea 522 feet. The lowest ground is about the canal along the west side of the parish, only 53 feet. The highest is in the south end of the parish in the townlands of Cullintrough, Carrickbrack, Skigatallagh. Carrickbrack Fort is 522 feet above the sea, a hill in Cullintrough 518 feet, one in Shigatallagh 449 feet. The ground there falls off to the east and west and to the north. In the townland of Tullynacross it is only 175 feet but rises again to 464 feet at Lisseraw Fort. Babylon hill in Mullaghglass townland is 452 feet and commands an extensive view. Glebe hill in Drumnally is 399 feet and a hill in Ballyshielmore is 401 feet. From Glebe hill the ground falls towards the canal on the north east to 53 feet.

Lakes

In the north end of Aughlish townland there is a small lake called Scarvagh lough, 64 feet above the sea. It contains about 7 acres. Another in the north end of Demone at its junction with Aughantaraghan and Federnagh contains about 11 acres. Another in the north west side of Crubeg at its junction with Ballyargin and Curlusk contains about 14 and a half acres. Lough Shark, partly in this county and partly in the county of Down, is 80 feet above the sea and is the summit level of the Newry Canal. 33 acres of the lake are in this parish and county.

Rivers

The principal river in this parish is the Cusher river, which enters the parish at its most western point in the townland of Maymacullen and becomes the parish boundary in the west for little more than a mile. It then takes a direction through the parish, being the boundary for various t[ow]nlands, for about 6 miles. It is very crooked but its general bearing is north east. Its height above the sea on entering the parish is 175 feet and on leaving it 53 feet. It varies in breadth, the average, perhaps, is 40 feet and depth 1 to 7 feet. Between the townlands of Clare, Moodge [Moodoge] and Druminure and between Cargans and Tullyhue its banks are thickly wooded. It is well adapted for mills, of which there are the following: in the townland of Clare a corn mill with kiln adjoining and a flax mill; in Ballyshielbeg a flax mill; in Druminure a corn mill; in Moodoge a corn and flax mill; in Mullinteer a spade foundry <foundary>; in Derryallen a flax mill and in Tullyhue a corn and flour mill. These mills are idle about 2 months in the year from the scarcity of water. It is subject to floods in winter when the low grounds through which it runs become flooded. The water of this river likewise supplies the Newry Canal by means of a feeder, an artificial cut commencing at the most eastern bridge near Tanderagee on the north side of the river. It runs through the centre of Cargans townland and enters Terryhoogan, where it crosses the ravine by means of an aquaduct 237 feet in length, supported on 12 arches about 20 foot rise. It enters the canal at the Wash bridge, its whole length being about 3 miles. The other small streams in the parish are not worth noticing in detail.

Bogs

There are about 100 acres of spent or worn out bog in this parish, but very little fuel is obtained from it. It is in small places scattered here and there through the parish.

Woods

There are no natural woods in this parish. It, however, contains about 403 acres of forest trees, of which 95 acres are in Derryallen, 75 in Skigatallagh, 16 in Demone, 50 in Brannock, 40 in Clare, 25 in Cargans, 20 in Druminaleg, 14 in Tullyhue, 12 in Moodoge and 12 in Druminure.

Geology

The soil is only tolerable in this parish as the clay is too much mixed with sand or gravel. Greywacke projects in many places and seems to be only substratum.

Modern Topography

Towns: History of Tanderagee

Tanderagee, formerly called Tanrygee, situated in the north west corner of the parish on the side of a very steep hill. It is 10 miles from Armagh, 10 from Banbridge, 11 from Newry and 61 from Dublin. It is now the property of Lord Mandeville, but at the time of Tyrone's defeat in 1603 it (the surrounding land) belonged to the O'Hanlons, but this, together with 1,500 acres belonging to Sir Oliver StJohn, was declared confiscated under James I, AD 1619. At this period government designed to make it a corporate town, for in an act of James I we find "a grant of 1,200 acres to 4 corporate towns viz. 300 to Armagh, 300 to Mount Norris, 300 to Claremount, and 300 to a corporate town to be erected at Tanrygee" (Harris).

Ecclesiastical Buildings in Tanderagee

It contains a handsome church, situated on the summit of the hill 238 feet above the sea, built in 1642 and rebuilt in 1812. It affords accommodation for 900 persons. It likewise contains a Seceding meeting house, built by subscription in 1828 for 600 pounds and capable of containing 600 persons. Likewise, 2 Methodist meeting houses, one Wesleyan, built in 1770 costing about 150 pounds and capable of containing 150, the other built in 1821, the cost and size the same as the preceding. They were both built by subscription.

Productive and Social Economy

Fairs and Courts

There are 2 fairs in the year, one on the 5th of July, the other the 5th of November. They are well attended for the sale of black cattle, sheep, pigs. The market is held on Wednesday when pork, grain, butter, potatoes, meat are brought in abundance. On an average 35 cartloads of pork, of say 200, are sold every market day in winter. There are no tolls or customs demanded; no weights or measures differing from the statute ones are allowed by the seneschal.

A manor court is held on the first Friday of every month, seneschal Mr Hunt, now Lord Mandeville's agent. The jurisdiction of the court extends to debts, fines and damages under the value of 1 pound 16s 11d. No magistrates attend the court. There is also a court leet once a year, generally either in April or May, to regulate trespass, poundage, fences and other local arrangements. It consists of the seneschal and 24 resident jurors.

Modern Topography

Mandeville Castle

The only resident magistrate is Lord Mandeville. Mandeville Castle is a handsome building in the Tudor style of architecture, situated on the verge of a steep declivity to the south east and west and sloping gradually to the north. It is close to the town and is surrounded by extensive plantations both old and new. The building is not yet completed. The stone used is greywacke brought from a quarry about a mile to the east.

Social Economy

Schools

There are 4 schools in the town, 2 built and supported by Lord Mandeville. One, called Tanderagee male and female school, was built in 1819 costing 800 pounds, is attended by from 80 to 120 boys and 100 to 130 girls. This school retains the books [and] system supplied by the Kildare Street Society. The other is an infant school established in 1825 by Lady Mandeville, who allows a salary of 35 pounds a year to a mistress for instructing from 60 to 140 children. The Reverend Mr Hawthorn, a Seceding clergyman, keeps a day school for 50 pupils and Miss Atkinson keeps a female boarding school and has 26 pupils.

Dispensary

There is a dispensary maintained by about 50 subscribers who give a guinea each annually, and they get 50 pounds more from the county. The days of attendance are Tuesdays and Fridays, when medicine and attendance are given by Dr Patton to any person recommended by a subscriber.

Coaches and Cars

The communications are a coach to Belfast every day through Portadown, a car to Armagh every Tuesday and one to Newry every Thursday, the market days at those places.

Modern Topography

Market House

The market houses generally are known by the name of the Shades. It is 2-storeys high, with excellent lofts which are used as stores from one market day to another for merchandize which has not met with a market.

Village of Poyntzpass

The village of Poyntzpass is situated on the east boundary of the parish in the townlands of Fedemagh and Tullinacross, and derived its name from Sir Toby Poyntz of Brannock Hall, Acton, who was appointed to watch this pass as well as those of Scarva and Jerrett <Gerrard> in the reign of William III. It is now the property of Colonel Close of Drumbanagher. It contains a small plain church with a turret and would accommodate about 300. It was built in 1796. There is a schoolhouse in the east end of the village, purchased by Colonel Close in 1828 assisted by the Kildare Street Society, whose books and system are still retained. There are 60 males and 50 females instructed in it. Colonel Close gives a yearly salary to the master and mistress.

Poyntzpass: Courts

A manor court is held on the first Saturday of every month, seneschal Mr Mitchell, Markethill. The jurisdiction of the court extends to debts, fines, and damages under 5 pounds. There is also a court leet once a year, generally in April or May, to decide on trespass, poundage, local improvements; the seneschal attends. The townlands in the manor are half of Carrickbrack, Corcreen, Ballinaleck, Ballyreagh, Tullinacross, Federnagh, half of Tannyokey <Tamyokey>, Tullylime, Crewmore, Acton, Brannock, Glassdrummond, Ballynagreagh and 8 townlands in the parish of Loughgilly.

Acton Village

The village of Acton, situated in the townland of that name or as it is sometimes called Curryotragh, is the property of Colonel Close. It contains the school formerly under the Kildare Street Society but now supported by the scholars and by Colonel

Close, who gives 5 pounds annually. The poor receive medicine and attendance from Poyntzpass dispensary by tickets from subscribers. This village has a wretched appearance: there is neither market nor fair.

Public Buildings

Besides those already mentioned as belonging to the towns, there are 2 Presbyterian meeting houses: 1 in Clare townland built in 1828 for 500 pounds, and capable of containing 500 persons; another in Derryallen townland would contain about 400. There are 3 Seceding meeting houses: 1 in Clare for 400 persons, 1 in Lisnagree for 400, was built AD 1765, the third is in Tamyokey for about 300 persons. 2 Roman Catholic chapels: 1 in Brannock, close to Poyntzpass, for 500 persons and the other in Mullaghglass, called Ballyargin chapel, for 800 persons. The latter was rebuilt in 1806 at cost of 600 pounds.

Gentlemen's Seats

Mandeville Castle, the seat of Viscount Mandeville, has already been mentioned when speaking of Tanderagee. Acton House, in the north east end of Brannock townland, is the residence of C.R. Dobbs Esquire. The ornamental ground is of trifling extent. Harrybrook, in Clare townland, is the residence of R. Harden, J.P., and the Glebe House, the residence of the present incumbent of this parish and the Reverend Carter, Dean of Tuam.

PRODUCTIVE ECONOMY

Manufactories and Mills

There are in this parish 7 corn mills, 1 flour mill and 6 flax mills besides 1 spade foundry and an old bleach mill in ruins.

The following table shows the situation and power of the various mills in the parish: [table gives name of townland, description of mill, type, diameter and breadth of wheel, fall of water].

Brannock, corn mill, breast wheel, 15 feet by 2 feet, 14 feet.

Ballyshielmore, flax mill, overshot, 13 feet by 3 feet, 14 feet.

Ballyshielbeg, flax mill, overshot, 14 feet by 2 feet, 8 feet.

Clare, flax mill, breast wheel, 13 feet by 2 feet 10 inches.

Clare, corn mill, both are turned by one wheel.

Demone, corn mill, breast wheel, 13 feet 9 inches by 2 feet, 16 feet.

Druminure, corn mill, breast wheel, 2 feet 6 inches by 3 feet 5 inches, 8 feet.

Derryallen, flax mill, breast wheel, 15 feet by 2 feet 4 inches, 4 feet.

Moodoge, flax mill, breast wheel, 12 feet by 3 feet, 7 feet 6 inches.

Moodoge, corn mill, breast wheel, 12 feet 6 inches by 2 feet 6 inches, 8 feet.

Mullinteer, spade foundry, breast wheel, 13 feet by 3 feet, 2 feet.

Tullynacross, corn mill, breast wheel, 15 feet by 2 feet, 18 feet.

Tullynacross, flax mill, breast wheel, 15 feet by 2 feet, 12 feet.

Tullyhue, corn mill, breast wheel, 24 feet by 6 feet, 18 feet.

Tullyhue, flour mill, breast wheel, 24 feet by 6 feet, 18 feet.

MODERN TOPOGRAPHY

Communications

The roads from Tanderagee to Portadown, Banbridge, Newry and Armagh are tolerably well laid out and are kept in good repair. There are also numerous by-roads connecting these. The Newry Canal runs contiguous to the eastern boundary of the parish for 8 and a quarter miles. The bridges over the canal are at Poyntzpass, a wooden one at the Tallyho Locks, Scarva and Madden bridge, in all four. Bridges over the Cusher river are 5 in number and 3 wooden bridges for the convenience of the proprietors of mills. None of these bridges deserve particular note.

ANCIENT TOPOGRAPHY

Ancient Remains

On the western side of Lisnagree townland the parish boundary is a ditch or trench, said to have been cut by the Earl of Tyrone as a defence in the year 1660. It still goes by the name of "Tyrone's Ditches", though now it is merely a drain. In the townland of Aughlish, near the north west point on the road from Tanderagee to Loughbrickland, is the site of an old church, a portion of the ruins of which are still visible. There are 2 circular burying grounds attached to it, having the appearance of Danish forts: one called Ballynaback is used exclusively by Protestants, the other called Relicairn is devoted to Catholics. In this latter they show a tomb or rather walls where they say the famous robber Redmond O'Hanlon was buried.

In the north west of the townland of Brannock, a quarter of a mile from Acton there are the ruins of an old church and on a stone in the burial ground is the following inscription: "This church was built at the sole expense of Sir Toby Poyntz, Knight, the son of Charles Poyntz, Knight, of Acton, Anno Domini 1684 and dedicated to the" the remainder is unintelligible. Besides the above the parish contains a number of forts but none worthy of particular remark.

Modern Topography and Productive Economy

Newry Canal and Cultivation

The Newry Canal is of considerable benefit to this and the surrounding parishes, as opening an export for grain. The parish is well cultivated except the bog tracts already mentioned. The low grounds are generally used as meadow.

Social Economy

Dispensary

There are 2 dispensaries, one in Tanderagee, the other in Poyntzpass, from whence medicine and attendance are issued by tickets from subscribers. Besides these Lord Mandeville maintains a surgeon and supplies medicines for the use of his own tenantry.

Local Government

Lord Mandeville, R. Harding Esquire of Harrybrook, C.R. Dobbs Esquire of Acton are magistrates residing within the parish. Colonel Close on the confines of this parish is also resorted to by the parishioners. All pecuniary matters such as wages, debts, fines, trespass, poundage, fences are settled by the manor courts and courts leet held in Tanderagee and Acton, but matters of more serious importance are referred to the sessions at Portadown.

Schools

The annexed table will show their situation: [Table contains the following headings: name of townland, Protestants, Catholics, males, females, how supported, when established].

Acton, 35 Protestants, 34 Catholics, 35 males, 34 females, 69 in total, Colonel Close 5 pounds per annum and scholars also pay, 1819.

Brannock, 20 Protestants, 40 Catholics, 40 males, 20 females, 60 in total, National Board, 1824.

Tanderagee, 150 Protestants, 80 Catholics, 110 males, 120 females, total 230, Lord Mandeville, 1819.

Tanderagee, 60 Protestants, 40 Catholics, 30 males, 70 females, 100 in total, Lady Mandeville allows 35 pounds to mistress per annum, 1825.

Tanderagee, 50 Protestants, all male, 50 total, scholars pay, 1830.

Tanderagee, 26 Protestants, all female, total 26, scholars pay, 1829 [this and the above school are bracketed together as private schools].

Corlusk, 25 Protestants, 5 Catholics, 22 males, 8 females, 30 in total, a hedge school.

Corenmar, 125 Protestants, 65 males, 60 females, 125 in total, Lord Mandeville 20 pounds to master, 10 pounds to mistress and part by scholars, 1825.

Clare, 29 Protestants, 6 Catholics, 25 males, 10 females, 35 in total, 6 pounds from London Hibernian Society and 1d ha'penny to 3d per week by scholars, 1830.

Cargans, 110 Protestants, 10 Catholics, 70 males, 50 females, 120 total, Lord Mandeville and the scholars a trifle, 1825.

Drumanaleg, 38 Protestants, 12 Catholics, 38 males, 12 females, 50 in total, 7 pounds from Society for Discountenancing Vice, 2 acres from Dean Carter and 1d per week from the scholars, 1829.

Lisnagree, 40 Protestants, 10 Catholics, 30 males, 20 females, 50 in total, 7 pounds from Hibernian Society and 1d per week from scholars, 1828.

Poyntzpass, 65 Protestants, 45 Catholics, 60 males, 50 females, 110 in total, Colonel Close and scholars, 1828.

Habits of the People

There is no provision for the poor. About five-eighths are Protestants, the remainder Catholics. The southern part of the parish has not so rich an appearance as the northern. Lord Mandeville as a landlord deserves the highest praise. He gives to his tenants time to whitewash their houses, he lends money to farmers of small capital to labour and crop their land and takes their labour in return for payment. He keeps a surgeon to visit them, supplies them with medicines and a dispensary, and maintains numerous schools in this and the adjoining parishes in which his estates lie, for the education of their children. The houses throughout the parish are for the most part mud, but the larger farmers have comfortable dwellings. Amongst these Maymount in Maymacullen townland, Violet Hill in Cargans, Cullentrough Lodge and Fairgrove, Infant Lodge and Mr Black's in Mullaghglass, Crossvale in Lisseraw, Cooley Hill, Atholl Cottage and Mr Cassidy's in Aughantaraghan may be considered as the best. The fuel is in general turf, which is brought from Braccagh in Kilmore, but the parish may be said to be supplied from the Montiaghs <Montaghs> by means of the canal. There are no prevailing customs and the language of the people is in general a tolerable good English with a Scotch accent.

Productive Economy

Fairs

Fairs and markets are mentioned under the head of Towns. They lead to much immorality.

Size of Farms

The farms vary in size from 2 to 100 acres. The old leases are let at from 3d to 18s per acre, the new from 20s to 40s, but 26s may be considered as a mean throughout the parish. Life leases and tenants at will are the general methods of letting at present. The proprietors are as follows: Colonel Close 15 townlands, Lord Mandeville 7 townlands, primate land 5 townlands, R. Harden 3 townlands, churchland 2 townlands, Lord Gosford 2 townlands, Mr Quin 2 townlands, Mr Loftie 1 townland, Mr Lucas 1 townland, Mr Bousley 1 townland, Mr Broomer [Boomer] 1 townland, Miss Cherry 1 townland. The remaining 7 are divided among different proprietors as will be seen in the descriptive remarks on each townland.

Townland Divisions

Aghantarahan Townland

Aghantarahan, pronounced Agh[stress]antar[stress]aghan[stress] from Ahigh-a-tarvan "the bull's hide." Is in the barony of Lower Orier and bounded on the north by Federnagh, west by Demone and Federnagh, east by county Down and south by Killevy parish. Proprietor Colonel Close, agent Mr Blacker of Armagh. It contains [blank acres], of which 6 are marsh and 4 are a portion of a lake. Farms from 3 to 19 acres, rent 17s to 25s, soil light, lime brought from Drumbanagher kilns at 1s 8d per barrel, cess 1s to 2s per acre. Market towns Newry and Tanderagee, the former 8 miles distant and the latter 4.

Aughlish Townland

Aughlish, pronounced Aug[stress]lish[stress] and Aiglis from Aghliss "the battle fort." It is bounded on the east by Muntclone and county Down, west by Mullaghglass and north by Terryhoogan. It is primate land attached to the see of Armagh and let to D. Lucas Esquire of Drumhergall House. Contains [blank] acres, farms 4 to 20 acres, tenure 19 years, rent 20s to 25s. In the north end there is a small lough known by the name of Scarva lough containing 7 acres. There is likewise about 15 acres of marsh. Near the north west point is Ballinaleck graveyard and site of an old church in the graveyard. There are none buried but Protestants. There is an old fort in the south, but no tradition of a battle having been fought. Cess 10d to 1s half yearly. The centre of this townland is 200 feet above the sea and the north part of it 70 feet. Market Tanderagee, 2 and a half miles distant.

Acton Townland

Acton, pronounced Act[stress]on[stress]. It is bounded on the north by Shanenglin [Shaneglis], north east by Druminnegall, south by Brannock and west by Ballnareagh. Curryo[stress]tragh is considered by some of the inhabitants to be the most proper name. Proprietor Colonel Close, agent Mr Blacker, it contains [blank] acres. It is nearly all divided into gardens attached to the houses of the village; the land is let at 40s per acre. There is a school which was formerly under the Kildare Street Society. It is 175 feet above the sea. Market Tanderagee, 3 and a half miles [distant].

Ballinaleck Townland

Ballinaleck, pronounced Bal[stress]enaleck[stress] from Boilyanleac "the town of great stone." It is bounded on the east by Ballyreagh, south east by Tullinacross and Federnagh, south by Corcreen, north by Tannyoky, west by the parish of Mullavilly. Proprietors Colonel Close, Counsellor Bell and the Reverend J. McCrate of Caledon, agents Messrs Black, Murphy and Kelly. It contains [blank] acres, nearly all out of lease. Farms from 5 to 12 acres, rent 20s to 25s 6d per acre, cess 7d to 10d half yearly. Market Poyntzpass and Tanderagee, 1 and a half miles distant from the former and 4 and a half from the latter.

Brannock Townland

Brannock, pronounced Bran[stress]ock from Branenoc "the black hill." It is bounded on the east by county Down, the Newry Canal forms a part of this boundary on the south by Poyntzpass village and Tullinacross, east and north east by Glassdrummond and Ballynareagh, north by Acton and Druminargall townlands. Proprietor Colonel Close, agent Mr Blacker, farms 3 to 20 [acres], rent 2s to 3s, it contains [blank acres]. In the north east is situated the residence of C.R. Dobbs Esquire called Acton House, and the Glebe in the south west occupied by the Reverend Daily, perpetual curate.

Lough Shark is on the north east point. There are about 50 acres of planting in this townland. It contains a Roman Catholic chapel in the south end and a school under the National Board, a corn mill in the south west corner and in the north west the ruins of an old church. For particulars see under their different heads.

Ballyreagh Townland

Ballyreagh, pronounced Balereagh[stress] from Baile-reigh "town of the plain <plane>." It is bounded on the north by Crubeg, south by Tannyoky and Ballinaleck, east by Lisseraw, west by Tannyokey. Proprietor Colonel Close, agent Mr Blacker. It contains [blank] acres, of which 23 are bog and 13 and a half marsh, farms 2 to 30 acres, rent 16s to 25s and some old leases at 8s, cess 10d ha'penny half yearly. [Markets at] Markethill, distant 3 and a half miles, Poyntzpass, 2 miles.

Ballinareagh Townland

Ballinareagh, pronounced Ballinagreagh[stress] from Baile-an-reigh "town of the plain." It is bounded on the east by Acton, south east and south by Brannock, south west by Glassdrummond, west by Lisseraw and north by Shaneglish. Proprietor Colonel Close, agent Mr Blacker, contains [blank] acres, farms 3 to 15 acres, rent 11s to 35s. It is a hilly townland, the highest part is 341 feet above the sea. Market Tanderagee, 4 miles distant.

Ballyargin Townland

Ballyargin, pronounced Baleargin[stress] from Baile-marghan "the border town." It is bounded on the north by Ballyshielmore, south by Crubeg, east by Corernagh, west by Corlusk. Proprietor Lord Gosford, agent Mr Mitchell of Markethill, contains [blank] acres, of which 3 are marsh, 5 water, part of a lake on the south. Farms from 2 to 30 acres, rent from 16s to 23s, cess 1s 1d. Soil of a cold sandy nature and won't bear wheat. Fuel brought from Clady, 6 miles distant. Lime from Kilmore and Armagh at 1s per barrel and 4d a load for the raw stone.

Ballyshielmore Townland

Ballyshielmore, pronounced Balleshill[stress]more from Bailesealb-more [Baileseall-more] "great field tower." It is bounded on the north by Druminure, north east by Cloghoge, west by Ballyshielbeg, south by Ballyregin and Corlusk. Contains [blank] acres, proprietor R. Harden, J.P., Harrybrook, who receives his own rent. Farms 5 to 25 acres, rent 25s to 27s 6d, tenants at will, employment generally farming and linen weaving. Lime got at Kilmore, fuel at Clady. It contains 4 and a half acres of marsh, two old forts and a flax mill (see Manufactories). Market town Tanderagee, 3 miles distant.

Ballyshielbeg Townland

Ballyshielbeg, pronounced Bale-shile-beg from Baile-sealb-beg "the little field tower." It is bounded on the south by Curlusk and Mullinary, west by Moymacullen and Clare, north by Druminure, east by Ballyshielmore. Proprietor R. Harden, J.P. of Harrybrook in this townland. It contains [blank] acres, farms 3 to 47 acres, rent 25s to 27s 6d. Lime got from Kilmore. It contains a flax mill, the ruins of an old bleach mill and 2 forts. Market Tanderagee, 3 miles distant.

Ballymore Townland

Ballymore, pronounced Bal[stress]emore[stress]. It is bounded on the west and north by the parish of Kilmore, east by Tullyhue and south by Derryallen. Proprietor Viscount Mandeville, agent Mr Hunt, it contains [blank] acres. The town of Tanderagee is situated in this townland as is also Mandeville Castle and a part of the demesne. There is likewise an old Danish fort in the centre of it. Farms from 4 to 30 acres, rent 16s to 25s, cess 7d ha'penny to 1s half yearly (for further particulars see under head of Towns).

Cullintrough Townland

Cullintrough, pronounced Corlintra[stresses] from Cullintraigh "foot of holly." It is bounded on the north by Lisnagree, east by Carrickbrack and on the south and west by Killevy parish. Proprietors Mr Dunbar near Belfast and Mr McCartney, Clady, middlemen Mr Black of Cullintrough Lodge and Mr Bittles of Fairgrove. 2 neat residences in this townland at 1s 6d per acre, who relet it in farms of 5 to 20 acres at 42s the Irish acre, tenure 21 years or 3 lives. It contains [blank] acres, cess 7d to 1s half yearly. 3 and a half miles distant from Poyntzpass [market].

Carrickbrack Townland

Carrickbrack, pronounced Carrickbrack[stresses] from Carrig-breac "the speckled rock." It is bounded on the north by Corcreem, east by Skigatallagh, south by Killevy parish and west by Cullintrough and Lisnagree. Proprietors Colonel Close and Mr McCullough, Clady, agents Mr Blacker and Mr Mitchel, contains [blank] acres, all under cultivation. Colonel Close's part is let to tenants at will at 20s per acre, the remainder is leased for 21 years at 26s to 30s, cess 6d to 1s half yearly. 3 miles distant from Poyntzpass [market].

Corcreem Townland

Corcreem, pronounced Corcreem[stress] from Corcrom "the crooked stone." It is bounded on the north by Federnagh, north west by Ballynaleck, east by Demone, south by Carrickbrack and Lisnagree. Proprietor Colonel Close, agent Mr Blacker, contains [blank] acres, farms 3 to 15 acres, rent 22s, tenants at will. A large crooked stone formerly stood in this townland but is now removed to Colonel Close's demesne. There are about 20 acres of spent bog, cess 7d to 10d half yearly. 2 miles distant from Poyntzpass [market].

Crewmore Townland

Crewmore, pronounced Crumore[stresses] from Cruadmore "the great stone." It is bounded on the north by the townland of Mullinary, east by Tullylinn, south and west by the parish of Loughgilly. Proprietor Colonel Close, agent Mr Blacker, it is let at 25s per acre. The houses are nearly all mud. It contains [blank] acres of spent bog. Market at Tanderagee, distant 4 miles.

Crubeg Townland

Crubeg is bounded on the north by Ballyargin, south by Tullylinn and Ballyreagh, east by Lisseraw, west by Corlusk. Proprietor Viscount Mandeville, agent Mr Hunt, contains [blank] acres, of which 3 are bog and 4 and a half lake (portion of). Farms from 2 to 20 acres, old leases 8s, new 20s, soil light. Limestone brought from Kilmore, cess 8d ha'penny half yearly. It is derived from the Irish Crobeg "the little fortress."

Curlusk Townland

Curlusk, pronounced Curlusk[stresses] from Corlosgan "the frog's pool." It is bounded on the north by Ballyshielmore and Ballyshielbeg, east by Ballyargin and Tullylinn, south by Crewmore and west by Mullinary. Proprietor Lord Gosford, agent Mr Mitchel, contains [blank] acres let at 23s per acre. The houses are chiefly built with mud. It contains a fort near the north west corner. There is likewise a hedge school in it (see Schools) and about 5 acres of a lake. Market Tanderagee, distant 3 and a half miles.

Corernagh Townland

Corernagh, pronounced Cor[stress]renar[stress from Correarnagh "the iron pit." It is bounded i the north by Tullymacan, east by Shaneglish an Lisseraw, on the west by Ballyargin and south b Crubeg. Proprietors Viscount Mandeville, agen Mr Hunt. Contains [blank] acres, of which 4 and half are marsh, farms 3 to 50 acres, rent from 10 to 25s. There is a school near the centre of thi townland, for which see Schools. Cess 8d to 1s hal yearly, market Tanderagee, distant 2 miles.

Cloghhoge Townland

Cloghoge, pronounced Cloghoge[short stresses from Cloghoiche "the water stone." It is bounde on the south east by Corernagh and Ballyargin an south west by Ballyshielmore. Proprietor Mr Lofti of Tanderagee who receives his own rents. I contains [blank] acres, of which 2 are marsh; 3 lif leases are let at 25s per [annum] and 1 life or 2 years from 20s to 25s. Employment farming an linen weaving. Lime brought from Kilmore, fue from Bracca. Market Tanderagee, 3 miles distant

Clare Townland

Clare, so pronounced, from Clier "clergy." Bounded on the south by Moymacullen, west b Mullabrack, north by Cooleyhill and Drumina gluntagh and east by Moodoge, Druminure an Ballyshielbeg. Proprietors R. Harden, J.P., Har rybrook, Mr J. Loftie and the heirs of the late A McCreight of Tanderagee. Contains [blank acres] of which 40 are thriving plantations. Rent 20s t 25s, tenure 3 lives or 31 years and part is held b tenants at will. It contains a Presbyterian and Seceding meeting house, a schoolhouse, a cor and flax mill and kiln and the ruins of Clare Castle Market Tanderagee, distant 1 and a half miles Employment farming and linen weaving.

Cooleyhill Townland

Cooleyhill, pronounced Cool[stress]ehill[stress from Coile "the wood hill." It is bounded on th west by Mullabrack parish, north east and north b Kilmore parish, east by Drumnagluntagh and sout by Clare. Proprietors Mr R. Hardy, who occupie his own part about 33 and a half acres, and J Hardy, who has his part let to tenants at will i small farms at 30s per acre. Lime obtained a Kilmore and fuel at Bracchagh bog. Employmen principally farming, market Tanderagee, 1 and quarter miles distant.

Cargans Townland

Cargans, pronounced Carregans[stresses] and Cargans[stresses] from Carriachan "the rocks." It is bounded on the north west by the townland of Tullyhue, north east by county Down, south east by Terryhoogan, south by Mullaghglass and south west by Lisbane. Proprietor Viscount Mandeville, agent Mr Hunt. It contains [blank] acres, of which 25 are planted with forest trees, 28 of marshy ground, farms 3 to 30 acres, rent 20s, cess 9d half yearly. The artificial cut already mentioned for feeding the canal runs through this townland. A planted fort in the south west end is 206 feet above the sea and in the northern end along the canal which runs contiguous to the boundary is 58 feet. It contains a school, principally supported by Viscount Mandeville. This townland is of a very rocky nature, the greater part of which is brought into cultivation, but towards the west rocks project above the surface. At the south end is Violet Hill, the residence of Mr Abraham Hardy. 1 and a half miles from Tanderagee [market].

Demone Townland

Demone, pronounced Demoan[stresses]. It is bounded on the north by Federnagh and Aghantaraghan, east by Aghantaraghan and county Down, south by Skigatallagh and Killevy parish and west by Corcrum. Proprietor Colonel Close, agent Mr Mitchell of Markethill. It contains [blank] acres, a part of which is walled into Drumbanagher demesne and the remainder let to tenants at will at 23s, only 2 or 3 farmers having leases, and they pay only 10s per acre. It contains about 60 acres of fir plantation, also a fort on the west side, 3 acres of a lake on the north side and a corn mill in the south. Markets Newry and Tanderagee, the former 5 miles, the latter 7 distant.

Druminargall Townland

Druminargall, pronounced Drum[stress]inar[stress]gan from Druminaigh "the milk ridge." It is bounded on the east by county Down, south by Brannock, south west by Acton, west by Shanegarish, north west by Mullaghglass and north by Muntclone. It is primate land attached to the see of Armagh and in possession of D. Lucas Esquire, who resides in the townland, and is relet in farms of from 2 to 31 acres at from 20s to 23s, cess 7d half yearly. In the north point there is 3 acres of a lake and a fort in the north east. Fuel obtained partly from bits of spent bog and partly from Montiaghs <Moyntagh> by [a] canal which passes through the townland near its eastern boundary, and there is about 33 acres of Lough Shark in it. A hill in south west of the townland is 208 feet above the sea and a stream in the south 127 feet. Market Tanderagee, 3 and a half miles distant.

Druminure Townland

Druminure, pronounced Druminyour[stresses] from Drumaneer "the heathy ridge." It is bounded on the south by Cloghoge and Ballyshielmore, west by Clare, north by Clare and Moodoge and east by Moodoge and Tullymacan. Proprietor R. Harden, J.P., Harrybrook receives his own rent. It contains [blank] acres, an old fort, a corn mill and kiln, 3 and a half acres of marsh and 12 thriving plantations. Farms 3 to 14 acres, rent 21s to 27s 6d, tenants at will. Occupations principally farming and linen weaving. Lime obtained at Kilmore, fuel at Bracchagh. Market Tanderagee, 2 and a half miles distant.

Druminaleg Townland

Druminaleg, pronounced Drumenalig[stresses] from Drumaleag "ridge of the great stone." It is bounded on the south by Tullymacan and Mullaghglass, west by Lisnakee and Mullintur, north by Derryan and east by Lisbane. Churchland, possessed by the resident incumbent Dean Carter, rector of the parish. He owns about half the townland in his own hands, in which is the Glebe House and about 20 acres of thriving plantation, and the remainder is let to tenants at will from 25s to 27s 6d. Occupations chiefly farming. It contains [blank] acres and a school. 1 mile distant from Tanderagee [market].

Druminagluntagh Townland

Druminagluntagh, pronounced Druminaglunch[stresses]er and is bounded on the south by Clare, west by Cooleyhill and Kilmore parish, north east by Deryallen and south east by Moodoge. Proprietor Miss Cherry, agent Mr Orr of Loughgall, contains [blank] acres, farms 3 to 12 acres, rent 30s, tenants at will. Lime obtained at Kilmore at about 1s per barrel, fuel at Braccagh, 3 miles distant. Market Tanderagee, 1 mile [distant].

Derryallen Townland

Derryallen, pronounced Derre-allen[stresses on last 2 syllables] from Druimaluin "the fair ridge." It is bounded on the north by Ballymore and Kilmore parish, east by Tullyhue and Drumenalig, south by Mullintur and Meedoge and west by

Drumnaglunter and parish of Kilmore. Proprietor Viscount Mandeville. The northern part of this townland is walled into Viscount Mandeville's demesne. It contains [blank] acres, a meeting house, a school and flax mill in its extreme south point. The remainder of this townland is let in farms of from 3 to 30 [acres], rent 15s to 25s, cess 2s annually. Market Tanderagee, half a mile [distant].

Federnagh Townland

Federnagh, pronounced Fethherner[stresses] from Feada-erinach "the Irishman's wood." It is bounded on the north by Tullynacross, east by Aghantaraghan and the county Down, south by Demone and Corcrum and west by Tullynacross. Proprietor Colonel Close, agent Mr Blacker. It contains [blank] acres, of which 4 is lake, farms 2 to 20 acres, old leases 12s 6d, new 28s. It contains a part of the village of Poyntzpass and an old fort. Lime brought from Kilmore, Armagh and Drumbanagher. Markets Tanderagee and Newry.

Glassdrummond Townland

Glassdrummond, pronounced Glassdrummun-[stress on last syllable] from Glassdrummond "the green furze edge." Is bounded on the east and north east by Ballinareagh and Brannock, on the south by Tullynacross and west by Lisseraw. Proprietor Colonel Close, contains [blank] acres, farms 4 to 30 acres, rent 10s 9d to 29s. Chief market Tanderagee, 4 miles [distant]. In the south end of this townland there are several plantations.

Lisseraw Townland

Lisseraw, pronounced Lisraw[stresses] from Lisrath "the fine fort" and is bounded on the north by Shaneglish, south by Ballyreagh and Glassdrummond, on the east and west by Crubeg. Proprietor Colonel Close, agent Mr Blacker and ex-agent Mr Mitchell, Markethill. It contains [blank] acres, 100 of which are held by Mr Moody at 12s, farms 2 to 20 acres, rent 25s, cess 10d ha'penny half yearly. It contains 3 acres of spent bog, soil bad and of a cold nature, not capable of bearing wheat. Markets Tanderagee and Poyntzpass, the former 4 miles and the latter a quarter mile distant.

Lisnagree Townland

Lisnagree, pronounced Lisnaygre[stresses] from Lisnagreech "the nut fort." It is bounded on the north west by Loughgilly and Killevy parishes, south by Cullintrough and east by Carrickbrack. Proprietors Mr Dunbar, near Belfast and M McCartin, Clady, agent Mr Murphy, Rathfriland It contains [blank] acres, of which 3 farms [are] o 12 acres, each are leased for ever at 1s 6d per acre The remainder is set in farms of from 7 to 30 acre at from 20s to 30s, cess 7d to 10d half yearly. I contains a meeting house and a school, and nea the meeting house at the parish boundary a dee trench said to have been cut by the Earl of Tyron as a means of defence. It has ever since gone by th name of Tyrone's Ditches. 3 miles distant fro Poyntzpass [market].

Lisnakee Townland

Lisnakee, pronounced Lisneykey[stresses on las 2 syllables] from Lisaceal "the fort of death." It i bounded on the south by Tullymacan, west b Moodoge, north by Mullintur and east by Drum naleg. Proprietor Mr Quinn, Newry, agent M Magill, Tanderagee. Contains [blank] acres, farm 3 to 16 [acres], rent 25s to 27s 6d, tenants at will cess and tithe paid by the landlord. There is a for in the centre of this townland on top of the hill Roads very bad. Lime got at Kilmore, fuel fro Bracchagh bog and Montiaghs. Market Tander agee, 1 and a half miles distant. Employmen farming and weaving.

Lisbane Townland

Lisbane, pronounced Lisbann [? Lisbaun] [stres on last syllable], from Lisban "the white fort." It i bounded on the north east by Cargans, south an south east by Mullaghglass, west by Drumnaleg and the Cusher water on the north north wes divides it from Tullyhue. Proprietor Viscoun Mandeville, agent Mr Hunt, contains [blank] acres of which 15 acres in the north east end is fi plantation. Farms 3 to 30 acres, rent 20s to 25s new leases 21 years, cess 8d to 1s half yearly. Th ground in the northern end is 140 feet above the se and rises towards the fort which is planted to 40 feet. In the south end are 2 limekilns and the [lim ?] obtained from Anahugh in the adjoining paris of Kilmore is burnt here and costs about 1s 1d barrel. Fuel obtained from Braccagh and Mon tiaghs by canal. Chief market Tanderagee, 1 mil distant.

Mullinary Townland

Mullinary, pronounced Mull-enar[stress]ry fro Mullanarach "brier hill." It is bounded on the wes by the parish of Loughgilly and Maymacullen north by Ballyshielbeg, east by Carlusk and sout by Crumore. Glebe land, occupied by the present incumbent Dean Carter. It contains [blank] acres, farms 3 to 20 [acres], rent 20s to 24s, cess 1s 1d per acre. It contains 3 forts. Market Tanderagee, distant about 3 and a half miles.

Maymacullen Townland

Maymacullen, pronounced May-ma[stress]cullen[stress] from May-macquillian "Macquillian's plain." It is bounded on the south west by Loughgilly parish, west by Mullaghbrack parish, north by Clare and east by Ballyshielbeg and Mullinary. Proprietor Mr Boomer, Belfast. It contains [blank] acres and let at 23s per acre. In the northern part is a neat farm house called Maymount and in the south is an old fort. Houses chiefly mud, nearest market Tanderagee, 3 miles distant.

Muntclone Townland

Muntclone, pronounced Munt[stress]lone[stress] from Meatcluain "the mead park." It is bounded on the west and north by Aughlish, east by Aghaderg <Aughaderg> parish, south by Druminargall and south west by Mullaghglass. Primate land, attached to the see of Armagh, and is let to D. Lucas Esquire of Druminargall House. It contains [blank] acres, of which 8 is worn out bog. Farms from 4 to 20 [acres], rent 20s to 25s, tenure 19 years, cess 9d to 1s half yearly. In the north end is a fort and in the south is a cluster of houses known by the name of The Close, and in the north east point is the village of Scarva. The northern end is 120 feet above the sea and the southern 200 feet. The Newry Canal skirts the eastern boundary. Market Tanderagee, 3 miles distant.

Mullaghglass Townland

Mullaghglass, pronounced Mullaghglass[stresses] from Mullochglass "the green height." It is bounded on the north east by Terryhoogan, east by Aughlish, south by Shaneglish, west by Tullymacan and north by Lisbane and Cargans. Proprietor Viscount Mandeville, agent Mr Hunt. It contains [blank] acres, of which 2 are marsh. Farms 4 to 20 [acres], rent 20s, tenure 1 life or 21 years, cess 8d to 1s half yearly. The road at the northern boundary is 95 feet above the sea and Babylon hill in the south end. The highest [point] in this or any of the adjoining townlands is 452 feet; most likely this is the height the name of the townland implies. It contains a Roman Catholic chapel which was rebuilt in 1806 at expense of 600 pounds and is capable of containing 800 persons. Mr Black's and Infant Lodge are the only respectable houses at it. [Market] Tanderagee, 2 and a half miles distant.

Moodoge Townland

Moodoge, pronounced Maydoge[stresses] from Muadh-oiche "good water." It is bounded on the north by Derryallen, south by Druminure, west by Clare and Drumnaglunter and east by Mullintur, Lisnakee and Tullymacan. Proprietors Mr Bansley and Mrs Smyth, Donaghadee, agent Mr Trotter, Tanderagee. It contains [blank] acres, 12 of which are plantation. It is all held by tenants at will, but 1 farm of 44 acres on which are a corn mill and a flax mill, rent 25s, lease 4 lives. Farms at will are from 3 and a half to 15 acres, rent 20s. Occupations farming and linen weaving. This townland is badly accommodated with roads. It contains an old fort. Market Tanderagee, 1 and a half miles distant.

Mullintur Townland

Mullintur, pronounced Mullintur[stresses] from Mulliontyr "Mullin's land." It is bounded on the north by Moodoge and Derryallen, east by Druminaleg and south by Lisnakee. Proprietor Mr Quinn, Newry, agent Mr J. Magill, Tanderagee. It contains [blank] acres, farms 2 and a half to 13 acres, rent 25s to 27s 6d, cess and tythe paid by proprietor. On the north of the townland is a spade foundry on the Cusher river. Lime obtained at Kilmore, fuel at Bracchagh, Montiaghs and Drumcree. [Market] Tanderagee, 1 mile distant.

Skigatallagh Townland

Skigatallagh, pronounced Skighatalher[stresses] from Sgeichawallaigh "the wild or snail's thorn." It is bounded on the north by Corcrum and Demone, west and south by Killevy parish and east by Carrickbrack townland. Proprietor Colonel Close, Mr Murphy, Rathfriland, agent. Contains [blank] acres: one half of it is Colonel Close's demesne, of which 75 acres are planted; the other is let in farms of from 5 to 7 acres, rent 20s to 22s, cess 7d to 10d half yearly. There are several small quarries opened by Colonel Close to build walls round his demesne. [Market] Poyntzpass, 2 miles distant.

Shaneglish Townland

Shaneglish, pronounced Shaneag[stress]lish from Sean-eglis "the old church." It is bounded on the south by Lisseraw, west by Corernagh, north by Mullaghglass and east by Druminargall. It is primate land attached to the see of Armagh and in possession of D. Lucas Esquire, who relets it in farms of from 2 to 34 acres, rent 20s to 24s. It is very hilly and well supplied with roads. Principal market Tanderagee, 3 miles distant.

Tullynacross Townland

Tullynacross, pronounced Tul-enacros[stresses] from Tullchanacross "hillock of the cross." It is bounded on the north by Ballyreagh, Lisseraw, Glassdrummond and Brannock, east and south by Federnagh and west by Ballynaleck. Proprietor Colonel Close, agent Mr Blacker. Contains [blank] acres, farms 3 to 14 acres, rent 18s to 25s, tenants at will, cess 1s 8d annually. It contains the greater part of the village of Poyntzpass. Quarter of a mile west of the village [is] a corn mill and a little higher up the stream a flax mill, in the north east end an old windmill stump.

Tannyoky Townland

Tannyoky, pronounced Tan-eo[stresses]key and Tineokey from Tainaoiche "the herd's waters." It is bounded on the north by Tullylinn and Ballyreagh, south by Ballynaleck and parish of Loughgilly, east by Ballynaleck and west by Loughgilly parish. Proprietor Colonel Close, agent Mr Mitchell, farms from 2 to 25 acres, rent 16s to 25s, a few old leases at 8s per acre, cess 1s. It contains a Seceding meeting house and about 1 acre of marsh. Fuel obtained at Clady, 5 miles distant. Market Markethill, 3 and a half miles distant. Contains [blank] acres.

Tullylinn Townland

Tullylinn, pronounced Tul-e-lin[stress] from Tullochlinn "hill of the pool." It is bounded on the north by Crubeg, south by Tannyoky, east by Ballyreagh and west by Crewmore. Proprietor Colonel Close, agent Mr Mitchell, Markethill. It contains [blank] acres, farms 2 to 20 acres, rent 16s to 25s and cess 8d ha'penny. It contains about 13 acres of marsh. Limestone from Kilmore and Armagh. Principal market towns Tanderagee and Markethill, the former 4 and the latter 4 and a half miles distant.

Tullymacan Townland

Tullymacan, pronounced Tul-emack[stress]an. It is bounded on the south by Corernagh, west by Cloghoge, Druminure and Moodoge, east by Mullaghglass and north by Lisnakee and Drumnaleg. Proprietor Mr Lucas, Acton, agent Mr Hill, county Antrim. It contains [blank] acres, farms from 3 and a half to 30 [acres], rent 20s to 22s for 19 year leases and some farms held by tenants at will at 25s per acre. Chief employment farming and linen weaving. Lime obtained at Kilmore, fuel at Montiaghs and Drumcree. Market Tanderagee, 2 miles distant.

Terryhoogan Townland

Terryhoogan, pronounced Ter[stress]-e-hoogan[stresses]. It is bounded on the north west by Cargans, east by Tullylish and a small portion of Aghaderg parish, county Down, south by Aughlish and south west by Mullaghglass. It is primate land attached to the see of Armagh and let in perpetuity to D. Lucas Esquire (at 3s 6d per acre renewable). It is let in farms of from 4 to 20 acres [at] from 20s to 25s, leases 19 years, cess 8d to 1s half yearly. It contains [blank] acres, of which 48 are of a boggy nature, flooded in winter in the northern end, and in the southern there are 10 acres subject to the same. The Newry Canal runs to the east end of it, on which are 2 locks and a wooden bridge. The canal feeder already mentioned in Cargans runs through this townland and enters the canal at the Wash bridge. At the south west end is a graveyard known by the name of Relicairn, in which, it is said, the Irish robber Redmond O'Hanlon is buried. None but those belonging to the Roman Catholic persuasion are buried here. Between this and the Tallyho Locks are a few old houses known by the name of the Barrack. The most respectable looking farm house is occupied by Mr Whiteside, who carries on the manufacturing of linen. The road through Terryhoogan moss in the north end is 60 feet above the sea, in the east is 116 feet, west 131 feet and south 75 feet. Market Tanderagee, 2 miles distant. Lime obtained at Annahugh in Kilmore parish at 1s a barrel of 4 bushels, 10 miles distant, soil tolerably good.

Tullyhue Townland

Tullyhue, pronounced Tul[stress]-e-hue[stress], is bounded on the north by Kilmore parish, east by county Down, south by Cargans, Lisbane and Drumnaleg and west by Derryallen and Ballymore townlands. Proprietor Viscount Mandeville. Contains [blank] acres, of which 25 are spent bog or marsh in wedge and 14 of fir plantation along the banks of the Cusher river. The Newry Canal passes through the east side along the banks of this river and nearly parallel to it. Farms 3 to 35 acres, rent 20s, cess 2s per acre annually. The south end of Tanderagee is in this townland, which is its market town. There is a fort situated in the south end near the Cusher. Madden bridge over the same river in the eastern point and McCreery's flour and corn mill in southern point wrought by water from the Cusher. Signed George A. Bennett, Lieutenant Royal Engineers, 2 June 1835.

Parish of Ballymyre, County Armagh

Brief Notes on Corn Mill, Church and Chapel

Modern Topography

Gentleman's Seat

Ballymyre House in the townland of Ballymyre, the residence of Marcus Synnott <Marquis Synod>.

Corn Mill

In the townland of Lurganna, belongs to Captain Reed, diameter 33 feet, breadth 4 feet, fall of water 16 feet, breast wheel.

Church

Adjoining the plantation of Ballymyre House, erected in the year 1821, dimensions 51 feet by 27, expenses paid by subscription. 25 seats, would hold 6 persons in each, about 76 attend on Sunday. In the interior there is a neat monument to the memory of Sir Walter Synnott.

Chapel

In the townland of Knockavannon, erected in 1835 but not yet finished, dedicated to St Malachy <Malychy>, the patron saint of the archdiocese of Armagh. Dimensions 66 feet by 33, there are not any seats. Cost about 300 pounds, which was paid by public subscription.

Parish of Clonfeacle, County Armagh

Memoir for the Northern Part of the Parish by J.R. Ward, January 1838

NATURAL STATE AND NATURAL FEATURES

Locality

There are 2 detached portions of the parish of Clonfeacle, situated in the north west corner of the county Armagh, for which, in order to prevent any mistake or confusion, 2 distinct memoirs are furnished. The north part of Clonfeacle is situated in the extreme west of the barony of Oneilland West. It is bounded on the north and north east by the parish of Killyman, on the south and south east by the parish of Loughgall and on the west by the county Tyrone. Its extreme length is 3 miles and extreme breadth 2 miles; it is 2,312 acres 2 roods 12 perches in content, of which [blank] are uncultivated. It is divided into 6 townlands and is valued at [blank] pounds to the county cess.

Hills

The hills in this part of the parish are small islands surrounded with bog. The highest is in the townland of Derryscollop, 147 feet above the level of the sea. The average height is 90 feet and the lowest ground along the Blackwater, 50 feet above the level of the sea.

Lakes and Rivers

Lakes: none. The Blackwater river runs along the west boundary and separates this portion from the county Tyrone for 1 and three-quarter miles. It is navigable for boats of 30 tons burden <burthen>.

The Callan river forms the south west boundary for 1 and a half miles. Its average breadth is 30 feet. For further particulars see Memoir of the parish of Loughgall.

The Tall river forms the south and south east boundary for 3 and a quarter miles. Its average breadth is 20 feet. For further particulars see parish of Loughgall Memoir.

Bogs and Woods

The north east part of the parish is, with the exception of a few islands of cultivated land, all bog. The average height of it above the sea is 75 feet, and above the Blackwater river 26 feet. The bog is used for fuel. The depth of it in the centre is not known. In those parts where it is cut it averages from 3 to 10 feet. Timber is found indiscriminately scattered through it, oak, fir and birch, of which the 2 latter is most predominant. No natural woods.

MODERN TOPOGRAPHY

Village of Derryscallop

The village of Derryscallop, situated in the townland of Derryscallop, is 2 and a half miles from Charlemont and 7 and a quarter miles from Armagh. It is merely a collection of about 30 mud cottages, all thatched, and a 2-storey brick house which is slated. In the latter resides the general merchant of the village.

Meeting House

In the townland of Tullyroan there is [a] meeting house belonging to the Wesleyan Methodists. It is a mud and stone building, thatched, it is 35 feet long and 20 broad. The inside has much the appearance of a barn. It has forms for seats and a kind of reading desk. The accommodation is for 130 persons, the average attendance is 20.

Schoolhouse

Derrycaw schoolhouse, situated in the townland of Derrycaw, is [a] neat brick building, 60 feet long and 30 feet broad. It was built by John McGeogh Bond of Derrycaw House Esq.

Gentleman's Residence

Derrycaw House, a residence of John McGeogh Bond Esquire, is situated in the townland of Derrycaw.

Communications

The Blackwater river is navigable for boats of 30 tons burden. There are no main roads in the parish, but there are several useful by-roads which are kept in repair by the county.

General Appearance and Scenery

The hills are well cultivated and apparently fertile, but being generally surrounded by bog their appearance is not very favourable to a stranger. The scenery is not very picturesque, nor are the views around extensive.

Social Economy

Education

[Table of schools contains the following headings: name, situation and description, when established, income and expenditure, physical, intellectual and moral education, number of pupils subdivided by age, sex and religion, name and religion of master or mistress].

Derrycaw, a brick cottage in the townland of Derrycaw, established September 1832; income: [from] John McGeogh Bond Esquire, 12 pounds, 5 pounds from pupils; expenditure: none; intellectual education: no society book read, the *Dublin reading book* mostly used; moral education: no visits from clergy, Authorised Version [of Scriptures]; number of pupils: males, 2 under 10 years of age, 2 from 10 to 15, a total of 4; females, 7 under 10 years of age, 7 from 10 to 15, 3 above 15, a total of 17; total number of pupils 21, all Protestants; mistress Anne Reading, Protestant.

Fair Sheets for Southern Part of the Parish by Thomas McIlroy

Natural State and Natural Features

Locality

The lower part of the parish of Clonfeacle is situated in the western side of the county Armagh, nearly due north of the city of Armagh. It is in the barony of Armagh and is bounded on the north by the parish of Loughgall, on the east by the parishes of Loughgall and Grange, on the south by the parish of Eglish and on the [west] by the county of Tyrone and the parish of Eglish. Its extreme length is 3 miles and extreme breadth 2 miles. Its content is 2,323 acres 1 rood 33 perches, of which [blank] are uncultivated, and it is valued at [blank] pounds to the county cess.

Hills

The highest point in this part of the parish is in the townland of Mullanary, 142 feet above the level of the sea, and the lowest ground is along the bank of the River Blackwater, 58 feet above the sea. The average height of the hills is 100 feet above the sea. They are well cultivated and fertile.

Rivers

The River Blackwater forms the western boundary line of this part of the parish for 1 mile. It runs due north, its average breadth is 110 feet and average depth is 7 feet. It is navigable to Blackwatertown for boats of 20 tons burden.

Bogs

There is a bog situated in the townland of Kilmore. Its extreme length is 1 and a quarter miles and extreme breadth three-fifths of a mile. The depth is not known. Timber is found imbedded, oak and fir. It is 70 feet above the level of the sea and 12 feet above the River Blackwater.

There is a bog situated in the townlands of Mullanary and Kilmore. Its extreme length is half a mile and extreme breadth one tenth of a mile. It is 66 feet above the level of the sea and 8 feet above the River Blackwater.

Woods

No natural woods in this parish.

Climate and Crops

No register of climate kept in the parish. Crops the same as those of the parish of Loughgall.

Modern Topography

Communications

The Ulster Canal runs through this parish for 2 miles in a south west by south direction. Its average breadth is 25 feet and depth 5 feet. Expense defrayed by the Ulster Canal Company.

The main road from Armagh to Blackwatertown runs through this parish in a westerly direction for 1 mile; its average breadth is 30 feet. It is a well laid out road and is kept in good repair by the county.

The main road from Charlemont to Caledon runs through this parish in a south west direction for 2 miles; its average breadth is 35 feet. It is a well laid out road and is kept in good repair at the expense of the county.

There are a few by-roads also, which are kept in repair by the county.

Blackwatertown

Blackwatertown, 68 miles distant from Dublin, in latitude [blank] and longitude [blank], is in the diocese of Armagh, the province of Ulster, the county of Armagh and the parish of Clonfeacle. Its extreme length is 440 yards and extreme breadth 240 yards. The surrounding country is rather pretty. It is well cultivated and fertile.

Blackwatertown Bridge

Blackwatertown bridge, over the River Blackwater, is 110 feet long and 25 feet broad. It is built of limestone and consists of 3 arches, expense of building and when erected not known.

Streets

The town consists of 1 principal street and 2 smaller ones which branch off from and form a triangle with the main street. The greater number of the houses are old. They are built of stone. The town consists of 27 of 1, 37 of 2 and 8 of 3-storeys; 54 of these are slated and the remainder thatched. The town is neither lighted nor watched.

Social Economy

Habits and Occupations of People

There are [no ?] scientific or literary institutions. The people have no amusements except in attending the markets held in Armagh and the fairs held in Moy.

Statistical Report of the Parish of Clonfeacle <Clonfeckle> by Lieut C. Bailey, 27 January 1835

Natural State

Name

The name of the parish is spelled Clonfeckle in Beaufort's map of Ireland, in McCrea's and Knox's map of county Tyrone and in McEvoy's *Statistical survey*; Clonfeakle in Carlisle's *Topographical dictionary*, in the *Irish ecclesiastical register*, in Archdall's *Monasticon Hibernicum* and in the House of Commons'*Report on the population of Ireland*; Clonfecle in the House of Commons' *Report on the survey and valuation of Ireland* and again Clonfeacle in Archdall's *Monasticon Hibernicum* and in the House of Commons' *Report on the population of Ireland*. "St Leyud or Lugaid, the son of Tailchan, was abbot of Cluain-fiacul, that is 'the church of the tooth', so named from a tooth of St Patrick which was said to have been preserved there", see Archdall's *Monasticon Hibernicum* p33.

Locality

The county Armagh part of the parish consists of 2 distinct portions: the northern portion is in the barony of Oneiland West and bounded on the north west, north and north east by the parish of Killyman and on the south east, south and south west by Loughgall parish. The southern portion is in the barony of Armagh and bounded on the north by the parish of Loughgall, east by the parishes of Loughgall and Armagh, south by the parish of Armagh and on the west by the parish of Armagh and by that part of Clonfeacle parish which is in the county Tyrone. It is divided into 18 townlands containing 4,636 statute acres, of which 3,714 are cultivated, 900 uncultivated and about 22 of water.

Natural Features

Hills

There are no hills of any consequence. The highest ground in the parish is Siulliliggan hill near Blackwatertown, which is 160 feet above the sea at low water, and about 100 feet above the adjacent country.

Lakes

There is a small lake close to Dartry Lodge and on the right of the road from Blackwatertown to Charlemont, containing about 9 acres.

Rivers

The Blackwater river forms the western boundary of the parish, dividing the counties of Armagh and Tyrone. It flows north and empties itself into Lough Neagh. It is from 30 to 100 feet broad, from 6 to 10 feet deep, and navigable for lighters of 40 or 50 tons burden. It is by no means a rapid river, but very subject to floods, which, however, soon subside.

The Tall river is a small river about 20 feet broad [which] flows west dividing the parishes of Clonfeacle and Loughgall. It unites with the Callan river at Fairlawn bridge, which then becomes the boundary between the above parishes, and empties itself into the Blackwater at about a mile below Charlemont bridge. These rivers have very little fall and are subject to floods which inundate the adjacent country during a great part of the winter.

Bogs

There are about 900 acres of bog, the greater part of which is in the northern portion of the parish, 75 feet above the sea at low water. Fir and oak timber, and occasionally pieces of yew, are found imbedded in the bogs. The fir timber occurs at about 6 feet under the surface, broken off at the same height, the roots and stumps remaining upright.

The oak is found at the bottom of the bogs with its roots to it, and generally lying in a north east direction. The bogs are about 3 feet deep round the edges, but in the centre the depth is not known: it is very considerable. The substratum is clay. There are several insulated hills of diluvial formation rising through the bogs.

Woods

There are no natural woods, but the quantity of roots and stumps of trees found in many parts of the parish (but more particularly in the northern portion) are evidences of its having been formerly a thickly wooded country.

Natural History

Zoology

Pike and eels are sometimes taken in the Tall river, but they are not by any means plentiful. Trout used to be caught in this river, but they have entirely disappeared of late years.

Geology

The country is wholly diluvial, consisting of small round gravelly hills. The valleys being bog are most[ly] moory pasture. There are no rocks whatever in situ.

Productive Economy

Blackwatertown: Commerce

Blackwatertown, situated on the eastern side of the Blackwater river, from which it derives its name, is a small post town containing a few good houses and several large corn stores. A cattle fair is held on the second Wednesday of every month. It is very badly attended, and scarcely deserves the name of a fair. A weekly grain market is held every Monday. A great quantity of corn is sold during what is called "the grain season", bought up by merchants for exportation. Rather an extensive trade is carried on in timber, slates and coals, imported from Belfast or Newry and brought up the river in lighters of 40 or 50 tons burden.

The following table shows the average quantity of some of the principal articles imported in the course of a year, viz. grain 1,080 tons, timber 600 tons, slates 500 tons, coals 550 tons, deal planks 1,000 in number. Most of the wheat imported is carried on in carts to the Caledon mills, in return for flour and bran which is exported to Belfast and Newry. It is thought that the Ulster Canal, which will pass close to the town, is likely to injure the trade in timber and coals, but will not affect the corn trade.

General Remarks

The day coach from Dungannon to Dublin passes through the town every Monday, Wednesday and Friday, and returns on the alternate days. The dispensary is supported by annual subscriptions. A small force of police is stationed in the town.

Modern Topography

Place of Worship

There is a Methodist meeting house in the townland of Tullyroan, which will accommodate 100 persons.

Gentlemen's Seats

Derrycaw, the residence of W. McGeogh Bond Esquire, situated on the banks of the Blackwater river, is a handsome modern house built with cut stone, with extensive office houses and large garden. There are about 92 acres of wood and young plantation.

Dartry Lodge, the residence of W. Olpherts Esquire, is situated in the townland of Drumark, commanding a view of a small lake. There are 2 large orchards and about 10 acres of plantation near the house.

Manufactory

There is a pottery in the townland of Derrycaw, at which large black crocks and bricks are manufactured. It is not constantly at work and is much out of repair.

Communications

The principal roads passing through the parish are those leading from Blackwatertown to Armagh, to Loughgall and to Charlemont, and from Armagh to Verner's bridge. They are kept in tolerably good order at the expense of the county, and are repaired with gravel, except the main road from Charlemont to Armagh which is repaired with broken stone. The Ulster Canal will pass for a distance of 2 miles through the parish. There is a ferry called Goodlatte's ferry across the Blackwater river near Derrycaw House, which opens a direct line of communication between Dungannon and the country about Loughgall. The charges are for a loaded cart 6d, horse and gig 8d, horse 2d, foot passenger 1d. There is very little communication across the ferry at present compared with what used to be the case a few years since.

Ancient Topography

Forts

There are several forts or raths, but none in any way remarkable. They generally consist of a circular bank of earth and small ditch.

Modern Topography

General Appearance and Scenery

The general appearance of the country is very bleak and miserable, with very little wood or trees to enliven the scenery. The northern portion is particularly flat, containing a large tract of bog with insulated hills rising through it.

Social Economy

Local Government

The only resident magistrate is W. Olpherts of Dartry Lodge, Esquire.

Dispensary

The only dispensary is that in Blackwatertown.

Schools

[Table gives townland in which situated, religion, sex, total number of pupils, remarks as to how supported, when established].

Derryscollop: Protestants 44, Roman Catholics 1, total 45; Mrs Reynolds gives 3 pounds annually towards its support, the scholars pay from 3s to 5s per quarter; established 1833.

Canary: Protestants 8, Roman Catholics 17, total 25; supported entirely by the scholars, who pay from 1d ha'penny to 2d each per week; established 1828.

Derrycaw: Protestants 35, Roman Catholics 8, males 16, females 27, total 43. There are 2 distinct schools, one for adults, the other for infants, taught by females who receive one 24 pounds, the other 18 pounds from Mr Bond; established 1832.

Poor

There is no permanent provision whatever for the poor, aged or infirm.

Religion

About equal numbers of Protestants and Roman Catholics. The greater portion of the inhabitants in the southern part of the parish are Roman Catholics.

Habits of the People

The cottages are of mud, 1-storey high, thatched, glass windows and divided into 2 or 3 small rooms, and in general very dirty. Potatoes form almost the only article of food. Turf is used as fuel. It is in great abundance and easily procured.

Emigration

Very few persons emigrate from this part of the country.

Productive Economy

Manufacturing

The principal occupation of the people is in weaving coarse cambric or very coarse linen (the coarser the more profitable). Hand spinning is not carried on to any great extent in the cottages, as the yarn may be purchased at a cheaper rate than they are able to prepare it. A weaver can earn from 3s 6d to 4s 6d and a spinner not more than 1s 6d to 1s 3d per week.

Fairs and Markets

The only fairs or markets in the parish are those held at Blackwatertown. The cloth markets usually attended are at Armagh or Dungannon. The coarse linens sell at 2d ha'penny a yard. The cambrics are generally woven on commission for merchants in Belfast, Portadown and other places. They are worth from 8d to 9d per yard.

Rural Economy

The chief proprietors are Lord Cremorne, Colonel Verner, Major Molesworth and W. McGeogh Bond Esquire. The latter resides in the parish. The size of farms varies from 3 to 30 statute acres. The average size would be about 12 acres, although a few contain as many as 40 or even 50 acres each. Leases are granted for a term of 1 life or 21 years, in some cases for 3 lives or 31 years. The leases on Lord Cremorne's estate are made for 4 years only, which is the term of his minority. The average rent per acre of the best land is from 1 pound 5s to 1 pound 10s, of the middling from 1 pound to 1 pound 1s and of the worst 10s 6d to 16s. The farmers appear to farm for subsistence only. It is not a profitable investment of money. The fields are very small, badly shaped and enclosed with banks of earth. There are not many quicks. The farm buildings are very small and are kept in order by the tenants. The soil is clay, sand and gravel, with a great quantity of bog. Manure used is stable dung, or bog mixed with lime brought from the neighbourhood of Loughgall, purchased at 10d per barrel. There are but few improved implements of husbandry. Mr Olpherts of Dartry Lodge has erected a threshing machine on his premises. Carts and wheel cars are in general use. Horses are employed in agriculture, 1 in a cart or car and 2 in a plough.

Crops and Cattle

The rotation of crops is potatoes, wheat, oats, grass seed and clover, then rest for a year or two. Quantity of seed sown, 2 cwt of wheat or 6 bushels of oats to the acre; average produce per acre, wheat 12 cwt, oats 45 bushels, potatoes 200 to 300 bushels, flax 4 to 5 stone to the peck of seed. Average price of wheat 7s 6d per cwt, oats 7d ha'penny to 9d per stone. The common breed of cattle and pigs are kept. Green feeding is not practised.

Uses made of the Bogs

The bogs are used wholly as fuel which is consumed in the neighbourhood, let at the yearly rate of 1 pound 10s to 2 pounds per acre. The bog timber is employed in building, the oak principally for roofing. The yew is sold to cabinet makers. The fir stumps are cut up for fuel.

General Remarks

The height of the cultivated land above the sea is 60 to 160 feet. The bogs are from 55 to 75 feet above the sea and might possibly be drained to a certain extent, but in some parts of the parish they are more valuable as fuel than they would be if brought under cultivation. Much the best crops of oats are grown upon reclaimed bog. The aspect of the country is bleak, from its low situation and from the quantity of bog and marshy ground it contains. It is damp and considered rather unhealthy. The prevailing soil is clay or gravel. The nearest place at which lime can be procured is at the Ballygawsey kiln near Loughgall, 4 or 5 miles distant. It is the manure best adapted to the land, but the inhabitants are in general too poor to purchase it. The land is only applicable to tillage, being too wet for pasture.

Parish of Lower Creggan <Cregan>, County Armagh

Notes on Crossmaglen by John Heather, 16 March 1838

Modern Topography and Social and Productive Economy

Crossmaglen: Houses and Occupations

Lower Creggan <Cragan>, town of Crossmaglen. This town is of late origin. There are many people still living who only remember a few houses scattered promiscuously over a large space. Indeed properly speaking it is nothing more yet, but it is still improving. The houses are greatly scattered over a large space. There is a good square in the centre of the town, but [th]is has a bad appearance from its being surrounded by a number of dirty houses. Although this part of the village is reckoned the most respectable, the number of 1-storey houses thatched are 23, of 2-storeys slated 85 and 1 3-storey house. The number of tradesmen are as follows, viz. 5 shoemakers, 1 tailor, 2 nailors, 4 blacksmiths, 6 carpenters, 3 whitesmiths, 1 painter, 4 hacklers, 2 bakers, 11 spirit shops, 1 woollen draper, 8 grocers and 4 [? doctor's] shops.

Local Government

There are 7 police stationed here in consequence of the country being in rather a disturbed state. There is also a chief constable resident here.

Fairs and Markets

There is a fair held here in the last Friday in every month, and is very well supplied with cattle. At these fairs there are many disturbances arisen which take some time to settle, and many receive promised beatings which they never get over till released from their earthly sufferings. There is also a market held here on Fridays which I believe is also well supplied.

Schools and Chapel

This school, which is a mixed one of boys and girls, is held in the gallery of the chapel. It contains 7 girls, all of whom are Catholics, [and] 36 boys, 1 of whom is a Protestant. It is under no board of education nor yet receives any contributions. The master teaches some of the boys classics, but on an average he receives 3s per quarter.

The chapel, which is styled <stiled> Bucklawn, is very old, being built in 1817. It resembles more a barn than a place of worship. There is a new one in progress of building. This old chapel would hold 800: there are 500 parishioners.

This school is held in a mud cottage. It is a small house but well filled with scholars. There are 10 girls and 46 boys, all of whom are Catholics. It is under no board of education nor receives any contributions for its support. The master receives [? 10d] per quarter from each pupil, [signed] John Heather, Carrickmacross, 16 March 1838.

Meeting House

There is a Presbyterian meeting house in the townland of Freeduff. Its shape and dimensions are as follows: [ground plan, main measurements 48, 24 and 12 feet, "T" shape]. It has been built upwards of 100 years. It will accommodate about 300.

School

In Tullynavall there is a school having 94 pupils, 48 males and 46 females. It was established in the present year (1837) and is supported entirely by the pupils, who pay from 1s 6d to 2s 6d per quarter.

Mill

In the townland of Dorsy is a corn mill with a breast wheel 14 feet in diameter and 4 feet in breadth.

Parish of Drumcree, County Armagh

Fair Sheets for Memoir by Thomas McIlroy and J. Cumming Innes, November 1837

Natural State

Locality

The parish of Drumcree is situated in the northern part of the county of Armagh and is in the barony of Oneilland West. It is bounded on the north by the parishes of Tartaraghan and Montiaghs, on the east by the parish of Seagoe, on the west by the parishes of Tartaraghan and Kilmore and on the south by the parish of Kilmore. Its extreme length is 8 and quarter miles and extreme breadth 4 and quarter miles. Its content is 13,385 acres 2 roods 52 perches, including 93 acres 3 roods 37 perches of water, [blank acres] of which are uncultivated. It contains or is divided into [blank] townlands and is valued at [blank] to the county cess.

Natural Features

Lakes and Rivers

Lakes: none in the parish. The River Bann, forming the east boundary line of this parish, runs due north for about 5 English miles. It then runs north west for 2 miles. It winds much in its course, its average breadth is 150 feet and average depth 20 feet. It rises in the parish of Clonduff, county of Down. It is navigable to Portadown for boats, none of which exceed 60 tons burden. The mouth is intercepted by a bar through which the boats have dredged a passage. It is usefully situated for drainage and navigation. There are no falls or rapids in this parish and the average fall is not more than 6 inches in the English mile. It generally overflows its banks in August and the waters do not subside until the April following. The present year, 1837, the waters did not rise until the middle of November owing, it was supposed, to the dryness of the season. The water leaves a very slight deposit of slime. The bed of the river is soft and the banks are flat and uninteresting.

Bogs

There is a bog situated nearly in the centre of this parish, 1 and a half miles north west of Portadown. Its extreme length is 1 English mile and extreme breadth three-quarters of a mile. The highest point in the bog is at the north west side, 118 feet above the sea and 68 feet above the River Bann. Timber is found embedded, mostly oak and fir. In the centre the depth is not known: it deepens in gradually from the margin. There is a bog situated in the townland of Ballyworken, 2 miles south of Portadown. Its extreme length is 1 mile and extreme breadth is half a mile. It is 55 feet above the level of the sea and 5 feet above the River Bann. It is 10 feet deep in the centre which is the deepest part. Oak is found embedded. The north of this parish is nearly all bog. The highest point in it is 76 feet above the level of the sea and 26 feet above the River Bann. Its extreme length is 2 miles and extreme breadth 1 and three-quarter miles. In the central parts the depth of the bog is not known. It is light on the top but found more solid the deeper you descend. Oak and fir are found embedded, which is used for firing and often in building.

Climate and Crops

The climate of this parish is considered healthy, many persons arrive at a very advanced age. The following journal of the state of the weather was kept in Portadown by T.C. McIlroy from the 7th October to the 27th November 1837 [see end of this report]. The crops are the same as those in the parish of Shankill <Shankhill>, for which see parish of Shankill.

Modern Topography

Communications

The main road from Armagh to Belfast passes through the southern part of this parish for 2 and three-quarter miles. Its average breadth is 38 feet. It is a well laid out road and is kept in good repair.

The main road from Loughgall to Portadown runs through the parish in an easterly direction for 2 miles. Its average breadth is 30 feet. It is a well laid out road and is kept in good repair.

The main road from Dungannon to Belfast runs through this parish in a southerly direction for 4 and a quarter miles. Its average breadth is [blank] feet. It is a well laid out road and in good repair.

The main road from Rich Hill to Portadown runs through this parish for 2 and three-quarter miles in a north east direction. It is a good road and in good repair. All the above are kept in repair at the expense of the county, [signed] T.C. McIlroy.

Church

Drumcree church, situated in the townland of Drumcree, is a plain stone building, roughcast and whitewashed. The form and dimensions of the building are represented by the following figure: [ground plan, main dimensions 62 and a half, 31 and 19 feet, rectangular shape with projection at north end]. There is accommodation for 500 persons and the general attendance is 400. The interior is neat, having a gallery at the north end. On the wall to the left is a tablet of black slate stone bordered with freestone, on which is the following inscription: "Here lies the body of Mrs Dorothy, who departed this life the 31st day of October 1729, aged 65 years; also Mrs Mable Bolton, died the 25th December 1734, aged 53." [Signed] J. Cumming Innes.

Chapel of Ease

Portadown chapel of ease, situated at the west end of Portadown in the townland of Corcrain, is a neat stone building, stuccoed in imitation of cut stone. The form and dimensions of the building are represented by the following figure: [ground plan, length 63 feet, rectangular shape with projection at both ends]. It was built in 1826 and cost 1,600 pounds. There is accommodation for 500 persons and the general attendance is 350. The interior is neat, having a gallery at the east end.

Wesleyan Chapel

The Wesleyan chapel, situated on the west side of Portadown in the townland of Tannagh, is a neat whinstone building corniced with freestone. It is 60 and a half feet long and 40 and a half feet broad, having 2 minarets in front and a portico projecting 18 inches. It was built in 1832 and cost 1,000 pounds, of which sum the late Mr John Johnson of Lurgan gave 150 pounds and the rest was raised by public subscription. There is accommodation for 700 persons and the general attendance is 400. The interior is neat, having instead of pews, benches with a rail across the back. There is a gallery at the east end. On the wall at the right hand side is a monument with the following inscription: "As a memorial of undying affection the trustees of this chapel have erected this tablet to perpetuate a grateful recollection of their late friend and brother Thomas Shillington, who exchanged mortality for life, 15th April 1830, aged 63. He was the nursing father of Methodism in this town and neighbourhood for nearly 40 years. An epistle of Christ known and read of all men."

Ministers' Salary

The ministers are Robert Masaroon and Arthur Darby, the former of whom receives 100 pounds and the latter 42 pounds per annum salary.

Chapel

St Patrick's chapel, situated on the west side of Portadown in the townland of Tannagh, is a neat stone building corniced with freestone and having 4 minarets in front and 2 in the rear. It is 73 feet long and 39 feet broad, built in 1835 and cost 700 pounds, raised by public subscription. There is accommodation for 2,500 persons, the general attendance not known as a service has only been performed once. The interior is very plain, having a mud floor and no ceiling. There is a gallery at the east end. The windows are Gothic. On the front of the chapel is a tablet on which is the following inscription: "Glory to God in the highest, St Patrick's chapel, erected AD 1835, Reverend James O'Neill, pastor, and on earth peace to men of good will."

Roman Catholic Chapel

Drumcree Roman Catholic chapel, situated in the townland of Selshion, is a plain stone building, roughcast and whitewashed. It is 63 feet long and 28 and a half feet broad. It was built in 1783, the cost not known. There were repairs done in 1831 which cost 90 pounds, raised by public subscription. There is accommodation for 2,000 persons and the general attendance is 1,500. The priest of the parish is the Reverend James O'Neill, who receives 100 pounds salary. The interior of the chapel is plain, it has a mud floor. There is a large gallery. Over the altar is a painting of the Virgin and Child. At the east end is a wooden tablet on which is the following inscription: "Sacred to the memory of the Reverend John Coyne, STP, faithful father of Drumcree, who departed this life AD 1803, aged 44. Consummatus in brevi explevit tempore multa, constant in prayer, in meditation high, removed from earth and tending to the sky, wise, gentle, humble, modest and kind, grace in his speech and virtues in his mind. Erected by his brother Revd Father Michael Coyne, Ord. Prod., STP, who also departed this life February 1815, aged 48. Requiescant in pace."

Schoolhouses

Derrycory schoolhouse, situated in the townland of Derrycory, is a neat stone cottage, slated. It is 48 feet 6 inches and 20 feet broad. It was built in 1827, not known what cost or how defrayed.

Breagh schoolhouse, situated in the townland of Breagh, is a neat stone cottage, slated. It is 58 feet long and 21 feet broad and was erected in 1829, not known what cost. There is an apartment in one end which is used by the master as a dwelling.

Scotch Street national school, in the townland of Richmond, is a stone cottage, roughcast and slated, not known when built. The cost was defrayed by subscriptions.

Drumgoose school, situated in the townland of Drumgoose, is a good stone cottage, slated. It is 42 feet 6 inches long and 24 feet 6 inches broad. Not known when built, said to have cost about 84 pounds. There is an apartment in the east end which is used as a dwelling by the master.

Ballyworken schoolhouse, situated in the townland of Ballyworken, is a stone cottage, whitewashed and thatched. It is 91 feet long and 22 feet broad. It was built in 1828 and cost 24 pounds, 5 pounds of which sum was defrayed by the Kildare Society. The remainder was defrayed by the master, Woolsley Haddon, [signed] Thomas C. McIlroy, 14 November 1827.

Methodist Meeting Houses and Chapel

There is a Primitive Wesleyan Methodist meeting house situated in the townland of Richmount, adjoining Scotch Street. It is a plain whinstone building, slated, 39 feet 6 inches long and 22 feet 6 inches broad. It was erected in 1831, not known what cost or how defrayed. The interior is plain, it is unceiled; the windows are Gothic. The accommodation is for 200 persons and the general attendance is 100.

Timakeel Wesleyan Methodist meeting house, situated on the road leading from Scotch Street to Loughgall in the townland of Timakeel, is an old plain building, whitewashed and slated. It is 43 feet long and 22 feet 6 inches broad, not known when built or what cost. The interior is very plain, it is unfloored and unceiled. The windows are rectangular. The accommodation is for 200 persons and the general attendance is 50. Neither of the above houses have a resident preacher.

There is a Primitive Wesleyan Methodist meeting house situated in the townland of Derryanvil. It is a plain rectangular stone building, roughcast, whitewashed and slated. It is 43 feet long and 25 feet broad, not known when built or what cost. The inside is very plain, the windows are rectangular. The accommodation is for 200 persons and the general attendance is 50. No resident preacher.

Drumnakelly Wesleyan Methodist chapel, situated in the townland of Drumnakelly, is a small plain rectangular stone building, 39 feet 6 inches long and 24 feet broad. It was built in 1828 at the expense of Mr Henry Ripley, not known what cost. In the north east gable end is the following inscription: "A gift from the late Henry Ripley to the Primitive Wesleyan Methodist Society, AD 1828." The interior is very plain. There is a gallery at the north east end. The windows are Gothic. The accommodation is for 250 persons and the general attendance is 200. No resident preacher.

Bridges

There is a very fine bridge at present building over the River Bann at Portadown. It is of granite and will consist of 3 semi-elliptical and 2 smaller semicircular arches. It was commenced in 1834 and will be finished, it is supposed, next year. The architects are Arthur Williams and Sons, Dublin. They are contracted to erect it for 8,000 pounds, but it is supposed that it will cost 9,000 pounds when finished. It is at the expense of the county.

The old bridge is still made use of, but it is supposed that it will be taken down early in the next year.

Schoolhouses

Portadown infant school is at present kept in an old Methodist meeting house, but there is a neat house at present finishing which is [blank] long and [blank] broad. Refused the necessary information by Thomas Gay, schoolmaster, by order of Mr Porter, Lord Mandeville's moral agent.

Mullantine schoolhouse is a neat stone house, roughcast and whitewashed and slated. It is 41 feet long and 20 feet broad. Refused the necessary information by the same order as above stated, [signed] J. Cumming Innes.

Natural Features and Modern Topography

Town of Portadown: Locality

Portadown is situated in the southern part of the parish of Drumcree and is 72 miles distant from Dublin. It is in latitude [blank] and longitude [blank], in the diocese of Armagh, parish of Drumcree and townlands of Corcraine and Tavanagh. It is situated on the River Bann and the main road from Armagh to Belfast runs through it. It is 696 yards long and its greatest breadth is 320 yards. It is situated on the side of a hill looking east. In the winter months when the Bann overflows its banks the surrounding country looks dreary. In

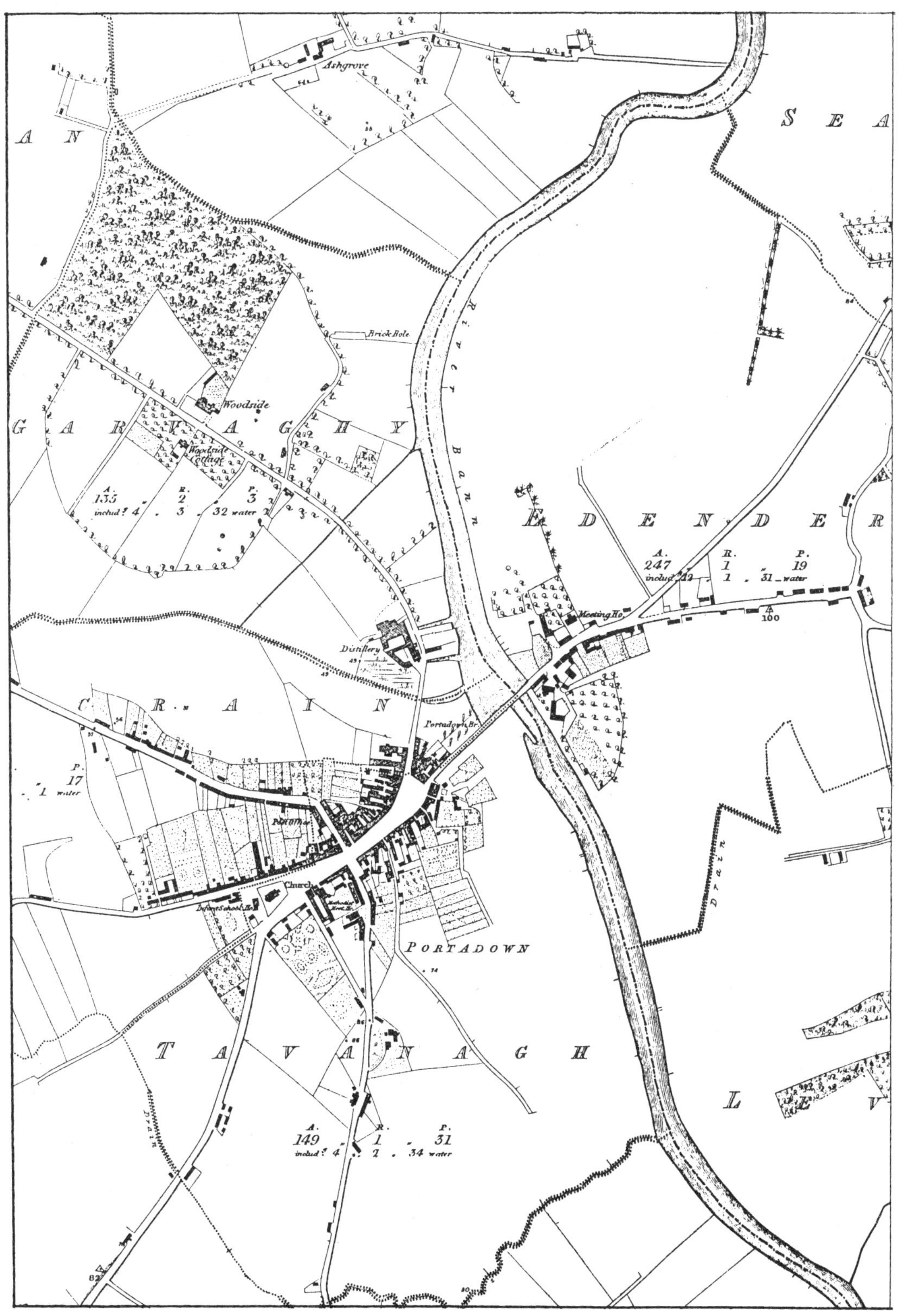

Map of Portadown from the first 6" O.S. maps, 1830s

summer the extensive flats on each side of the Bann are covered with numbers of black cattle and are surrounded with highly cultivated hills. These, combined with the air of business which is perceptible about the quay of Portadown, convey to the spectator a flourishing and fertile appearance.

River Port

The extreme breadth of the River Bann on the north side of Portadown bridge where the boats load and unload is 360 feet, and the average depth is 20 feet.

PRODUCTIVE ECONOMY

Port Dues

The port dues are collected by trustees, gentlemen and merchants of the town who were appointed to that office by the commissioners for carrying into effect an act of George IV Chapt. [blank] entitled "An act for providing for the lighting, cleansing and watching of market and other towns in Ireland." The proceeds of dues are applied to keep the quay in good repair, but the amount is very small owing to a private individual having a more commodious quay at which the same charges are made.

Imports and Exports in 1836

Imports for the year 1836: iron 250 tons, coal 600 tons, timber 500 tons, slates 200 tons, flour 50 tons, oatmeal 100 tons, total 1,700 tons.

Exports for the year 1836: wheat 2,250 tons, oats 2,500 tons, barley 250 tons, total 5,000 tons. Inclusive of the above were 90 tons of pork sent to Belfast on carts.

The imports are all for the consumption of the town. They are carried on in boats belonging to merchants of the town. There are 18 boats belonging to the town, varying from 45 to 60 tons burthen, [signed] T.C. McIlroy. Three-quarters of the timber is imported from Newry by the Newry Canal. The remainder is brought from Belfast through the Lagan Navigation Canal, Lough Neagh and the River Bann. 200 tons of coal are imported from Coalisland annually. The remainder of the imports are from Newry. There are a few direct importations of salt from Liverpool through the Newry Canal. Exclusive of the above, large quantities of merchandize are brought hither from Belfast on carts, viz. sugars, teas, hardware, tallow, woollen and cotton goods. There are no building docks.

Import Dues

Port or quay dues for wares discharged or shipped. Timber saw'd: for every boat of 5 tons and not exceeding 10 tons, 3d; for every boat of 10 and not exceeding 20 tons, 6d; for every boat exceeding 20 tons 1d [1s ?]. Turf: for every load not exceeding 50 guages, 8d; for every load exceeding 50 guages, 1d [1s ?]; for every load exceeding 100 guages, 1s 6d. For all other goods, wares or merchandise discharged or shipped not exceeding 5 tons, per ton 2d; exceeding 5 and not 10 tons, 1d ha'penny [?]; exceeding 10 and not 24 tons, 1s; exceeding 24 tons, 2s. Small boats laden with grain for the market are free of toll; every boatload of limestone 1s.

SOCIAL AND PRODUCTIVE ECONOMY

Habits and Occupations

There are no scientific or literary societies in Portadown. The inhabitants take up newspapers: The *Ulster Times* seems to be a favourite. The people have no amusements except in attending the fairs and markets held in Portadown and Lurgan.

Fairs and Markets

There is a very good weekly market in Portadown on Saturdays and a fair on the [blank] of every month.

Bank

There is a branch of the Ulster Bank which was established in 1836.

Table of Mills

[Table gives townland, proprietor, tenant, date built, dimensions and type of water wheel, fall of water, material of which made, number of pairs of stones or sets of scutches <skutches>, remarks].

Artabrackagh, Mrs Kelly, Armagh, James Robinson, 12 feet by 3 feet, breast, wood, one pair of stones, a very old stone building, slated.

Ballyfodrin, Honourable Charles Brownlow, John and Robert Hyde, 1834, wood and iron, 8 sets of scutches, worked by steam engine equal to 8 horse power.

Drumnakelly, Sir Francis McNaghten, John Cummins, 12 by 3 feet, breast, wood and iron, 1 pair of stones, 4 sets of scutches and 1 pair of rollers, a stone and mud house, right of water disputed by George Kipley.

Table of Schools

[Table of schools contains the following headings: name, situation and description, when established, income and expenditure, physical, intellectual and moral instruction, number of pupils subdivided by age, sex and religion, name and religion of master or mistress, date on which visited].

Derrycory, a neat cottage situated in the townland of Derrycory, established 1827; income: from the Reverend Charles Alexander 4 pounds per annum, 5 pounds per annum from pupils; intellectual instruction: Kildare and Hibernian Society Books; moral instruction, catechisms taught by the master on Thursday, Authorised Version of Scriptures read daily; number of pupils: males, 46 under 10 years of age, 16 from 10 to 15, a total of 62; females, 12 under 10 years of age, 28 from 10 to 15, 1 over 15, a total of 41; total number of pupils 103, 95 Established Church, 1 Presbyterian, 7 Roman Catholics; master James Atkinson, Established Church, visited 7th November 1837.

Breagh, a cottage in the townland of Breagh, established 1829; income: from the Reverend Charles Alexander 4 pounds, and an acre of ground from the Honourable Charles Brownlow, 10 pounds from pupils; intellectual instruction: Kildare Society's books; moral instruction: visited by the Reverend David Babbington, catechisms taught by the Reverend David Babbington, assisted by the master, on Wednesdays, Scripture lessons read daily; number of pupils: males, 53 under 10 years of age, 57 from 10 to 15, 5 over 15, a total of 115; females, 40 under 10 years of age, 12 from 10 to 15, a total of 52; total number of pupils 157 [crossed out], 50 Established Church, 14 Presbyterians, 40 Roman Catholics, 63 other denominations, Methodists, [author's insertion: some mistake ?]; master Joseph McGerr, Roman Catholic, visited 10 November 1837.

Scotch Street national school, a cottage in the townland of Richmond, established 1822; income from pupils 4 pounds; intellectual instruction: books of the Education Board; moral instruction: Scripture read on Monday, catechisms taught on Monday; number of pupils: males, 46 under 10 years of age, 10 from 10 to 15, 3 above 15, a total of 59; females, 22 under 10 years of age, 7 from 10 to 15, a total of 29; total number of pupils 88, 8 Established Church, 40 Presbyterians, 30 Roman Catholics, 10 other denominations, Methodists; master James Thomson, Presbyterian, visited 10 November 1837.

Drumgoose, a cottage in the townland of Drumgoose, established 1823; income: from the Reverend Charles Alexander 10 pounds and 1 and a half acres of ground, 5 pounds per annum from pupils; intellectual instruction: visited by the Reverend Charles Alexander and the Reverend David Babbington, Scriptures read daily, catechisms taught by the master daily; number of pupils: males, 39 under 10 years of age, 20 from 10 to 15, a total of 59; females, 14 under 10 years of age, 8 from 10 to 15, a total of 22; total number of pupils 81, 28 Established Church, 1 Presbyterian, 23 Roman Catholics, 29 other denominations, Methodists; master William Richards, Established Church, visited 9 November 1837.

Ballyworkan, a cottage in the townland of Ballyworkan <Ballyworkin>, established 1828; income: from the Reverend Charles Alexander 5 pounds per annum, 9 pounds per annum from pupils; intellectual instruction: Kildare Society books; moral instruction: visited by the Reverend Charles Irwin, catechism taught on Mondays by the master, assisted by the Reverend Charles Irwin, Authorised Version of Scriptures read daily; number of pupils: males, 28 under 10 years of age, 14 from 10 to 15, a total of 42; females, 22 under 10 years of age, 8 from 10 to 15, a total of 30; total number of pupils 72, 61 Established Church, 4 Presbyterians, 7 Roman Catholics; master Woolsley Hadden, Established Church, visited 21 November 1837, [signed] T.C. McIlroy.

Weather Journal kept in Portadown

[Weather between October 17 and November 27 1837, recorded each morning, noon and afternoon, with wind direction].

October: 17th, fine, fine, fine, west wind; 18th, fine, fine, fine, south west; 19th, fine, fine, fine, north; 20th, wet, wet, wet, south west; 21st, fair, fair, fair, west; 22nd, fair, fair, fair, west; 23rd, showery, showery, showery, west; 24th, showery, showery, showery, west; 25th, fair, fair, fair, west; 26th, showery, showery, showery, south west; 27th, showery, showery, showery, north; 28th, showery, showery, showery, north; 29th, fine, fine, fine, west; 30th, wet, wet, wet, west; 31st, showery, showery, showery, north west.

November: 1st, fair, fair, fair, north wind; 2nd, fair, fair, fair, north; 3rd, showery, showery, showery, south west; 4th, fine, fine, fine, north; 5th, fine, fine, fine, north; 6th, fair, fair, fair, west; 7th, fair, fair, fair, west; 8th, fair, fair, fair, south west; 9th, fine, fine, fine, north west; 10th, wet, wet, fine, changeable; 11th, fine, showery, showery, south; 12th, fine, fair, fair, north; 13th, wet, wet, wet, south; 14th, fine, wet, fair, north west; 15th, fine,

fine, fine, west; 16th, wet, wet, wet, south; 17th, fair, fair, fair, south; 18th, fair, fair, fair, north; 19th, fair, fair, fair, north; 20th, showery, showery, showery, north west; 21st, fair, fair, fair, north; 22nd, wet, wet, wet, south; 23rd, fair, fair, fair, south west, stormy; 24th, fair, fair, fair, north; 25th, fair, fair, fair, north; 26th, fair, fair, fair, north; 27th, fair, fair, fair, north, [signed] Thomas C. McIlroy, January 4 1838.

Memoir by Lieut G.A. Bennett, 20 February 1835

Natural State

Name

This parish in Armstrong's *Survey of the county* is spelt Drumcree, and in all other documents the same.

Locality

It is situated in the north east end of the county Armagh and in the barony of Oneiland West, and is bounded on the north west by the parish of Tartaraghan, on the north and on the north east by the Montiaghs <Montaghs>, on the east by Seagoe, on the south and south east by Kilmore and on the south west partly by Kilmore and partly by Upper Grange, a detached townland of the lordship of Newry. Its greatest length is 80 and a half English miles from its extreme south point near an old fort in Ballyworken townland to its most northern point in Muckery townland, where the River Bann is the boundary with the Montiaghs. Its greatest breadth is 4 miles from east to west. It contains 13,385 acres 2 roods 32 perches, divided into 65 townlands. Of these 2,486 acres are bog, 17 acres rocky ground, 52 acres of wood and 94 acres of the portion of the River Bann that is in this parish. There is no other water.

Natural Features

Hills

The country is generally low and may be considered as flat, especially the northern end which is nearly all bogland and which varies in altitude above the sea from 57 to 70 feet. The highest ground is nearly in the centre of the parish, in the townlands of Cornamucklagh, Richmond and Drumenagh. Cornamucklagh hill is 177 feet above the sea, Carrick hill in Richmond 159 feet and Drumenagh 160 feet. These hills have but little command over the adjoining country, the low ground about Cornamucklagh being about 110 feet. Besides these the hills in Canagolabeg (147 feet), Crocket's hill in Leganny (133 feet), Oak hill in Foy-Beg (141 feet), Farra hill in that townland (150 feet) and the hill in Kilmarerty (146 feet) are the principal. They are merely undulations of the ground and should scarcely be termed hills.

Rivers

There is no lake in the parish. The River Bann enters this parish about 1 and one eighth miles above Portadown bridge at its junction with the Newry Canal. For 8 and a half miles it becomes the boundary of the parish to the east and north, separating it from the parishes of Seagoe and the Montiaghs. It is navigable throughout, being of an average depth of 30 feet. It is on the line of communication between Lough Neagh and the Newry Canal, nearly, if not quite, a dead level from that canal to the lough. Its summer level is 47 feet, its average breadth 150 feet. It overflows its banks after heavy rains and in the winter the low meadow grounds, not only on its banks but in the interior of the parish, are always under water, nor does it seem practicable to prevent this periodical inundation until some method is taken to lower Lough Neagh.

The Cusher river enters from Kilmore parish in the south east, and is the eastern boundary of Ballyworken townland and parish for about three-quarters of a mile when it meets the Bann at the junction of the parishes of Kilmore, Seagoe and Drumcree.

The Toll water, a small and insignificant stream, becomes the boundary between this parish and Upper Grange for about half a mile. This river, as well as the Cusher, is nearly level as is also Ballibay river, a small stream which enters from Kilmore parish at the south west and, after being the western boundary of the parish for a mile, takes a north east direction and enters the Bann a few perches below Portadown bridge. From the want of a fall on these rivers there are no mills on them, except one on the last mentioned where the fall is obtained by damming up the river.

Bogs

The parish contains 2,480 acres of bog: the principal part is in the southern end in the townlands of Muckery, Derryniskin, Derrgal, Derrycaw, Derrymarfal. There is one large bog in the centre of the parish (Cornamucklagh bog) and another in the south in Ballyworkan townland, containing about

427 acres. Oak is the principal tree found in these bogs; fir is also found. The roots are in position as when growing, the trunks apparently broken off by violence. The bogs in the north vary from 57 to 73 feet. Cornamucklagh is 110 and Ballyworken 59 feet.

Woods

There are no woods in the parish, which altogether contains only 52 acres of forest trees, 21 of which are in Garvaghey townland, 20 in Mahon and 11 in Drumnakilly.

Natural History

Geology

The country in general is covered with a deep clay and few rocks project above the surface. Where they do project, they are found to be graywacke or greenstone.

Modern Topography

Town of Portadown

Portadown is said to be derived from Port-na-dun "the pool of the fort." It is situated in the south east end of the parish and on the River Bann. It is 2 miles from the south extremity of the parish, 5 from its northern and 4 from its western. It is on the high road from Belfast to Armagh, to which places there are excellent roads. The town is built on a rising ground above the river, about 200 yards from it and 38 feet above it. It is 68 miles from Dublin by Banbridge, to which place it is distant 8 miles. It is [blank miles] from Belfast, 9 to Armagh, and 5 to Lurgan. It contains a church or rather chapel of ease erected in 1826, which cost 1,300 pounds, 900 pounds of which were given by the Board of First Fruits and the remainder paid by the parish. It would accommodate from 400 to 500 persons.

It contains also a Methodist meeting house built by public subscription in 1832, which cost 1,200 pounds. There is a school taught in this house and there is also an infant school in the town, both are under the jursidiction of Lord Mandeville.

An old and narrow bridge connects the town with a number of houses built on the opposite bank of the river in Seagoe parish, on the road to Lurgan. It has been long contemplated and, I believe, is now decided that a new one is to be built, the estimated expense of which is 8,640 pounds. There is a tolerably good inn, and 2 coaches run daily through the town from Armagh to Belfast, passing through Lurgan.

Social and Productive Economy

Commerce, Markets and Fairs

Corn-factors have established this place as a depot from its facility of communication with England by the Newry Canal. In consequence, it is the grain market for the surrounding country. Coals, both English and Irish, are kept by merchants for the supply of the town and surrounding neighbourhood. Turf is obtained in abundance from the bogs in this parish and is brought up the river from the Montiaghs.

The regular market day is Saturday, though there are few days on which grain is not brought in. The town has a fair every third Saturday of every month, also one on Easter Monday, one on Whit Monday and one on the 13th November.

Local Government

A manor court is held on the second Monday of February, May, August and November. The seneschal is Charles Hunt, agent to Lord Mandeville. The petty sessions are held every Saturday; the presiding magistrates are T. Atkinson Esquire and Curran Woodhouse Esquire.

Dispensary

A dispensary, supported by Lord Mandeville, is exclusively for the use of his own tenants. He also maintains a surgeon to visit his tenantry at their houses.

Distillery

A little north of the town on the river is a distillery of about 9 years standing, the property of B. Smith and Co., who distil annually about 13,000 gallons.

Modern Topography

Village: Scotch Street

Scotch Street is a small village on the old road from Portadown to Armagh. It is 3 miles from the former place. It consists of but a few houses and contains a Methodist meeting house and a school.

Public Buildings: Portadown

Besides those already mentioned as belonging to the town, there is the parish church, a plain building in the south east end of Drumcree townland and nearly in the centre of the parish. It would contain about 600 persons. The ground on which this church stands is 97 feet above the level of the sea, and the top of the spire 207 feet. The other places of worship are a Methodist meeting house in Drumnakilly, Derryanvil and Timnakeel townlands and a Roman Catholic chapel, capable of containing about 800, in Silshion.

Gentlemen's Seats

The Glebe House in Cornalack townland and Ballyworken House, [blank] Popper Esquire, are the best houses in the parish and are surrounded by a few trees.

Manufactories and Mills

The distillery has already been mentioned as connected to the town of Portadown. It affords employment to about 100 persons. There are throughout the parish 4 corn mills turned by water and one by wind, 3 flax mills and a corn kiln. There is so little fall of water in the streams throughout this parish where mills do exist [that] the water is obtained by damming up and overflowing the adjoining meadows for 6 months in the year. From this want of water a flax mill is now building to be turned by steam. The remainder of the year the meadows are used for pasture. There is a tanyard in Clownagh townland, where 6 men are employed.

Communications

The principal road is from Portadown to Armagh, a new road (turnpike) passing within half a mile of Rich Hill. The roads to Dungannon, Tanderagee and Markethill are all in good repair and tolerably well laid out. The principal by-road is from Portadown to Loughgall, passing by Scotch Street, and there are numerous lanes in every direction. The only communications across the River Bann are by the bridge in Portadown, by a ferry called Robb's ferry, 4 miles below this bridge and by Rush's ferry a mile below the other. The latter is for foot passengers only.

ANCIENT TOPOGRAPHY

Forts

A few old forts still exist in different parts of the parish, but they contain nothing remarkable.

PRODUCTIVE ECONOMY

Newry Canal and Cultivation

The Newry Canal is of considerable benefit to this and the surrounding parishes as opening an export for grain. The parish is nearly all well cultivated except the bog tracts already mentioned, and the low grounds which are generally used as meadow.

SOCIAL ECONOMY

Dispensaries

Some of the northern townlands obtain medicine and attendance from the Loughgall dispensary, and there is another established in Portadown for the tenantry of Lord Mandeville and supported solely by him.

Religion

The inhabitants are nearly equally divided between the Protestant and Catholic religion.

Schools and Poor

Schools are established throughout the parish in the following townlands: 1 in Richmond townland in the village of Scotch Street, male and female, attendance 50; 1 in Drumgoose townland, partly supported by the Society for Discountenancing Vice and partly by the Reverend Mr Alexander, the rector of Drumcree; the attendance is about 46; 2 schools already mentioned in the town of Portadown and 1 in Mullentin, all supported by Lord Mandeville; 1 in Derryconey townland, attendance about 40; 1 in Derryvane townland, attendance about 40; 1 in Breagh townland, partly supported by C. Brownlough Esquire and partly by the Reverend Mr Alexander, attendance about 100; 1 in Drumherriff where the attendance is about 100; 1 in Ballyworken townland. There is no provision for the poor, the aged or the infirm except the small amount collected on Sundays in the churches.

Habits of the People

In the north end of the parish the houses are nearly all mud and look most wretched, but towards the centre and south they assume a better appearance. Food and dress are the same as in the surrounding country. Their fuel is turf, of which there is an abundance. A few houses belonging to the most opulent farmers consist of 1-storey and are slated, but except those in the town of Portadown and village of Scotch Street there are probably not a dozen. The remainder in general consist of the ground floor divided into 2 or 3 apartments, and are thatched. The magistrates presiding in the parish are Curran Woodhouse Esquire of Mount Prospect and Corcraine townland, and T. Atkinson Esquire, but William Hancock Esquire of Lurgan occasionally presides at the bench in Portadown.

There is no prevailing name or any peculiar custom, and the language of the people is generally a tolerably pure English with a few Scotticisms and rather a Scottish accent. Weaving is followed as an occasional employment in every townland. The market for it is Lurgan. This, with agricultural pursuits, occupy the men; the women add spinning to their domestic duties.

Productive Economy

Farms

The farms vary in size from 2 to 60 acres, old leases being from 14 to 16s per acre, new leases from 25 to 35s; 28s per English acre would perhaps be the mean throughout the parish.

Manures and Proprietors

Bog when set for cutting for sale fetches 6 pounds per acre in Ballyworken townland. The greater part of the parish belongs to C. Brownlow Esquire, who possesses 24 townlands. Lord Mandeville is proprietor of 11. The remaining 30 are divided among different proprietors, which will be seen in the descriptive remarks on each townland. Lime is the principal manure, mixed with that of cattle. It costs to lay down lime in a field 1s per barrel of 4 bushels.

Apples

The apples obtained from the numerous orchards in the parish are generally of an inferior quality, though the young trees now planting promise a better description. The greater part of the produce is exported to England.

Modern Topography

General Appearance and Scenery

Upon the whole the parish is rich and prosperous. In the centre and south the houses, though of mud, are dashed and whitewashed, and when seen through the orchards with which nearly every house is surrounded, the scenery, though of a home, is of a very pleasing description.

Townland Divisions

Aughanergill Townland

The parish is divided into 65 townlands viz. Aughanergill, pronounced Aghaner[stress]gill, but is generally called by the inhabitants Corglass. Proprietor is Lord Dungannon, agent R. Tebb Esquire, farms from 2 to 13 acres, rent from 12 to 16 [pounds ?], soil good and well cultivated, lime for manure brought from Anahugh townland, parish of Kilmore, houses chiefly mud. County cess 3 pounds 10s. The nearest market Portadown, distant 3 and three-quarter miles. Medicine and attendance from Loughgall dispensary on Monday and Friday each week, by tickets from subscribers. Area 93 acres 1 perch.

Cushenagh Townland

Cushenagh, pronounced Cushany, proprietor C. Brownlow of Lurgan, agent W. Hancock Esquire, Lurgan. A hill in this townland 122 feet above the sea, farms from 2 to 10 acres, old leases about 16s per acre, new 28s. Market Portadown, distant 4 miles, county cess 3 pounds 9 shillings, area 83 acres 2 roods 35 perches.

Annagouragh Townland

Annagouragh, pronounced Anago[stress]ra, proprietor C. Brownlow, agent W. Hancock Esquire. Farms from 5 to 20 acres, rent 30s per acre, new leases, contains 4 acres of bog, county cess 5 pounds 10s. [Market] Portadown, 2 and a half miles distant. [Area] 92 acres 2 roods 17 perches.

Cohair Townland

Cohair, so pronounced. Proprietor C. Brownlow Esquire, agent W. Hancock. Farms from 3 to 25 acres, new leases at 28s per acre. Portadown is 3 miles distant. County cess is 4 pounds 4 shillings, area 110 acres 2 roods 25 perches.

Kingarve Townland

Kingarve, so pronounced, contains 82 acres of bog. Proprietor C. Brownlow, agent W. Hancock, farms from 6 to 30 acres, rent 26s to 28s. Portadown 3 miles distant. Area 180 acres 17 perches.

Diviny Townland

Diviny, pronounced Div[short stress]in[long stress]y[short stress], proprietor C. Brownlow Esquire, agent W. Hancock Esquire. Farms from 5 to 30 acres, rent 28s to 30s. Contains the village of Scotch Street, in which is a corn mill and kiln. The mill is only used for the 6 months from 1 April to 30 September, as the land which is kept flooded during this period is used as meadow the other 6 months. There is also a windmill in the south end of the town and for corn. Portadown is 3 and a half miles distant. County cess 7 pounds, area 157 acres 1 rood 13 perches.

Richmond Townland

Richmond or Richmount, proprietor C. Brownlow Esquire, agent W. Hancock Esquire. Carrick hill is 159 feet above the sea. Farms from 5 to 30 acres, old leases 14s to 18s, new 28s to 30s. There is a national school in Scotch Street, partly in this townland, average attendance 50. The schoolmaster receives 8 pounds per annum from the board and 1d a week from each scholar. Contains a Methodist meeting house, built by subscription in 1829, would hold 100 persons. Houses are generally stone. Portadown is 3 miles distant. [Area] 123 acres 1 rood 13 perches.

Legannagh Townland

Legannagh, pronounced Leg[long stress]an[short stress]ny[short stress]. Proprietor is C. Brownlow, agent W. Hancock. Crocket's hill is 133 feet above the sea. Farms from 4 to 13 acres, mostly old leases at 15s per acre. Houses generally stone. Portadown is 2 and a half miles distant. [Area] 58 acres 5 perches.

Cornamucklagh Townland

Cornamucklagh, so pronounced. Proprietors C. Brownlow Esquire, agent W. Hancock. A hill in this townland is 177 feet above the sea, the highest in the parish. Contains 50 acres of bog, farms from 3 to 12 acres, rent 28s. Houses are of stone. Portadown is 2 and a half miles distant. [Area] 130 acres 38 perches.

Annakeera Townland

Annakeera, proprietor Mr Strongman of Waterford, agent C. Wakefield. Farms from 2 to 30 acres, old leases 14s, new 28s. Portadown is 2 miles distant. Contains 36 acres of bog, [area] 150 acres 2 roods 21 perches.

Clanmartin Townland

Clanmar[long stress]tin, proprietor P. Greer of Randlestown, agent J. Wilson of Lurgan. Farms from 4 to 18 acres except Mr Bell's, which is 37. Rent 14s to 21s, houses mud. Portadown 3 miles distant. [Area] 97 acres 2 roods 2 perches.

Clanmola Townland

Clanmo[stress]la is glebe land, Reverend C. Alexander, rector. Farms from 3 to 16 acres, rent 20s to 25s. Portadown is 2 miles distant. [Area] 60 acres 2 roods 15 perches.

Druminalduff Townland

Called Druminally[long stress on last vowel], proprietor is Mr Strongman, agent is C. Wakefield of Moyallen. Farms from 4 to 20 acres, rent 27s 6d, houses generally stone. Portadown 1 and a half miles distant. [Area] 96 acres 3 roods 15 perches.

Drumgoose Townland

Drumgoose, glebe land. Contains Drumgoose cottage, the residence of the curate of the parish. Farms from 2 to 16 acres, rent 30s, which if paid on the appointed day is subject to an abatement of 3s in the pound. This arrangement is made for all the glebe lands under the Reverend Mr Alexander. Houses chiefly mud. Contains a school under the Society for Discountenancing Vice, average attendance 46. The schoolmaster receives 10 pounds a year from Mr Alexander, 1 and a half acres of land and a house rent free. The society allow him 7 pounds per annum and some trifle from the scholars. Portadown is 2 miles [distant]. [Area] 5 acres 2 roods 37 perches.

Drumcree Townland

Drumcree, proprietor Captain Acheson of Portnorris. Farms from 2 to 30 acres; Captain Acheson holds about 90 himself and has built a large and commodious range of stabling and offices. Rent from 30s to 40s. Contains a church with a spire. The spire was added in 1800. Portadown is half a mile distant. [Area] 62 acres 17 perches.

Cornalack Townland

Cornalack, glebe land and contains the Glebe House, a good plain building. The rector holds it all in his own hands except 28 acres which are let at 25s. Portadown is 1 and a half miles distant. [Area] 21 acres 24 perches.

Selshon Townland

Selshon, proprietor Lord Mandeville, agent C. Hunt of Moyallen. Contains 13 acres of bog, farms 3 to 20 acres, rent 24s. It contains a Roman Catholic chapel which holds about 800. It is the only Roman Catholic chapel in the parish. Contains a school supported by the scholars alone. Portadown is about 1 mile distant. [Area] 172 acres 22 perches.

Muckery Townland

Muckery, property of Miss Reid, Dublin. Contains 119 acres of bog. Houses mud, rent 17s to 20s. Portadown 5 and a quarter miles [distant]. 22 acres

9 perches of water, [area] 349 acres 2 roods 6 perches.

Derryniskin Townland

Derryniskin, proprietor [blank] Burgess of Castle Caulfield. Farms from 10 to 20 acres, rent 15s, contains 144 acres of bog, houses mud. Portadown is distant 4 and a quarter miles. [Area] 214 acres 2 roods 18 perches.

Derryall Townland

Derryall, proprietor Mr Wallace, Captain Acheson of Portnorris middle landlord, who sublets it very high. Houses mud. It is bounded on the east by the River Bann, contains 221 acres of bog. Portadown is distant 4 and a quarter miles. 7 acres 2 roods 28 perches of water, [area] 363 acres 1 rood.

Derrycaw Townland

Derrycaw, proprietor C. Brownlow, agent Mr Hancock Esquire. Contains 78 and a half acres of bog, houses mud, new leases 20s per acre, old 10s. Portadown is 3 and three-quarter miles distant. [Area] 172 acres 2 roods 17 perches.

Derrymacfall Townland

Derrymacfall, proprietor Mr Burley Esquire of Carrick. Let at 20s per acre, contains 315 acres of bog and 9 acres 3 roods 24 perches of water. Portadown is 3 and three-quarter miles distant. [Area] 431 acres 3 roods 38 perches.

Derrybroghus Townland

Derrybroghus, proprietor C. Brownlow, agent W. Hancock. Contains 82 acres of bog and 14 acres 2 roods 5 perches of water, rent 26s. Robb's pottery in this townland. Portadown is 3 and a half miles [distant]. [Area] 252 acres 2 roods 6 perches.

Derrycorey Townland

Derrycorey, property of the heirs of the late H. Ruston Esquire of Ardee. Contains 53 acres of bog, 15 acres 3 roods 13 perches of water. It contains a school, formerly under the Kildare Street Society, now the master is paid by the scholars alone; average attendance 40. Portadown is 2 and three-quarter miles distant. [Area] 196 acres 2 roods 2 perches.

Derryvane Townland

Derryvane, glebe land, contains 101 acres of bog. Rent 25s to 30s. A schoolhouse, formerly under the Kildare Street Society, now supported by the scholars alone; average attendance 40. Portadown 3 and a quarter miles [distant]. [Area] 190 acres 1 rood 33 perches.

Derrymattry Townland

Derrymattry, proprietor [blank] Dobbin Esquire, Armagh. Rent 25s, contains 3 and a half acres of bog, houses mud. Portadown 2 and three-quarter miles distant. [Area] 118 acres 3 roods 18 perches.

Drummanagh Townland

Drummanagh, proprietors [blank] Craig Esquire and Miss Waugh of Armagh, rent 17s to 20s. Portadown is distant 2 and a quarter miles. Nearly the highest ground in the parish, 160 feet above the sea. [Area] 160 acres 2 roods 16 perches.

Kilmagarnish Townland

Kilmagarnish is glebe land, rent 25s to 30s, houses are of mud. Portadown is 2 and three-quarter miles distant. [Area] 177 acres 23 perches.

Corbracky Townland

Corbracky, proprietor [blank] Moorewood Esquire of Bushmills and [blank] McCann Esquire. Rent 27s to 30s, contains 78 acres of bog, houses mud. Portadown 2 and a half miles distant. [Area] 302 acres 1 rood 32 perches.

Derryanvill Townland

Derryanvill, proprietor [blank] Thompson Esquire of Dublin. Rent 28s, contains 51 acres of bog, houses mud. A Methodist chapel in this townland, would hold about 200, and 3 acres 2 roods 15 perches of water. [Area] 217 acres 1 rood.

Derrycarran Townland

Derrycarran, Lord Dungannon, proprietor, Mr Cullen of Armagh a middle landlord from whom the tenants hold. Contains about 158 acres of bog, houses mud. Portadown is distant 3 and a half miles. [Area] 251 acres 2 roods 10 perches.

Drumlellum Townland

Drumlellum, proprietor C. Brownlow Esquire, agent W. Hancock Esquire. The largest farm is Groove Hill, 100 acres at 23s. Farms in the south are about 16 acres at 13s. Contains about 55 acres of bog. To Portadown 4 miles. County cess 7 pounds, [area] 231 acres 38 perches.

Derrylettiffe Townland

Derrylettiffe, proprietor C. Brownlow Esquire, agent W. Hancock Esquire. Cess at 25s, farms 2 to 7 acres, houses mud, county cess 9 pounds. To Portadown 4 miles. Mulholland's hill is 125 feet above the sea. [Area] 182 acres 17 perches.

Timnakeel Townland

Timnakeel, proprietor C. Brownlow Esquire, agent W. Hancock Esquire. At the south east end is the village of Scotch Street, a few houses among which is one Methodist chapel. Farms from 10 to 30 acres, average rent 20s, county cess 9 pounds, houses stone. To Portadown 3 and a half miles. [Area] 199 acres 23 perches.

Drumkerriffe Townland

Drumkerr[long stress]iffe, proprietor C. Brownlow Esquire, agent W. Hancock Esquire. Farms from 12 to 30 acres, rent 23s to 29s. Mullen's hill is 129 feet above the sea. County cess 6 pounds. A school in this townland is supported by the pupils. To Portadown 4 miles. [Area] 136 acres 1 rood 20 perches.

Roughan Townland

Roughan, pronounced Ruffan, proprietor C. Brownlow Esquire. Barn hill farm is 71 acres at 34s, the rest are from 2 to 7 acres, houses are stone. Barn hill is 146 feet above the sea. County cess 11 pounds 13s. To Portadown 4 miles. [Area] 228 acres 1 rood 19 perches.

Timulkenny Townland

Timulkenny, pronounced Tumblikenny. The agent is T. Hazleton Esquire, Lurgan. Largest farm is Spring Lane, 34 acres at 14s, the remainder are under 13, rent 33s, houses stone, county cess 4 pounds. To Portadown 4 and a half miles. Proprietors heirs of the late T. Hall of Lurgan. [Area] 54 acres 23 perches.

Cananeale Townland

Can[short stress]aneale[long stress], proprietor as in Timulkeeny, rent 33s, county cess 6 pounds, houses of stone and mud and comfortable appearance. The highest ground is 130 feet above the sea. County cess 6 pounds, [area] 113 acres 1 rood 3 perches.

Canagolabeg Townland

Canagol[stress]abeg, proprietor C. Brownlow Esquire. Largest farm is 25 acres at 14s, old lease, county cess 6 pounds 18s. To Portadown 4 and a half miles. The centre of the townland is 147 feet above the sea. [Area] 133 acres 1 rood 15 perches.

Foybeg Townland

Foybeg, property of Miss Waugh of Armagh, lets at 30s. Oak hill is 141 feet above the sea. It contains about 29 acres of bog, county cess is 4 pounds. To Portadown 4 miles. [Area] 214 acres 4 perches.

Foymore Townland

Foymore, proprietor C. Brownlow Esquire, contains 88 acres of bog. Foymount farm is 60 acres, Mr Carrick. To Portadown 4 miles. Highest ground at the south east is 140 feet above the sea. [Area] 216 acres 31 perches.

Breagh Townland

Breagh, proprietors C. Brownlow Esquire and Mr Boomer of Belfast. Farms from 3 to 20 acres, contains 22 acres of bog. A school to which Mr Brownlow gives 1 acre of ground rent free and Mr Alexander 2 pounds per annum; the remainder is paid by the scholars. Houses mud. To Portadown 3 and a half miles. County cess 9 pounds, [area] 240 acres 1 rood 17 perches.

Dromalis Townland

Dromalis, proprietor C. Brownlow Esquire. Largest farm is 24 acres, remainder are small, county cess 4 pounds. To Portadown 3 and a half miles. [Area] 88 acres 1 rood 9 perches.

Drumnevin Townland

Drumnevin, proprietor C. Brownlow Esquire. The largest farm is 43 acres at 24s, the remainder are small, houses stone. Highest ground 135 feet above the sea. To Portadown 3 and a half miles. County cess 3 pounds 16s, [area] 70 acres 1 rood 20 perches.

Farra Townland

Farra, proprietor C. Brownlow Esquire, farms from 10 to 30 acres, rent 20s, county cess 4 pounds. Farra hill 150 feet above the sea. To Portadown it is 3 and a half miles. [Area] 84 acres 3 roods 26 perches.

Ballyfodrin Townland

Ballyfodrin, pronounced Ballyfod[long stress]-rin[short stress], proprietor C. Brownlow Esquire, about 15 acres of rock and furze, farms small, the largest is 20 acres at 25s, the proprietor of which, T. Hyde, is about erecting a steam engine flax mill. County cess 5 pounds 11s, [area] 101 acres 10 perches.

Drumnasoo Townland

Drumnasoo, proprietor Mrs Cope of Loughgall, agent John Hardie of Loughgall, farms from 5 to 15 acres, houses mud. 2 and a half miles to Portadown. [Area] 221 acres 39 perches.

Mullintine Townland

Mullintine, proprietor Lord Mandeville, agent [blank] Hunt of Gilford <Guilford>, farms from 4 to 36 acres, rent 25s. Contains a school under Lord Mandeville's superintendence. Mean distance to Portadown 2 and a half miles. 2 roods 37 perches of water in a mill dam, [area] 276 acres 3 roods 22 perches.

Kilmarerty Townland

Kilmarerty, proprietor Lord Mandeville, but let for 999 years to the heirs of the late Mr Jones, whose agent is Mr Moore of Belfast. Contains about 7 acres of bog, the farms from 4 to 40 acres, rent 25s to 29s. Mean distance to Portadown 1 and a half miles. [Area] 326 acres 1 rood 30 perches.

Corcullentramore Townland

Corcullentramore, proprietor Lord Mandeville, farms from 5 to 30 acres, rent 25s. Contains 50 acres of bog, for which tenants are charged 8s per acre for cutting fuel for their own consumption. 1 corn mill and flax mill in the south east end of the townland, diameter of wheel 14 feet, fall of water 10 and a half feet. [Blank] hill in this townland 133 feet above the sea. 5 acres 2 roods 17 perches of a mill dam. [Area] 225 acres 2 roods 7 perches.

Corcullentrabeg Townland

Corcullentrabeg, proprietor Lord Mandeville, farms from 5 to 30 acres, rent 25s, contains 32 acres of bog. Mean distance to Portadown 1 and a half miles. [Area] 161 acres 2 roods 22 perches.

Clownagh Townland

Clownagh, proprietor Lord Mandeville, farms 4 to 12 acres, rent 25s. In the south west of the townland is a tanyard; 6 men are usually employed. Contains 22 acres of bog on the south east, 13 acres on the west, [area] 295 acres 2 roods 22 perches.

Baltylum Townland

Baltylum, proprietor Sir F. McNaughten, agent Mr Evans. Farms small, rent 30s to 38s, houses mud. A manor court is held every sixth Thursday in F. Lutton's public house, seneschal Curran Woodhouse Esquire. It contains 6 acres of bog, [area] 145 acres 3 roods 35 perches.

Tavenagh Townland

Tavenagh, chief proprietor Lord Mandeville. It contains the town and town parks, sublet at various rates, see Towns for further description of this townland. 4 acres 2 roods 34 perches of water, [area] 149 acres 1 rood 31 perches.

Corcrain Townland

Corcrain, proprietor Lord Mandeville. Contains part of the town and town parks, Mr Wakefield, Moyallen, holds the greater part, see Towns. 1 acre 1 rood 1 perch is water, [area] 200 acres 1 rood 17 perches.

Garvaghey Townland

Garvaghey, proprietor Lord Mandeville, it is held by 5 tenants at 38s. Contains the distillery already mentioned. About 21 acres of wood and 3 acres nearly of River Bann, 4 acres 3 roods 32 perches water, [area] 135 acres 21 roods 3 perches.

Ballyoran Townland

Ballyo[stress]ran, proprietor Lord Mandeville, farms from 3 to 40 acres, rent 20s to 30s. Mean distance to Portadown 1 mile. [Area] 136 acres 1 rood 6 perches.

Balynagone Townland

Ballynagone, part is churchland and except 1 farm of 40 acres is let to tenants at will at 25s. Contains about 37 acres of bog and 15 acres of the Bann river, [area] 127 acres 4 perches.

Annagh Townland

Annagh, proprietor Lord Mandeville, farms from 8 to 20 acres, rent 20s to 30s, contains 6 acres of the River Bann. Is three-quarters of a mile south of Portadown, [area] 236 acres 2 roods 3 perches.

Ballyworkan Townland

Ballyworkan, head proprietor Mrs Cope, let at 2s 6d per acre to Mrs Kelly of Armagh, farms from 5 to 20 acres, rent 26s to 30s. The bogland is let for cutting for sale at 6 pounds per acre. There are 422 acres of bog, 5 of marsh and 1 plantation. Contains a small school supported by the scholars. [Area] 978 acres 30 perches.

Drumnakelly Townland

Drumnakelly, the same proprietor as Ballyworkan, farms 5 to 20 acres, rent 26s to 30s. Contains a small corn and flax mill, and a Methodist chapel built in 1828. 11 acres are wood and 21 are spent bog. About 2 miles to Portadown. [Area] 484 acres 2 roods 23 perches.

Artebracca Townland

Artebracca, proprietor Sir F. McNaughten, held from Mrs Cope at 2s 6d per acre, farms 5 to 20 acres, rent 26s to 50s, contains 41 acres of bog. There is a small corn mill at the east side. The water wheel is 12 feet in diameter, an undershot wheel. 3 miles from Portadown. [Area] 547 acres 1 rood 15 perches.

Mahon Townland

Mahon, proprietor Sir H. McNaughten, farms from 5 to 20 acres, rent 20s to 26s, contains 20 acres of wood. About 1 mile from Portadown. [Area] 291 acres 17 perches.

Boundaries of Townlands

The boundaries of each townland are described in the Name Books, [signed] George A. Bennett, 20 November 1835.

Parish of Eglish, County Armagh

Notes towards a Memoir by Thomas McIlroy, January 1838

NATURAL STATE AND NATURAL FEATURES

Locality

The parish of Eglish is situated in the western side of the county of Armagh and north west of the city of Armagh. It is in the baronies of Armagh and Tiranny. It is bounded on the north by the county of Tyrone, on the east by part of the parish of Clonfeacle and the parishes of Armagh and Grange, on the west by the county of Tyrone and on the south by the parishes of Lisnadil, Derrynoose and Tynan. Its extreme length is 5 and a half miles and extreme breadth 4 and a half. Its content is 10,575 acres 1 rood 17 perches, including 11 acres 2 roods 12 perches of water, [blank] of which are uncultivated, and it is valued at [blank] pounds to the county cess.

Hills

The hills in this part of the parish of Eglish are not very highly cultivated. There is a gradual fall in a north east direction. The hills are connected in ridges which run north and south. Their average height is 250 feet above the level of the sea, and the lowest ground in this part of the parish is along the banks of the River Blackwater, 59 feet above the sea.

Lakes and Rivers

Lakes: none in this part of the parish. The River Blackwater separates this part of the parish from the county of Tyrone. It runs nearly due north for 2 and a quarter miles, then takes a south east by east direction for 3 and a half miles. Its average breadth is 100 feet and it is from 1 to 5 feet in depth. It rises in the county of Tyrone. It is not navigable in this parish. It is usefully situated for drainage and water power. There are no rapids of any consequence along this part of the parish. The general fall of the river south of Battleford bridge is 2 feet in the mile. When it passes the bridge the fall increases to 50 feet in the 2 next miles. The scenery of the banks is picturesque and beautiful. In the neighbourhood of Benburb, and from thence to Battleford bridge, the banks are steep. At Benburb the bed of the river is rocky and hollowed out into innumerable small basins. The remaining part of it has a gravelly bed.

MODERN TOPOGRAPHY

Towns

None in this part of the parish.

Bridges

Battleford bridge, over the River Blackwater 2 miles west of Benburb, is built of whinstone and limestone. It is 104 feet long and 25 feet broad. It consists of 4 semicircular arches, including the parapet walls. Expense of building or when built not known.

Benburb bridge over the River Blackwater close to Benburb: it is built of limestone and is 65 feet long and 25 feet broad. It consists of 2 arches, semicircular. There are 9 bridges in this part of the parish over the Ulster Canal, each of which consists of 1 arch, 14 feet long and 14 feet broad. They are built of limestone. They were erected in 1836, cost defrayed by the Ulster Canal Company.

Communications

There are no main roads through this part of the parish, except one from Benburb to Caledon. It runs in a southerly direction for 2 miles; it is not a well laid out road. It is kept in repair at the expense of the county. There are several by-roads also, which are kept in repair by the county.

Canal

The Ulster Canal runs through this part of the parish for 5 and three-quarter miles, close to the bed of the River Blackwater. Its average breadth is 25 feet and depth 5 feet.

General Appearance and Scenery

The general appearance of this part of the parish is wild and uncultivated. The hills are steep and the cottages are not numerous. The only picturesque part is in the neighbourhood of Benburb.

PRODUCTIVE ECONOMY

Table of Mills

[Table gives townland, proprietor, tenant, when built, dimensions and type of water wheel, fall of water, material of machinery, number of pairs of stones and sets of scutches <skutches>, remarks].

Tullymore estate, proprietor Bond McGeogh Esquire, tenant David McMullan, 3 mills: [1st] water wheel 16 feet diameter by 4 feet breadth, breast wheel, fall of water 7 feet, wooden machinery, 2 pair of stones, a good stone house, slated; [2nd] 1834, water wheel 14 feet diameter by 3 feet 6 inches breadth, breast wheel, fall of water 7 feet, wooden machinery, 8 stocks and 2 rollers, a good stone house, slated; [3rd] 1807, water wheel 16 feet diameter by 4 feet breadth, breast wheel, fall of water 7 feet, machinery of wood and iron, 1 pair of shears, a hammer and bellows, a good stone house, slated.

Maydown, proprietor Thomas Jackson Esquire, tenant Thomas Ayr; 1800, water wheel 16 feet diameter by 5 feet breadth, undershot, fall of water 7 feet, machinery of wood and iron, 8 sets of scutches, 1 set of rollers, a good stone house, slated.

Carrickaness, proprietor Leonard Dobbin, M.P. (agent for the Ashmore legatees), tenant Richard Cross, 2 mills: [1st] 1835, water wheel 15 feet 6 inches diameter by 2 feet 9 inches breadth, breast wheel, fall of water 7 feet, machinery of wood, 1 pair of rollers, a stone house, slated, close to the River Blackwater; [2nd] 1806, water wheel 15 feet diameter by 2 feet breadth, breast wheel, fall of water 7 feet, machinery of wood and iron, 1 pair of stones and 1 fanning machine; an old stone house, slated, close to the River Blackwater.

Parish of Forkhill, County Armagh

Notes by George Scott and Another, 1837

MODERN TOPOGRAPHY

Village of Forkhill

The village of Forkhill [is] situated in the townland of Shean, about 7 miles from Newry in a south westerly direction. It contains about 10 1-storey houses, of which 4 are slated; 15 2-storey houses, 11 of which are slated. The only public buildings are a Methodist meeting house, market house and mill. The village is in a wild district of country and not very likely to improve. A short distance to the north of the town on the Belleek road there is a church and a range of buildings consisting of their schoolhouse.

Church

The church was erected in 1767, principally at the expense of the late Richard Jackson. There are 26 seats, which would accommodate 6 persons each. There is also a small gallery in which there are a few forms. Dimensions 72 feet by 22. Average number attend on Sunday 70. The church is in good repair, situated in the townland of Shean. It is a plain building, neat and substantial.

SOCIAL ECONOMY

Schools

The range of building[s] in the townland of Shean, which is used as schoolhouses, was built for the purpose it is now applied to, the expenses paid by the late Richard Jackson Esq. By his will there is an annual sum of 350 pounds allotted to the support of schools on his estate. In the male school there are: male department, boys 120, girls 10, total 130, Protestants 80, Catholics 50, master a Protestant; the master receives 40 pounds a year from the sum appropriated to the support of schools by the will of the late Mr Jackson. Female department: girls 84, Protestants 25, Catholics 59, total 84; mistress a Methodist, receives 20 pounds a year from the above mentioned fund; over 15 years of age 30, over 10 years 39, under 10 years 15, total 84. Infant department: girls 60, boys 5, total 65, Protestants 15, Catholics 50; mistress a Protestant and receives 15 pounds a year from the same fund.

MODERN TOPOGRAPHY

Mill

In the village of Forkhill, it belongs to John Bellew. Diameter of the wheel 15 feet, breadth of wheel 2 feet 10 inches, fall of water 7 feet, is a breast wheel. There are kilns adjoining the mill belonging to the same person.

Market House

A small wretched building, erected about the year 1800 at the expense of Susanah Barton, dimensions 40 feet by 21 feet.

Methodist Chapel

Erected by subscription, cost about 30 pounds, dimensions 33 feet by 16 feet, would accommodate about 100 persons. There are not any seats. The house is of the plainest description, being merely 4 walls and a slated roof.

SOCIAL ECONOMY

School

[In another hand] In the townland of Carrigans there is a school at which there are at present 65 pupils, 58 males and 7 females. They are all Catholics but one. The school was established in the present year (1837) and is supported entirely by the contributions of the scholars.

Dispensary

There is a dispensary in the townland of Shanroe, which is open during 3 days in the week.

Parish of Jonesborough, County Armagh

Notes on Modern Topography by G. Scott

MODERN TOPOGRAPHY

Hamlet of Jonesborough

The hamlet of Jonesborough is situated half in the townland of Edenappa and Foughill Otra. It is rapidly going to ruin. In this place there is an unfinished chapel and old barracks now unoccupied, merely serving as a barn. The military have been withdrawn from the barracks about 12 or 14 years. There are 28 wretched 1-storey houses, 6 of which are slated; 5 2-storey houses, all slated.

Chapel

[The] chapel is not finished, built and expenses paid by subscription. [Ground plan, main dimensions 45, 24 and 21 feet, rectangular shape with projection at one side].

arish of Keady, County Armagh

Jotes on Modern Topography by John Heather, 6 March 1838

ODERN TOPOGRAPHY

orn Mill

ize of wheel of this mill is 18 feet in diameter, 4 eet across the buckets, 20 feet fall of water. There s a good supply of water both in winter and ummer. It is a breast wheel.

leach Mills

1] Size of wheel is 32 feet in diameter, 6 and a half cross the buckets, 24 fall of water. It is a breast vheel.

[2] Size of wheel 22 feet in diameter, 5 feet cross the buckets, 18 feet fall of water, breast vheel.

[3] Size of wheel is 18 feet in diameter, 4 and a alf feet across the buckets, 24 fall of water, breast heel.

[4] There is another mill close to the former, hich is a bleach mill, the size of which is the same s the former.

The 4 former mills belong to the one person and n the one stream. They have a plentiful supply of vater in winter, and in summer the stream comes om Aughnagurgan lough and has a good fall all e way.

This mill is a bleach mill: the wheel is 30 feet in iameter, 6 across the buckets, 20 feet fall of vater; it is a breast wheel. This person has another ill quite close to the former, the size of which is e same [as] those 2 last mentioned mills, and on e same stream as the former, and as well supplied vith water, there being no stoppage.

hapel

his building has an old appearance and is not in ny way remarkable for its architectural appearnce. It was built in the year 1804. The congregaon is large, but it is only capable of containing 00. The sum it cost I could not ascertain, nor how at sum was raised, but I rather supposed from oluntary contributions.

chool

his school, situate in the townland of Corran, is st established and contains 9 boys and 3 girls, all f whom are Catholics. It is under no board of eduation nor receives no aid from private contributions. The school house is a cabin. The mistress receives 8d per month from each pupil.

Mill

The bleach <blach> mill, situate in the townland of Dundrum, is a low dilapidated building. The size of the wheel is 12 feet diameter, 4 feet across the buckets, 28 feet fall of water; it is a breast wheel.

Seceders Meeting House

Seceders meeting house in the townland of Tullynamalloge. There are no galleries and in the aisle <isle> there are 52 seats. It is capable of containing about 500. There is a large congregation. It has lately gone under repair which cost 180 pounds. It was given by the members belonging to the meeting. It could not be ascertained when it was built, nor the cost, as it has been there time immemorial and has gone under a great number of repairs from time to time.

Notes on Modern Topography by M.M. Kertland, February 1838

Appearance of Keady

Keady is situated in the parish of the same name, in the diocese of Armagh and province of Ulster. The road from Dublin to Armagh passes through it. It is 6 Irish miles from the latter and 58 from the former. Its greatest length is not more than one-third of an English mile. Surrounded as it is by small hills it cannot be seen from any great distance. From the top of any of these hills it has the appearance of a handful of houses thrown into the valley, without much regularity as to size, materials or relative position.

Houses

There are about 250 houses in the town: of these 140 are thatched, the remainder are slated. 3 houses are 3-storeys in height, 39 are 2 and the rest 1. They are almost all whitewashed. The streets are tolerably broad and in dry weather have a tolerably clean appearance. The town is considered to be improving. 25 of the houses are licensed for the sale of spirits.

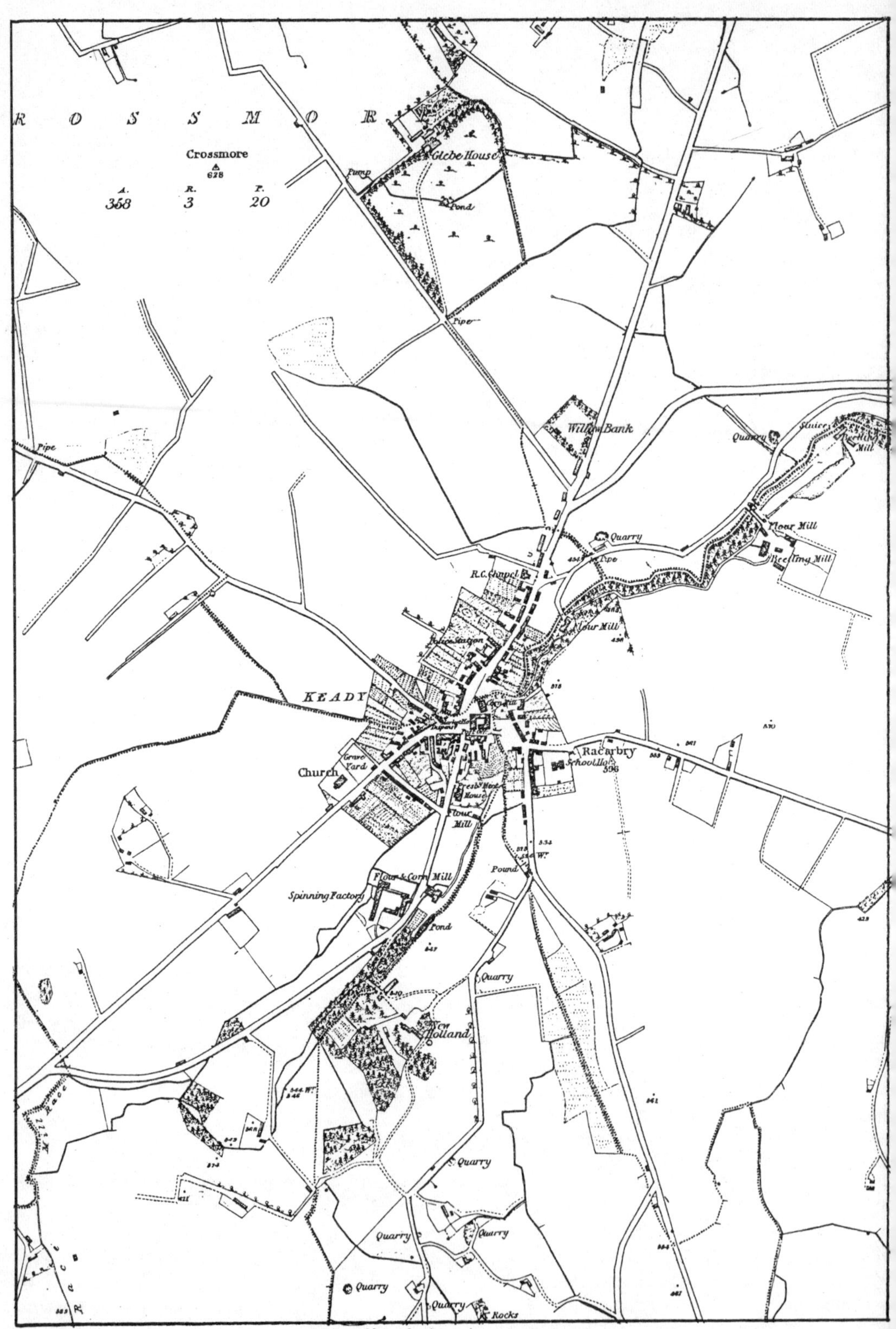

Map of Keady from the first 6" O.S. maps, 1830s

Church

The church stands on a high point at the western extremity of the town. It is a small plain building, measuring 63 feet by 30 and capable of accommodating 200 to 300.

Dispensary

There is a dispensary in the town which is open on 2 days in the week for the distribution of medicines.

Presbyterian Meeting House

The Presbyterian meeting house measures 66 feet by 36, and will accommodate between 300 and 400. It was built by subscription in the year 1803 at a cost of about 1,000 pounds. 300 pounds has recently [been] expended on it in repairs and alterations. The average attendance at this house on Sundays is 200.

Roman Catholic Chapel

The principal body of this building measures 55 feet by 20, and it has a lateral projection 15 feet by 25. It was erected in 1786, and would probably accommodate 400 or 500, though there are not seats for anything like that number. The weekly attendance at this place of worship is much larger than that at either of the above mentioned.

Market House

The only other public building in the town is the market house, a very small and insignificant erection, with no point deserving of observation about it.

PRODUCTIVE AND SOCIAL ECONOMY

Fairs and Markets

A fair is held on the second Friday in every month, and a market once in every week.

Schools

There are 5 schools in the town as follows: [Table gives number of pupils divided by sex and religion, how supported, date established].

Total pupils 20, males 6, females 14, Protestants 8, Catholics 12; supported entirely by the pupils, who pay from 1d to 2d weekly, established 1828.

Total pupils 91, all male, Protestants 57, Catholics 34; under the Association for Discountenancing Vice, and supported by the payments of the pupils, which vary from 1d weekly to 16s quarterly, established 1828.

Total pupils 38, all female, Protestants 24, Catholics 14; situated in the same house as the above, and under the same association, supported in the same manner, established 1828.

Total pupils 35, males 28, females 7, Protestants 30, Catholics 5; supported by quarterly payments of 6s 6d from each of the pupils, established 1837.

Total pupils 20, males 14, females 6, Protestants 3, Catholics 17; supported by the pupils, who pay from 2s 6d to 5s quarterly, established 1835.

Mills

The following mills are in or in the immediate vicinity of the town:

A spinning mill having 2 breast wheels, the first 30 feet in diameter and 4 feet in breadth, with a fall of 29 feet. The second is 21 feet in diameter, 4 feet 6 inches in breadth and has a fall of 20 feet. About 100 persons receive employment in this mill.

A corn mill with a breast wheel 20 feet in diameter, 5 in breadth and a fall of 17 feet.

A second corn mill with a breast wheel 16 feet in diameter, 3 in breadth and having a fall of 13 feet. There is a second wheel in this mill which is 14 feet in diameter and 3 in breadth.

A flax mill with a breast wheel 60 feet in diameter, 3 feet 6 inches in breadth; the fall of water is 12 feet.

A flour mill with a breast wheel 18 feet in diameter, 3 feet 6 inches in breadth, fall of water 15 feet.

Coach

The coach from Dublin to Armagh passes through the town at half past 4 p.m. on Mondays, Wednesdays and Fridays. At half past 6 a.m. it passes through the town on the intervening days on its way from Armagh to Dublin.

Police

3 men and a sergeant <sargeant> are stationed in the town.

MODERN TOPOGRAPHY

Mills

In the townland of Darkley there is a large spinning mill, with a breast wheel 30 feet in diameter and 6 feet in breadth. In the same townland a beetling mill with a breast wheel 18 feet in diameter and 4 feet in breadth.

Schools

In the townland of Clay there is a school having 62 pupils: 42 males and 20 females, 6 are Protestants, the rest are Catholics. It is supported entirely by the pupils, who pay from 1s 6d to 4s 6d a quarter.

In Tullyglush there is a school under the patronage of the Kildare Place Society. The total number of its scholars is 130; of this number 87 are males and 43 females, 44 are Protestants and 86 Catholics. The school is supplied with books from the society, but in other respects it is supported by the contributions of the pupils, who pay from 1d to 4d weekly. It was established in 1821.

Mills

In the townland of Racarbry is a flour mill with a breast wheel 18 feet in diameter and 4 feet in breadth, also a beetling mill with a breast wheel 20 feet in diameter and 4 feet in breadth.

In Tullynamalloge is a beetling mill with a breast wheel 24 feet in diameter and 4 feet in breadth, also a beetling and washing mill with a breast wheel 30 feet in diameter and 4 in breadth, and a steam engine of about 13 horse power which is used during dry seasons.

In Racarbry [is] a beetling mill with a breast wheel 22 feet in diameter and 6 in breadth.

In Tullynamalloge [is] a flax mill with a breast wheel 14 feet in diameter and 4 feet 4 inches in breadth.

In Tullyglush there is a large beetling and washing establishment employing the following wheels: 1, breast wheel 32 feet in diameter and 5 in breadth; 2, breast wheel 14 feet in diameter and 6 in breadth; 3, breast wheel 18 feet in diameter and 5 in breadth; 4, overshot wheel 18 feet in diameter and 2 feet 6 inches in breadth.

In the same townland is a beetling and washing mill with 2 breast wheels, the first 18 feet in diameter and 5 feet in breadth, the second 16 feet in diameter and 4 feet 6 inches in breadth.

In Tullynamalloge is a flax mill with a breast wheel 16 feet in diameter and 4 feet in breadth.

In Dundrum there is a corn mill with a breast wheel 16 feet in diameter and 4 feet in breadth.

Natural Features

Rivers

The Callan river has its origin in Tullynawood lake at the south of the parish, and runs in a northern direction till it joins the Clay river at a distance of about 4 miles from its source. Its average breadth is 20 feet. It runs between rather steep and cultivated banks, and is usefully situated for drainage and water power.

There is a stream called the Clay river, which runs from Clay lake in a north eastern direction to the parish boundary. Its length within the parish is about 3 miles. It runs between bold sloping cultivated banks, is usefully situated for drainage, and, though a small stream, taken great advantage of as a water power.

Hills

The above mentioned streams divide the surface of the parish by forming 2 principal valleys. The highest ground, generally speaking, lies at the south. The highest point, situated in the townland of Aughnagurgan, is 931 feet above the sea. From this point an elevated ridge runs northward, lying between the eastern boundary of the parish and the Callan river. Between the Callan river and Clay river there is another elevated district, the principal point of which is 863 feet above the sea. A third feature lying between the Clay river and the north western boundary of the parish, with a principal point 628 feet above the sea, completes the general form of the country, which taken more in detail is in some places cut up into little round hills and small features.

Lakes

Clay lake, in the townland of Clay on the western side of the parish, is the principal. It is about three-quarters of a mile in length. Its average winter level is 596 feet above the sea.

Tullynawood lake, at the south of the parish, is about three-quarters of a mile long and 661 feet above the sea.

Gentle Owen's lake, in the south west of the parish, is about half a mile in length and 650 feet above the sea.

Aughnagurgan lake, in the townland of the same name, is a little more than a quarter of a mile in length, and 670 feet above the sea.

Parish of Kilclooney, County Armagh

Notes on Glassdrumman Church and Schools by J. Hill Williams, 7 January 1838

MODERN TOPOGRAPHY

Glassdrumman Church

Glassdrumman church, situated in the townland of Glassdrumman on the road between Markcthill and Keady at a distance of 1 and a quarter miles from the former, is a plain rectangular building, slated and in good order, without a tower. It was built in the year 1788 and repaired last in 1836, a new roof and gable having been then added. It is 50 feet long and 25 feet broad. Rector the Reverend Doctor Blacker, curate the Reverend L.H. Robinson at Kilclooney Glebe.

SOCIAL ECONOMY

School

[Table contains the following headings: name, situation and description, when established, income and expenditure, physical, intellectual and moral instruction, number of pupils subdivided by age, sex and religion, name and religion of master or mistress, date on which visited].

Brackley male and female school, a good 2-storey house, situated partly in the townland of Brackly and partly in Ballymacully, 2 miles west south west of Markethill, established 1826; income: from London Hibernian Society 6 pounds per annum, from Lord Charlemont 5 pounds per annum, from Lord Gosford 2 pounds per annum, from pupils averages 5 pounds per annum; expenditure: total income of master averages 18 pounds per annum, poor scholars taught free; intellectual instruction: books furnished by the London Hibernian Society; moral instruction: visited by the Reverend L.H. Robinson, Protestant curate; number of pupils on the books: males, 18 under 10 years of age, 25 from 10 to 15, 17 over 15, a total of 60; females, 7 under 10 years of age, 15 from 10 to 15, 12 above 15, a total of 36; total number of pupils 96, 23 Established Church, 18 Presbyterians, 13 Roman Catholics, 42 other denominations, Seceders; master George Moore, Established Church, visited 22nd August 1837.

Sunday School

There is a Sunday school held in the above, at which the average attendance of pupils during the summer is 79, the number on the books being 86. The Sunday school pupils are of the following denominations: Established Church 21, Presbyterians 12, Seceders 41, Covenanters 3, Roman Catholics 9, a total of 86, [initiallcd] JHW [1838].

Notes on Mills by G. Scott

MODERN TOPOGRAPHY

Flax and Corn Mills

Flax mill in the townland of Ballylane, diameter 13 feet, breadth 4 feet, fall of water 5 feet, breast wheel.

Corn mill in the townland More [superscript: Cladymore], diameter 14 feet, breadth 2 and a half feet, overshot wheel, erected 1814.

Flax mill in the same townland, diameter 14 feet, breadth 3 feet, overshot wheel, belongs to William Gas.

Meeting House

Erected in 1835 in same townland [Cladymore], not yet finished, cost about 500 pounds, paid by subscription. Dimensions 60 feet by 25, 300 attend on Sunday.

Parish of Killevy, County Armagh

Notes on Modern Topography by John Heather

MODERN TOPOGRAPHY

School

Lower Killevy <Killavy> school has 64 boys, 9 of whom are Protestants, the rest Catholics. It is under the National Board and the master receives 13 pounds per annum, 1d per week from each pupil. The girls' school is under the same roof and in the same room. It numbers 38 girls, 11 of whom are Protestants. The mistress receives 5 pounds per annum from same board as the boys' school and 1d per week from scholars.

Church

This church has rather a new look for one built in 1731. It has lately gone under great repair at the expense of Colonel Close. It has 15 seats in the aisle <isle> and has 40 of [a] congregation and is capable of containing 130. The cost could not be made out from the great length of time since it was built.

School

This school, which is situated near Colonel Close's demesne, has rather a neat appearance. It is some distance from the road. Both the boys' and girls' school are under the same roof. The house cost 300 pounds. Kildare <Killaan> Place Society gave 100 pounds towards building, the rest was raised by contributions. It was established in 1826. There are 70 boys, 8 of whom are Catholics, the rest Protestants. In the girls' part there are 70, 9 of whom are Catholics. They receive 14 pounds per annum, Colonel Close gives 10 pounds.

Meeting Houses

This meeting house was built in 1797. I could not find what it cost, as some give lime and stones while others draw them. There are 43 seats, and is capable of containing 330. The congregation is nearly that number.

The other meeting house, which is quite close to this one, has much the newest appearance, being lately repaired. It was built in the year 1740 and has 50 seats. It is capable of containing 640, the amount of parishioners is 1,000.

Drumdannaher [Drumbanagher] House

Drumdannaher House, the seat of Colonel Close who commenced the building of it about 6 years back. The house has a humble appearance. It has no massy architecture about it. All seems light spacious and neat. At some distance the house has the appearance of a [?] strip cottage, but on a much larger scale. There is a great profusion of cut stone about it and the pleasure grounds. The stones have been all got in Scotland and brought over in a rough state. The pleasure grounds are not yet finished, but will be spacious and beautiful. The demesnes are very extensive and covered with fine grown trees, and some young plantation seems to be still extending its way along the cultivated soil.

Church

This church is situated within about 2 miles of Newry on the road leading between that town and Markethill. It has been lately built and is built in a plain manner, having at a distance more the appearance of a chapel.

Corn Mill

The wheel is 14 feet in diameter, 2 and a half across the buckets and 4 feet fall of water.

Chapel

This chapel is quite close to the town of Newtown Hamilton. [It] is a neat building. It has a neat exterior, but is yet unfinished. It was [built] by subscription in the year 1834 and cost 600 pounds. It is capable of accommodating 1,000. There are about 300 parishioners. There has been service performed for this some time back, though yet to be consecrated, [signed] John Heather, Carrickmacross, 16 March 1838.

Notes on Modern Topography by M.M. Kertland, 1837

Chapel

In the townland of Ellisholding there is a Roman Catholic chapel, which is 64 feet in length and 55 feet in its greatest breadth [ground plan, "T" shape]. It is capable of accommodating about 400.

Schools

In the same townland there is a school (close to the chapel) at which there are at present 218 scholars. They are all Catholics, 150 are males and 68 females. The school was established about the year 1831. It is under the National Board of Education, from which the master receives 10 pounds per annum. He also receives 1d weekly from each of the pupils.

Mills

In the townland of Aghayalloge there is a corn mill with an overshot wheel 13 feet in diameter and 2 feet 6 inches in breadth.

Gentlemen's Seats

Killevy Lodge, the residence of John Foxall Esq., is situated in the townland of Clonlum. It stands on the eastern base of Slieve Gullion and is built with considerable taste in a castellated style. It was completed during the present year (1837). The patches of fir plantation that rise above it take away in some measure from the wild and barren appearance of the mountains.

Hawthorn Hill, in the townland of Annahaid, is a rather small and plain building, also situated on the base of the mountain. It is the residence of Hunt Welsh Chambrey Esq.

Church

The church, in the townland [of] Meigh, is a small and neat building without a spire. It is built of granite, a good deal of which is hewn. It measures 60 feet by 30, and is capable of accommodating about 200.

Chapel

There is a chapel in the townland of Ballinlis. Its dimensions are [ground plan, dimensions 62, 35, 22 and 20 feet, "T" shape]. It was built in the year 1795, and is capable of accommodating about 400. It is in very good repair.

School

There is a school in the same townland [Ballinlis] close to the chapel. It has 87 pupils: 32 are males and 55 females, they are all Catholics. The school was established in 1832 and is supported by the Board of Education and the contributions of the pupils.

Mill

In Ballykeel is a corn mill with an overshot wheel 13 feet in diameter and 2 feet 6 inches in breadth.

Notes on Modern Topography by G. Scott

School

In the townland of Corrinshigo, supported by Lady Mandeville <Mandiville>. The house is neat and prettily situated. The master receives from Lady Mandeville 18 pounds a year, and not anything from any other source. The house is divided into male and female apartments. The mistress also receives an annual sum from Lady Mandeville, but declines stating the amount. The house is slated and in good repair. Total number of children 76, boys 76, Protestants 30, Catholics 46, children under 10 years 30, children between 10 and 15 years 33, children over 15 years 13; average attendance each day 50, master a Protestant.

Mill

Log wood mill, situated in the townland of Cloghreagh, belongs to William Atkinson. Diameter of wheel 18 feet, breadth 4 feet, fall of water 1 foot, overshot wheel.

Thread Mill

Situated in the townland of Clogharevan, belongs to Catherine Knox. Diameter 20 feet, breadth 6 feet, fall of water 25 feet, breast wheel.

Bleach Mill

In the townland of Glassdrummond, belongs to William Atkinson. Diameter 24 feet, breadth 5 feet, fall of water 6 feet, high breast wheel.

Corn Mill

In the townland of Mullaghglass, belongs to Alexander McAllister. Diameter 15 feet, breadth 2 feet 10 inches, breast wheel, fall of water 8 feet.

Flax Mills

Townland of Mullaghglass, belongs to Alexander McAllister. Diameter 17 feet, breadth 4 feet, fall of water 7 and a half feet, breast wheel.

In the townland of Mullaghglass, belongs to Samuel Frazier. Diameter 14 feet 6 inches, breadth 2 feet 6 inches, fall of water 5 feet, undershot wheel.

Thread Mill

In the townland of Clogharevan, belongs to John Nicholson and son. Diameter 40 feet, breadth 10 feet, fall of water 40 feet, high breast wheel.

Corn Mill

Townland of Derrymore, belongs to Isaac Smyth. Diameter 24 feet, breadth 6 feet, fall of water 6 feet, breast wheel.

Flax Mill

In the townland of Cross. Diameter 18 feet, breadth 5 feet, fall of water 16 feet, breast wheel. Belongs to Joseph Kelly.

Gentleman's Seat

Derrymore House, in the townland of Derrymore, the residence of Isaac Smyth.

Church

In the townland of Cross, erected about the year 1774, dimensions <diameter> 48 feet by 24, 28 seats, which would contain 6 persons each.

Hamlet of Camlough

Hamlet called Camlough, in which there are 16 2-storey houses, all slated. There are 3 police station[ed] in Camlough.

Flour Mill

In the townland of Lisdrumgullion, belongs to John Richey. Diameter 17 feet 6 inches, breadth 8 feet, fall of water 12 feet 5 inches, breast wheel.

Bleach Mill

In the townland of Mullaghglass, belongs to William Atkinson. Diameter 22 feet, breadth 4 feet, fall of water 10 feet, breast wheel.

Flax Mill

In the townland of Cloghreagh, belongs to John Bell. Diameter 20 feet 4 inches, breadth 5 feet, fall of water 2 feet, overshot wheel.

Dispensary

In the townland of Mullaghglass, erected in 1825, the expenses paid by Roger Hall Esq. of Narrow Water. There are 800 families in the district, about 600 of whom annually receive relief <relieve>. The health of the country people is supposed to be improved by the establishment of dispensaries.

Schools

In the townland of Mullaghglass, supported chiefly by Mrs Roger Hall, who is patron and contributes 5 pounds a year towards the support of the mistress. Girls 50, Protestants 46, Catholics 4, total 50. Mistress a Protestant and receives from the children from 1s 1d to 3s per quarter.

In the townland of Ernagh, under the London Hibernian Society. Master receives 6 pounds a year from the society and 2 pounds per annum from the Reverend Mr Hill and 1d per week from the children. The schoolhouse is kept in repair by the parents of the children. The house was erected in 1830. Total number 97, boys 60, girls 37, Protestants 75, Catholics 22. The master is a Protestant.

Chapel

In the townland of Corrackcroppan, originally very old, was rebuilt about the year 1816, expenses paid by subscription. There are 41 seats in the gallery, would accommodate 6 persons each; between 200 and 300 attend on Sundays. Dimensions 60 by 36 [feet].

School

In the townland of Lett, erected in 1827, cost about 150 pounds. Roger Hall Esq. paid the greater part, the Kildare Street Society gave the remainder. The master receives from the children from 1d to 3d per week. Total 121, boys 111, girls 10, Protestants 116, Catholics 5, master a Protestant; over 10 years 30, over 15 years 4.

Flax Mill

Belongs to Robert Ferret, in the townland of Lett. Diameter of wheel 15 feet, breadth 2 feet 8 inches, fall of water 4 feet, breast wheel.

Parish of Killyman, County Armagh

Part of a Memoir by J.R. Ward and Thomas McIlroy, January 1838

NATURAL STATE AND NATURAL FEATURES

Locality

The parish of Killyman occupies portions of the counties Tyrone and Armagh. That part which is in the latter is situated in the north west corner and is bounded on the north by Lough Neagh, on the east by the parishes of Tartaraghan and Loughgall, on the south by the north portion of the parish of Clonfeacle, and on the west by the county of Tyrone. Its extreme length is [blank] miles and extreme breadth [blank] miles, its mean length [blank] and mean breadth [blank] miles. Its content, including 49 acres 35 perches of water, is 3,154 acres 3 roods 6 perches, of which [blank] are cultivated. It is divided into [blank] townlands and is valued at [blank] pounds to the county cess.

Hills

The surface of the parish consists of a number of small conical hills rising out of bog. The highest is in the townland of Derrycorry, 115 feet above the sea. The average height is 80 feet and the lowest ground is along the banks of the River Blackwater and Lough Neagh, where it is only 50 feet above the level of the sea.

Lake

Annagariff lake occupies a portion of the townland of Derryhubbert in this parish, and a portion of Derrylee in the adjacent parish of Tartaraghan. It is 75 feet above the level of the sea, is 88 acres 2 roods 35 perches in content, of which 49 acres 35 perches are in this parish, and it averages 20 feet deep in the centre. It contains 2 small islands covered with brushwood.

River

The Blackwater river divides this part of the parish from the county Tyrone. It averages 120 feet broad and 15 feet deep. A more minute description of this river will be found in the Memoir of Loughgall parish.

Bogs

The greater part of the east side of this parish is bog. It averages 80 feet above the sea and 30 feet above the Blackwater river. Timber, viz. oak, fir and birch is indiscriminately scattered through it. The depth of the bog varies from 5 to 20 feet.

Climate

No register kept in the parish.

PRODUCTIVE ECONOMY

Crops

Same as Loughgall parish.

MODERN TOPOGRAPHY

Public Building: Roman Catholic Chapel

Towns: none. Clonmore Roman Catholic chapel, situated in the townland of Clonmore, is a neat stone building, slated. It is 44 feet long and 25 feet broad. It was built in 1834 and cost 180 pounds, which sum was raised by subscription. The interior is neat and has a large gallery neatly fitted up with pews, the lower part has only forms. The whole accommodates 500 persons, the average attendance is 400. The windows of the chapel are plain, rectangular. The Reverend John Montague P.P. is the officiating priest. He resides in the town [of] Dungannon, county of Tyrone.

Communications

The main road between Portadown and Dungannon by Verner's bridge crosses the parish in a north west direction for 2 miles. The average breadth is 26 feet. There are several by-roads useful for the farmer. They are all kept in good repair by the county, [signed] J.R. Ward.

Gentleman's Seat

Church Hill, the seat of Colonel William Verner, M.P. for Armagh county, is situated in the townland of Mullenakill. It was erected in 183[last figure blank]. It is a handsome rectangular stone building, stuccoed, 4-storeys high. The entrance through the demesne is pretty. The demesne and ornamental is extensive. The gardens are good and well laid out. There is a small collection of paintings, which are mostly portraits, and a good library.

Burying Ground

There is a burying ground situated in the demesne

of Churchill House. It is in an elevated situation and is surrounded by a low circular wall. There are a few old trees in it.

Bridge

Verner's bridge, situated in the townland of Mullenakill West over the River Blackwater, is composed of wood. It is 116 feet long and 21 feet 6 inches broad. When erected and cost of building not known. There are 5 open work supports. It was built by Colonel William Verner. There is a toll gate attached to it, [signed] Thomas C. McIlroy.

Parish of Kilmore, County Armagh

Fair Sheets for Memoir by Thomas McIlroy, 20 November 1837

NATURAL STATE

Name

The parish derives its name from a large church or monastery, which in former times occupied the ground adjoining the site of the present church.

Locality

The parish of Kilmore is situated 5 miles north east of the city of Armagh, in the county of Armagh, in the baronies of Oneilland West and Lower Orior. It is bounded on the north by a part of the parish of [sic] Newry and the parish of Drumcree, on the east by the county Down and parish of Mullaghbrack <Mullybrack>, on the west by the parish of Loughgall and on the south by the parishes of Mullaghbrack and Ballymore. Its extreme length is 7 and a half miles and extreme breadth 5 miles. Its content is 17,274 acres 2 roods 3 perches, including 13 acres 1 rood 32 perches of water, and it is valued at [blank] to the county cess.

NATURAL FEATURES

Hills

The hills in this part of the parish are highly cultivated. The highest point in this part of the parish is in the townland of Mullagdry, 207 feet above the level of the sea. The average height of the hills is 175 feet above the sea. There is a very gentle fall in a northwest direction.

Lakes

There are no lakes in this part of the parish of Kilmore.

Rivers

The Tall water runs through this part of the parish for 3 miles in a north west direction. Its average breadth is 5 feet and its depth from 1 to 3 feet. It rises in the parish of Mullaghbrack in the county Armagh. Its fall is 10 feet in the English mile. It is usefully situated for drainage.

Bogs

There is a bog situated in the townland of Derryhale. Its extreme length is two-thirds of a mile and extreme breadth one-third. It is 74 feet above the level of the sea and 24 above the River Bann. Its depth is from 1 to 6 feet. There is not much timber found imbedded. Formerly it was much deeper but is now nearly cut out.

MODERN TOPOGRAPHY

Church

The parish church is situated in the townland of Kilmore. It is a neat stone building, roughcast. It was rebuilt in 1814, except the tower, and cost 4,000 pounds, which sum was borrowed from the Board of First Fruits, to be defrayed by instalments of the parish. Part of the above sum still remains unpaid. The body of the church is 73 feet long and 39 feet broad, the tower is 20 feet long and 20 broad. The interior of the church is neat. There is a small gallery at the west end and a good organ. The windows are Gothic. The accommodation is for 700 persons and the general attendance is 500. In the tower is a belfry containing 1 bell on which there is the following inscription: "Made for the parish of Kilmore 1755 IP." The spire is of wood, coppered. It was erected in 1825 and cost 250 pounds. The total height of it is 282 feet above the level of the sea. Repairs done to the church in 1836 cost 9 pounds 7s 6d. Repairs done in 1837 cost 53 pounds 14s.

Glebe House

Glebe House is situated in the townland of Annaboe. It is a neat stone building, 2-storeys high. It is handsomely situated and the grounds have been much improved by the present rector, the Rev. Edward Chichester.

Meeting House

There is a Presbyterian meeting house situated in the townland of Ballintaggart. It is a stone building, whitewashed and slated, when built or what cost not known. The form and dimensions of the building are shown by the following figure: [ground plan, main dimensions 59, 27 and a half, 20 and 17 feet, "T" shape]. The interior is plain, the windows are Gothic. The accommodation is for 700 persons and the general attendance is 100. On the sacramental cup is a date, 1729. Repairs done in 1835 cost 20 pounds, defrayed by subscription. There is no resident preacher for the above house.

Schoolhouse

Bottle Hill schoolhouse, situated in the townland of Bottle Hill, is a neat stone house, 2-storeys, slated. It was built in 1826, not known what cost. It is 35 feet long and 17 feet broad. The upper part is occupied as a dwelling by the master.

Roman Catholic Chapel

There is a Roman Catholic chapel situated in the townland of Drumnahunshin. It is a plain rectangular stone building, 95 feet 3 inches long and 29 feet 6 inches broad. It was built in 1771 and cost (not known) defrayed by (not known). The interior is very plain. It has a small gallery at the east end, but it is not ceiled. There are no seats below but a few forms. The windows are Gothic. The general attendance is 550 persons and the accommodation is for 550. Improvements done in 1827 cost 50 pounds. The priest's income is 100 pounds per annum.

Schoolhouses

Kilmore schoolhouse, situated in the townland of Kilmore, is a stone building, 2-storeys high, whitewashed and slated. It is 50 feet 6 inches long and 16 feet 3 inches broad. Not known when built or what cost.

Annahugh schoolhouse, situated in the townland of Annaghugh. It is a good stone house, slated, 2-storeys high, not known when built or what cost. It is 34 feet long and 18 feet broad. The upper storey is occupied by the master as a dwelling.

Communications

The main road from Armagh to Belfast runs through this parish in a north east direction for 4 miles. Its average breadth is 40 feet. It is a well laid out road and is kept in good repair by the Commissioner of Turnpikes. The main road from Loughgall to Portadown runs through this parish in an easterly direction for 4 miles. Its average breadth is 35 feet. It is a well laid out road and is kept in good repair at the expense of the county. There are several by-roads also, which are kept in repair by the county.

General Appearance and Scenery

This parish is well cultivated and fertile. The country in the neighbourhood of the parish church is picturesque. It is well watered by many streams which empty themselves into the Rivers Bann and Blackwater.

Social Economy

Education

[Table of schools contains the following headings: name, situation and description, when established, income and expenditure, physical, intellectual and moral instruction, number of pupils subdivided by age, sex and religion, name and religion of master or mistress, date on which visited].

Bottle Hill, a good house situated in the townland of Bottle Hill, established 1826; income: 1 acre of ground from the Reverend Edward Chichester, 4 pounds per annum from pupils; moral instruction: visited by the Reverend Edward Chichester and the Reverend Edward Taylor, Scripture read daily; number of pupils: males, 24 under 10 years of age, 54 from 10 to 15, 6 above 15, a total of 84; females, 16 under 10 years of age, 30 from 10 to 15, a total of 46; total number of pupils 130, 106 Established Church, 12 Presbyterians, 12 Roman Catholics; master Absolam Hewitt, Established Church, visited 24th October 1837.

Kilmore, a neat house situated in the townland of Kilmore; income: from the Reverend Edward Chichester 4 pounds per annum, 3 pounds per annum from pupils; intellectual instruction: Kildare Society books; moral instruction: visited by the Reverend Edward Chichester, catechisms heard daily by the master, Authorised Version of Scriptures read daily; number of pupils: males, 33 under 10 years of age, 12 from 10 to 15, 1 above 15, a total of 46; females, 22 under 10 years of age, 10 from 10 to 15, a total of 32; total number of pupils 78, 26 Established Church, 2 Presbyterians, 38 Roman Catholics, 12 other denominations; master Thomas Loney, Established Church, visited 2nd November 1837.

Annatiugh, a house in the townland of Annatiugh, established 1826; income: from the Reverend Edward Chichester 6 pounds per annum, 3 pounds per annum from pupils; intellectual instruction: Kildare Society's books; moral instruction: visited by the Reverend Edward Chichester, Authorised Version of Scriptures read daily; number of pupils: males, 19 under 10 years of age, 26 from 10 to 15, 3 above 15, a total of 48; females, 19 under 10 years of age, 11 from 10 to 15, a total of 30; total number of pupils 78, 11 Established Church, 59 Roman Catholics, 8 other denominations; master James Bell, Established Church, visited 23rd December 1837, [signed] T.C. McIlroy.

Notes for Memoir by J. Heming Tait, 27 January 1838

Modern Topography

Town of Rich Hill

[The] town of Rich Hill is situated in the south west part of the parish of Kilmore, in the barony of Oneilland and in the county of Armagh. It contains 167 houses, of which 7 are of 3-storeys, 103 are of 2-storeys and the remaining 57 are cabins and cottages. There is a chapel of ease, an Independent meeting house (or Congregationalist), a Quakers' meeting house, a Presbyterian meeting house, a Methodist meeting house, a pound, a small market house and 2 schools, and also a police office. The number of trades in the town are as follows: publicans 5, doctors 3, tanner's men 6, shoemakers 7, grocers 9, gauger or excise man 1, carpenters 5, baker 1. There is very little business of any sort carried on in the town. There are no markets held, and fairs are only 4 times a year, viz. on [blank]. There is no support for the poor.

Congregationalist Meeting House

The Congregationalist meeting house of Rich Hill is 33 feet broad and 45 feet long. It will contain 350 persons. The congregation consists of 80 families, or 180 persons. The clergyman is the Rev. John Carroll, who is supported by [the] congregation. The building was finished in 1800.

Market House

The market house, a small hexagonal building of which each side is 9 feet in length, has not been used for 12 years, about which period the last markets were held. They died a natural death.

Chapel of Ease

The chapel of ease is situated at the north end of the town on the top of the hill. [It] was formerly an old session house, repaired in 1837 at a cost of 620 pounds by private subscription. It is 30 feet long and 27 feet broad. It will hold 450 persons. The rector is the Rev. Edward Chichester.

Social Economy

Religion

There are 8 sects of the Christian religion in this small town, viz. Episcopalians, Roman Catholics, Quakers, Presbyterians, Congregationalists, Wesleyans, Primitive Wesleyans, English Primitive Wesleyans. The 2 last sects have no houses of worship here.

Schools

[Table of schools contains the following headings: name, situation and description, when established, income and expenditure, physical, intellectual and moral instruction, number of pupils subdivided by age, sex and religion, name and religion of master or mistress, date on which visited. No expenditure nor physical education].

Erasmus Smith's school, north end of Rich Hill village, very neat and clean house; income: bequest of Erasmus Smith 57 pounds 10s; intellectual instruction: Scripture and *Dublin reading book*; number of pupils: males, 50 under 10 years of age, 30 from 10 to 15, 20 over 15, a total of 100; females, 71 under 10 years of age, 25 from 10 to 15, 4 above 15, a total of 100; total number of pupils 200, 146 Established Church, 24 Presbyterians, 18 Roman Catholics, 12 other denominations, Quakers; master and mistress: Joseph and Mary Anne Parker, Episcopalians, visited July 1837.

Private school, Cordra townland; income from pupils 1d a week; intellectual instruction: the Bible; number of pupils: males, 17 under 10 years of age, 3 from 10 to 15, a total of 20; females, 22 under 10 years of age, a total of 22; total number of pupils [sic] 42, 38 Established Church, 4 Roman Catholics, 42 other denominations; mistress Martha Bond, Episcopalian, visited July 1837.

Derryhead school, Derryhead townland, established 1829; income: 10 pounds per annum from Miss Richardson, 1d a week from pupils; intellectual and moral instruction: Bible and *Dublin reading book*, visited by the Reverend John Marks and the Reverend Maxwell Carpendale; number of pupils: males, 38 under 10 years of age, 12 from 10 to 15, a total of 50; females, 38 under 10 years of age, 18 from 10 to 15, 3 above 15, a total of 59; total number of pupils 109, 98 Established Church, 2 Presbyterians, 9 Roman Catholics; master and mistress: William Taylor and Margaret Murphy, Established Church, visited 26th July 1837.

Ballynahinch national school, Ballynahinch townland, established 1836; income: 10 pounds from National Board, 2d a week from pupils; intellectual instruction: *Dublin reading book*; moral instruction: Bible, visited by Reverend John Marks; number of pupils: 38 under 10 years of age, 20 from 10 to 15, 6 above 15, a total of 64, all male, 20 Established Church, 20 Presbyterians, 8 Roman Catholics, 16 other denominations; master Samuel Coyne, Episcopalian, visited 28 July 1837.

Mullavilly school, Ballylisk townland, established 1817; income: from the Count De Salis 8 pounds to mistress, 4 pounds to master, [from] Erasmus Smith 30 pounds to master, 20 pounds to mistress, [crossed out] none from pupils; intellectual instruction: *Dublin reading book*; moral instruction: Bible, [visited by] the Reverend John Marks and the Reverend Maxwell Carpendale; number of pupils: 105 males, 80 females, a total of 185; master and mistress: William Hoare and Anne McAlister, Episcopalians.

Modern Topography

Corn Mill

The corn mill belonging to Charlotte Langtry, situated at the village of Rich Hill, has 2 wheels: the largest is 16 feet in diameter and 2 and a half feet in breadth and is a breast wheel; the smaller is 14 feet in diameter and 2 feet in breadth and is an overshot wheel.

Dispensary

The dispensary of Mullaghvilly in the townland of that name is kept by Mr Richard Crozier. He receives from [the] county for his service 50 pounds per annum.

Roads

The principal roads which pass through this parish are the road from Armagh to Belfast. It is a mail coach road, is kept in excellent repair, is [blank] feet broad and runs in the parish for the distance of 4 miles, passing three-quarters of a mile to the north of the village of Rich Hill.

The road from Tanderagee to Rich Hill runs in the parish for 6 miles and is kept in good repair, but is rather hilly owing to the undulating nature of the country.

The road from Markethill to Rich Hill also runs in it for 1 and a half miles in a northern direction, as does also that between Tanderagee and Portadown at the eastern end of the parish. Both of these roads are hilly but are kept in good repair.

Corn Mill

Corn mill, townland of Lisnagree, built in the year 1834, belongs to Moses Greer. Has a breast wheel of the following dimensions: diameter 14 feet and breadth 1 foot 10 inches.

Flax Mills

Flax mill, situated in the townland of Aghore. It has a breast wheel of the following dimensions: diameter 20 feet and breadth 4 feet.

Flax mill, same townland, breast wheel, diameter 16 feet, breadth 3 and a half feet. Both of these mills belong to Mr Robert Williamson.

Memoir by Lieut G.A. Bennett, 2 June 1835

Natural State

Name

This parish in Armstrong's *Survey of the county* [is] spelled Killmore, but by the Rev. E. Chichester and all other authorities Kilmore. It is derived from the Irish kill "graveyard" and more "big", owing to a very large graveyard situated in the townland of the same name.

Locality

It is situated in the east side of the county in the baronies of Oneilland West and Lower Orier, and is bounded on the north by the parishes of Tartaraghan <Tartarahan>, Drumcree and Lower Grange, a detached townland of the Lordship of Newry, north east by Seagoe, east by Tullylish (county Down), south east by Ballymore, south by Mullabrack and west by Loughgall. Its greatest length is 6 English miles from its extreme south point near a fort in Rockmacreeny townland to its most northern point in Derryloughan, joining the parish of Tartaraghan. Its greatest breadth is 7 and a half miles from east to west. It contains 17,274 acres 2 roods 23 perches and is divided into 52 townlands, not including Upper and Lower Grange, containing 968 acres 1 rood 33 perches, which form no part of the parish of Kilmore but belong to the Lordship of Newry. Of these 166 acres are bog, 21 marsh, 16 and a half water, of which 13 and a half are portions of River Bann and canal on the east and north east of [the] parish, and about 49 of wood.

Natural Features

Hills

The surface of this parish is broken up into a large number of hills, which, however, do not exceed in height above the sea 407 feet, the lowest grounds about the River Bann 50. The highest ground is in the south west end of the parish in the townlands of Maynooth, Suez, Rockmacreeny and Liskeyborough: Maynooth, in townland of same name, 407 feet above the sea, a hill in Suez 391, one in Rockmacreeny 356 and a fort on top of a hill in Liskeyborough 360 feet. From Maynooth the ground falls easterly to 296 feet on the Ballynahinch range and north west to a hill on which the town of Rich Hill is situated, 270 feet. Besides these, Tamnavelton hill is 255 feet, Ahory 212 feet, Ballybreagh 223 feet, Kilmore hill in Kilmore townland 258 feet, Anna hill in Ballyleany townland 125 feet, which is a continuation of the Ballynahinch range, Diamond hill in Lower Grange 144 feet, Bottle hill 244 feet. The latter commands a most extensive view of the more northern parts of the county. The north east corner of the parish along the River Bann varies from 50 to 65 feet.

Lakes

There are no lakes in this parish.

Rivers

The River Bann enters this parish about quarter of an English mile below the Knock bridge at the north east corner of the townland of Mullahead. For 1 and three-quarter miles it becomes the boundary of the parish to the north east, separating it from the parish of Seagoe <Seago> to its junction with the Newry Canal. It is not navigable in this parish but becomes so on leaving it. There are no manufactories on this portion of it. Its breadth entering the parish is 62 feet but leaving it increases to 130 feet. It overflows its banks in the winter season, at which period the lowlands in the valley through it runs are nearly always under water, owing to the slight fall it has to Lough Neagh.

The Cusher river enters this parish at the south east corner of the townland of Mullahead from Ballymore, and runs parallel to the Newry Canal for half an English mile. It then becomes county and parish boundary on the east, separating it from Tullylish (county Down) for 1 mile. The boundary then leaves it for eight-ninths of a mile, then for seven-eighths of a mile becomes the boundary of the parish to the west and north west between Bracchagh townland and the parish of Drumcree, till it joins the River Bann and canal at the most northern point in the east end of the parish. Its average breadth is 42 feet and its depth from 3 to 6 feet. Its general direction in this parish is north west. The place where the Rivers Bann, Cusher and the canal meet is called White Coat Point, on account of a man who generally wore a white coat having drowned himself about a century ago.

The Ballybay river, a small insignificant stream, enters this parish at the most southern point of Ballyloughan townland and becomes parish boundary on the south between this parish and Mullabrack for three-quarters of a mile. Thence it bears through the parish, being a boundary for various townlands for 4 and a quarter miles, till it becomes parish boundary between the townland of Ballintaggart in this parish and Drumcree on the north east for 1 mile. It then enters Drumcree. Its general direction is north. There is one flax, also a corn mill on it, both in the townland of Ahory, immediately above which there is a fall of about 40 feet over a precipice of basaltic rock or whin <whyn> dyke. This is known in the country as the Ahory Leap.

The Tall water, another small stream, enters this parish in the most south westerly point, becomes parish boundary between the townland of Rockmacreeny and parish of Mullabrack for 2 miles. It then winds through the parish, its general bearing being north east, for 5 miles, then becomes parish boundary between Lower Grange and Drumcree, bearing north west for 2 and a half miles, again between Lower Grange and Tartaraghan for 2 and a quarter miles and lastly between the townland of Derryloughan and Tartaraghan parish for three-eighths of a mile, leaving the parish at the most north westerly point. There are 2 mills on it, a flax mill in Rockmacreeny and a corn mill in Rich Hill. The fall of this river is so trifling that it is impossible to apply the water power to any extent, and when mills happen to be built the river has to be dammed up to give a sufficient fall.

Bogs

This parish contains about 166 acres of bog, 63 of which are in the townlands of Derryhale and Lissavogue in the northern end of [the] parish and known by the name of Derryhale bog. Both fir and oak trees are found in this bog. In general the roots are in position as when growing, the trunks apparently broken off by force. There are likewise small portions of spent bog in the townlands of Ballyhagan, Ballytrew, Tullymore, Ballywilly, Castleraw, Anahugh, Ballynahuich, Cavan, Cloghan, Mooney, and Mullaletra, varying from 6 to 20 acres. The bog in Ballyhagan [is] 84 feet above the sea, in Ballytrew and Ballywilly 69 feet, in Tullymore 68 feet.

Woods

There are no natural woods in the parish, which altogether contains only about 49 acres of forest trees, of which 25 acres are in Bracchagh townland and the remaining 24 in Rich Hill.

Natural History

Zoology

Pike, trout, salmon, perch, dolaghan and eels abound in the River Bann. The latter are prized as being of a superior quality. The salmon come up this river from Lough Neagh. There is a species of fish found in Ballyhagan bog, but are considered dangerous food.

Geology

The soil of this country in general is a fair mixture of sand or gravel and clay, and is of a good quality. Few if any rocks project above the surface. The substratum is lime of a reddish <redish> hue.

Modern Topography

Town of Rich Hill

Rich Hill, formerly called Legacorry, is situated in the south west corner of the parish on the top of a hill, 1 and three-eighth miles from the south, 4 and five-eighth miles from the north and 1 [mile] from the west of the parish. It is the property of the family of the Richardsons <Richesons>, a member of which was in the Irish parliament early in the 17th century. It is 63 miles Irish from Dublin by Newry, 4 from Armagh, 5 from Portadown and 13 from Newry. The main road from Armagh to Belfast went through it formerly, but the new line of road passes five-eighths of a mile north of it and is very well laid out. On it there are 2 coaches running daily from Armagh to Belfast through Portadown. The roads in general are in good repair. It contains a Presbyterian meeting house built by the public subscription of Protestants and Dissenters in 1780, and capable of accommodating 300 hearers. The minister receives the Regium Donum. It likewise contains a Quaker meeting house built by subscription in the year 1793, capable of containing 500; likewise an Independent or Evangelical meeting house built by subscription in 1799 and capable of containing 400. There is a Sunday school taught in this house. The minister is supported partly by the congregation and partly by the Irish Evangelical Society. Also a Methodist meeting house built by subscription in 1726. There are 2 day schools in this town, one of Erasmus Smith's and the other under the National Board.

Productive Economy

Markets, Fairs, Court and Employment

About 50 years ago there was an excellent market in this town, the best in the county for linen cloth, and it is even said that the inhabitants of Armagh came here to purchase their wearing apparel and victualling, which would imply a great superiority in this market over their own. The market, which is held on Saturday, is now merely nominal, not more than 40 persons attending it, and their only dealing is in yarn. This falling off in the market of Rich Hill is said to be owing to the hostility of the Quakers, who resolved to desert the town in consequence of one of their members having been killed in some riot in the place. The market house has been a plain neat building but is in a rapid state of decay, and the general appearance of the town indicates the same. This may be attributed, besides the decay of the market, to the alteration of the road, as neither coaches nor carriers pass through it.

There are 3 fairs in the year, one on Shrove Tuesday, one on the 26th of July, one on the 15th of October: they are but badly attended.

A seneschal court is held on the first Monday of every month and can recover to the amount of 2 pounds. Mr H. Walker of Annahill is the seneschal.

There is one tanyard of about 25 years standing, employing 5 men constantly and prepares about 1200 hides annually. It takes 6 months to make it ready for use from its green state. The people in general are very poor, the greater portion of them living [by] labour and a few by weaving.

Modern Topography

Village of Kilmore

The village of Kilmore, in townland of same name, contains the parish church and a school, and is famed for its limestone.

Public Buildings: Churches

The parish church, a plain building with a neat spire, situated nearly in the centre of Kilmore townland and in the west side of the parish, is believed to have been originally built by St Patrick. The old tower still remains, but the body was rebuilt in 1814. It would contain about 700 persons. The ground on which it stands is 159 feet above the level of the sea and the top 262 feet. There is likewise a chapel of ease called Mullavilly church, situated in the east side of Mullavilly townland and east side of parish. It is quarter of a mile from the nearest northern point and seven-eighths from the western point of Kilmore parish. It was built in 1755 and is capable of containing 600. The ground on which it stands is 177 feet above the sea and the top 228 feet. It has no spire.

The other houses of worship are a Presbyterian meeting house in Ballintaggart, capable of containing 400; a Seceding meeting house in Ahory, containing 400; a Catholic chapel in Tamnavelton, built in 1717 and rebuilt in 1824, containing 500; and one in Drumnahuncheon containing 400; all built by subscription.

Gentlemen's Seats

On the top of the hill and connected with the town of Rich Hill is the seat of the family of the Richardsons, a very old and substantial building but of no particular beauty. It is surrounded by a demesne of 188 acres, enclosed within a stone wall 10 feet in height. The demesne contains some remarkably fine timber and about 24 acres of wood, chiefly young plantations.

The Glebe House, the residence of the rector the Rev. E. Chichester, is a plain solid building affording much comfort, but without any beauty. It is surrounded with trees and the ornamental grounds, though of trifling extent, are laid out with much taste.

Ballintaggart House, in the townland of that name, is a plain building commanding an extensive view on the surrounding counties. The ground and plantings are laid out with much taste, but it is uninhabited, the owner [blank] Todd Esq. being resident in England.

Manufactories and Mills

In this parish there is in the townland of Cordrain a steam engine, which is used for dressing the yarn for a check manufactory adjoining it. There are likewise 4 corn and 5 flax mills. The following table shows <shews> the situation and power of the various mills in the parish: [Table gives name of townland, type of mill, description, diameter and breadth of wheels, remarks].

Rich Hill, corn mill, overshot, 14 by 2 and a half feet, 13 by 2 feet.

Lissavogue, corn mill, overshot, 14 by 2 feet.

Ahory, corn mill, overshot, 13 by 2 feet.

Ahory, corn mill, undershot, 13 by 2 feet.

Ahory, flax mill, overshot, 14 by 2 and a half feet.

Ballyloughan, flax mill, overshot, 13 by 2 feet.

Rockmacreeny, flax mill, overshot, 13 by 2 feet.

Ballybreagh, flax mill, breast wheel, 10 by 1 and a half feet, very small.

Communications

The main road from Armagh to Belfast runs through this parish and within an eighth of a mile of Rich Hill for 4 and a half miles. Its average breadth is 42 feet, made at the expense of the county. It is a turnpike road and very well laid out, and is but 2 and a half years completed. The roads to Armagh, Portadown, Dungannon, Tanderagee and Markethill are all in good repair and tolerably well laid out. There are numerous by-roads and lanes joining the main roads through the parish. The only communication across the River Bann is by the Knock bridge, and the bridge across the canal adjoining it is likewise called the Knock bridge, on a by-road leading from Mullavilly church to Portadown.

Ancient Topography

Church, Well, Castle and Forts

The church was supposed to have been built by St Patrick as mentioned before. There was a monastery near the church, the foundation of which was visible about 70 years ago, and the graveyard seems to have been of great extent, judging from the skeletons which have been found in the surrounding fields. There is likewise a well in the garden of the old monastery, and now in the garden attached to the glebe, which has the reputation of sanctity, having been blessed some centuries ago by St Kyrue-na-gort and of which nothing more is known.

In the townland of Castleraw there are still some remains of an ancient castle, which formerly belonged to Hugh Roe O'Neill. It is likewise said Tyrone stopped 2 or 3 days in it on his retreat from Dungannon in 1602, and likewise that a number of Protestants were murdered in it in 1641. The country people have taken the greater part of it away to build houses.

Besides these the parish also contains a number of old forts, of which nothing remarkable is mentioned. Castle Raw or Roe is situated on top of a hill, having a gradual slope each way, and is surrounded by an entrenchment near the base of the hill. The entrenchment is 330 yards in circumference. The parapet is 12 feet in height, having the ditch in the inside, the outside being a continuation of the natural slope of the hill: see sketch [crossed out marginal drawing, triangular shape].

Social Economy

Improvements

The Newry Canal is of great utility as opening the communication with this and the surrounding parishes. The land is all well cultivated and a branch of the North East Farming Society, meeting twice a year in Rich Hill and distributing premiums, has tended greatly to the improvement of agriculture. There is a dispensary in the town of Loughgall in the adjoining parish, supported by a great number of gentlemen and farmers residing in different parishes. Any poor person getting a ticket from one of the members composing the society is entitled to medicine and attendance.

Local Government

There are no resident magistrates in this parish, but all pecuniary matters, such as trespass, wages and debts under 2 pounds, are settled by the seneschal court in Rich Hill, previously mentioned under the head of Towns; but all matters of more serious consideration are settled in the petty sessions in Armagh and Portadown.

Schools

This parish is very well supplied with schools, and the people are of a quiet and orderly disposition. The following table shows the situation of the schools: [table gives name of townland, number of Protestants and Catholics, males and females, how supported, when established].

Ballintaggart: Protestants 55, Catholics 25, males 45, females 35, total 80; 8 pounds per annum each to master and mistress from Miss Richardson and 1d a week from scholars, established 1828.

Ballynahinch: Protestants 55, Catholics 20, males 35, females 40, total 75; 18 pounds from National Board and 1d per week from scholars, established 1827.

Ballyloughan: Protestants 60, Catholics 25, males 60, females 25, total 85; 16 pounds from Miss Richardson, 20 free scholars and the remainder 1d ha'penny per week, established 1823.

Ballylick: Protestants 114, Catholics 44, males 108, females 50, total 158; Erasmus Smith's legacy, established 1814.

Bottlehill: Protestants 28, Catholics 12, males 30, females 10, total 40; supported by scholars, established 1824.

Bottlehill Sunday school: Protestants 80, Catholics 20, males 60, females 40, total 100; 2 pounds per annum from rector, established 1824.

Ballynahinch: Protestants 60, Catholics 20, males 45, females 35, total 80; national [school].

Brachagh: Protestants 30, Catholics 10, males 25, females 15, total 40; supported by scholars, established 1834.

Brachagh Sunday school: Protestants 16, Catholics 18, males 22, females 12, total 34; 2 pounds per annum from rector, established 1834.

Anahugh: Protestants 16, Catholics 53, males 44, females 25, total 69; 15 pounds donations and scholars, established 1825.

Anahugh Sunday school: Protestants 20, Catholics 49, males 39, females 30, total 69; 2 pounds per annum from rector, established 1825.

Derryhale: Protestants 55, Catholics 6, males 40, females 21, total 61; 12 pounds from Miss Richardson and 1d per week from scholars, established 1821.

Lower Grange: Protestants 38, Catholics 10, males 29, females 19, total 48; supported by scholars, established 1820.

Kilmore: Protestants 25, Catholics 11, males 21, females 15, total 36; 2 pounds from rector and 1d per week from scholars, established 1824.

Kilmore Sunday school: Protestants 22, Catholics 8, males 20, females 10, total 30; 2 pounds from rector, established 1824.

Mullahead: Protestants 20, Catholics 7, males 18, females 9, total 27; 15 pounds from Lord Mandeville, established 1819.

Mulladry: Protestants 25, Catholics 15, males 29, females 11, total 40; 8 pounds from Miss Richardson and 1d per week from scholars, established 1822.

Rich Hill: Protestants 115, Catholics 25, males 70, females 70, total 140; Erasmus Smith's foundation, established 1819.

Rich Hill Sunday school: Protestants 60, Catholics 20, males 50, females 30, total 80; 2 pounds from rector, established 1819.

Rich Hill day school: Protestants 20, Catholics 10, total 30, all male; national school, established 1824.

Poor

A number of the poor are maintained by the Richardson <Richison> family, but there is no legal provision for them. The amount collected in the churches on Sunday and the charity of individuals is their only support.

Habits of the People

The northern part of the parish has not so rich an appearance as the centre and the southern, the houses being for the greater part mud, but in the other parts of the parish the farmhouses generally assume a very comfortable appearance, and amongst these Wheatfield in Ballybreagh, Fieldmount in Drumard Jones, Mandeville Hall, Prospect House and Mount Pleasant in Mullahead, Laurel Hill in Ballylish, Glebe House in Ballyknock, Mullavilly House in same townland,

Sandymount in Cloghan, Broomfield, Bellview, Fruitfield and Annahill in Ballyleany, Courschill in Annareagh, Money House and Suez House in townlands of same name are the best, and the greater number of the farmhouses are slated. Food and dress are the same as in the surrounding country, and the poorest endeavour to appear clean on Sundays. Their fuel is in general turf, which is brought principally from Drumcree and Tartaraghan parishes. The prevailing names are Hutchison in Cloghan townland, Williamson in Creenagh and Adams in townlands of Bracchagh and Ballylisk. There are no prevailing customs, and the language of the people is in general tolerably good English with a Scotch accent, as is usual in the north.

Productive Economy

Occupations

Weaving is pretty extensively followed in this parish. The marts for it are Lurgan and Armagh, which together with agricultural pursuits employ the men, and the women add spinning to their housewifery <housewiffery>.

Farms and Economy

The farms vary in size from 2 to 100 acres, the old leases being let at from 10s to 20s per acre and new from 24s to 45s, but 30s may be considered as a mean throughout the parish. Life leases (equal to 31 years or 3 lives) and tenants at will, with a few exceptions, comprise the letting of the whole of this parish. The principal bog in the parish is in Derryhale townland, which is the property of Mr Bacon and let at a very trifling rate to the holders of the surrounding tenements. The proprietors are as follows: Mr Bacon 11 townlands, non-resident; primate land attached to the see of Armagh 9; churchland 3; Count De Salis, non-resident, 10; Mrs Cope 7; Miss Isabella Richardson 5; Miss Elisabeth Richardson 4; Colonel Verner 1; Lord Mandeville 1; Major-General Sir T. Molyneux <Mollyneux> 1; Lord Viscount Dungannon, non-resident, 1, and the Revd H. Caulfield 1, non-resident.

Lime is the principal manure and is found in abundance in the townlands of Kilmore, Anahugh and Ballyhagan, from which it can be had at 1s per barrel of 4 bushels and the raw stone may be had 1d per load and quarrying it. There are limekilns in all the large farms and the owners purchase the raw stone at Kilmore and Annahugh and burn it in their own kilns with equal parts of coal and turf. This parish abounds with orchards, which are generally of a good quality, the greater [part] of which is exported to England. Mr Bacon and the Misses Richardson keep a Scotch steward for the sole purpose of instructing their tenantry in agriculture.

Uses made of the Bogs

In the townland of Mulladry there is about 80 acres of meadow known by the name of Pulrawer bogs, supposed to be derived from the Irish pul "a hole or low ground" and rour "fat or fertile", as descriptive of the great quantity of milk obtained from the cattle fed upon them. It was formerly bog, and all the other portions of bog found in this parish, except in Derryhale, are used as pasture and are termed "spent bog."

Cattle

Green feeding is greatly practised in this parish. The cattle for the most part are fed in the house, in the winter with turnip and rape and in the summer with clover and vetches.

General Remarks

This parish may be considered rich and of a home pleasing scenery, much improved by the rich appearance of the numerous orchards which abound throughout the parish. It may in general be said to be in a high state of cultivation, and lime, the manure best suited to the soil, is easily obtained. The culture of the turnip has of late been introduced and is becoming general, although a few years since it was rarely seen.

Social Economy

Ecclesiastical Summary

Name Kilmore, diocese Armagh, province Ulster, rectory, not an union. A perpetual curacy with a district attached to it is established at Mullavilly. Patron the Archbishop of Armagh, incumbent the Rev. Edward Chichester; extent of glebe 700 English acres, all arable. Rectorial tithes belonging to the incumbent in all cases. The number of Established Protestants in the district belonging to the mother church is by the last census 3,679. The number of Established Protestants in the perpetual curacy of Mullavilly 3,781, total in the parish of Kilmore 7,460. The parish is divided into 54 townlands.

TOWNLAND DIVISIONS

Annaboe Townland

Annaboe, pronounced An-na-boe[stressed] from the Irish bo "cow" and agh "ford", in the barony of Oneiland West and is bounded on the north by the townland of Annahue, west by Mooney, east by Clonroot and south by Kilmore and Drumard Jones. Proprietor Mr Bacon, agent C. Brush Esq. It contains 3,511 acres 14 perches, farms from 6 to 40 acres, rent from 27s to 29s 6d, soil good and well cultivated. A part in the south side of this townland is allotted for a glebe and is occupied by the present incumbent, the Rev. E. Chichester. It is about 4 miles distant from Portadown, its nearest market town. Cess 1s 1d per acre.

Annarea Townland

Annarea, pronounced An-na-ray[stressed], in the barony of Oneiland West and is bounded on the north by the townland of Maynooth, west by Rockmacreany, east by Ballynahinch, north east by Ballyleany and south west by the parish of Mullahead. Proprietor Mr Bacon, agent C. Brush Esq. It contains 247 acres 5 perches, farms from 2 to 48 acres, rent 10s to 34s, soil good and well cultivated. Market Armagh, distant 4 and a half miles.

Annahue Townland

Annahue, pronounced An-na-hue[stressed], in the barony of Oneiland West and is bounded on the north by Upper Grange, east by Tullymore and Ballywilly, south by Mooney and west by Ballyhagan and Castleraw. Churchland in possession of the Rev. E. Chichester. It contains 293 acres 2 roods 7 perches, farms from 3 to 33 acres. The occupiers hold the land at will, rent 20s to 30s. The road from Loughgall to Portadown passes through this townland, and on the north side of this road are lime quarries and kilns belonging to Mr Hewitt. There is a good schoolhouse in the centre, the building of which cost 120 pounds in the year 1825 (for further particulars see under head of Schools). Agent Mr Scott. It is 6 miles distant from Armagh and 5 from Portadown. In the north end there are about 10 acres of spent bog. Cess 1s 6d per acre.

Ahory Townland

Ahory, pronounced A-ho[stressed]-ry, in the barony of Oneiland West and is bounded on the north by Ballybreagh, west by the parish of Mullabrack and townland of Ballyloughan, on the east by Cornerscube and on the south by the parish of Mullabrack. Proprietor Colonel Verner. It contains 463 acres 2 perches, of which 2 roods 10 perches is water; farms from 4 to 20 acres, rent from 20s to 25s. On the west side of the townland there is a corn and flax mill and on the east side a flax mill. Market Portadown, distant 3 miles. Cess 1s 4d ha'penny per acre. Colonel Verner is proverbial for being a good landlord.

Ballytrew Townland

Ballytrew, pronounced Bally-true[stressed], is situated in the barony of Oneiland West and is bounded on the north by Tullymore and Grange, east by Lurgancot, south by Ballywilly and west by Tullymore. Primate land attached to the see of Armagh, agent Mr. Isles. It contains 160 acres 1 rood 18 perches and of which about 20 acres are spent bog. Farms from 4 to 35 acres, rent 20s to 36s, tenancy perpetuity and at will, soil good and well cultivated. The road from Loughgall to Portadown passes through the south end of it. Market towns Portadown and Armagh, the former 4 miles, the latter 7 distant. Cess 2s 3d per acre.

Ballyhagan Townland

Ballyhagan, pronounced Bally-hay[stressed]-gan, is situated in the barony of Oneiland West and is bounded on the north by Castleraw, east by Annahue, south by Kilmacauly and Creenagh and west by the parish of Loughgall. Primate land attached to the see of Armagh, agent Mr Isles. It contains 156 acres 3 roods, of which about 20 in the south west corner are spent bog. Farms from 1 to 60 acres, rent 6s to 30s, tenure some in perpetuity, others at will and others who have renewable life leases pay only from 2s 6d to 6s 6d per acre. Soil good and well cultivated. Lime is the principal manure, which is found in abundance along the east side, 10 feet below the surface. Market towns Armagh and Portadown, equal distances 5 and a half miles.

Ballywilly Townland

Ballywilly, pronounced Bally-wil[stressed]-ly, is situated in the barony of Oneiland West and is bounded on the north by Tullymore and Ballytrew, east by Lurgancot and Anaboe and west by Anahugh. Primate land attached to the see of Armagh, agent Mr Isles. It contains 197 acres 2 roods 12 perches, of which 15 are spent bog and between 10 and 20 acres on the south east side are flooded in winter. Farms from 3 to 60 acres, perpetuities and renewable life leases 2s 6d, new [leases] 34s per acre. There is a slaughterhouse in this townland on the road from Loughgall to Portadown, where pig drovers get their pigs killed and thence cart them to the Belfast market. The charge for killing is 6d per pig and they frequently kill 100 a day. Market town Portadown, 5 miles distant.

Ballynahinch Townland

Ballynahinch, pronounced Bally-na-hinch-[stressed], is situated in the south end of parish and barony of Oneiland West. It is bounded on the north and north west by Ballyleany, west by Annareagh, south east by Ballyloughan, east by Mullalelish and south by Mullabrack parish. Proprietors Mr Bacon and Miss Elizabeth Richardson, agent C. Brush Esq. It contains 462 acres 2 roods 23 perches, of which 10 acres 2 roods are bog. Farms from 2 to 40 acres, rent from 25s to 35s, soil good and is in a high state of cultivation. Contains a national school, see head Schools. Portadown is 4 and a half miles distant.

Ballyloughan Townland

Ballyloughan, pronounced Bally-lough[stressed]-an, is one of the most southern townlands in the parish, in [the] barony of Oneiland West and is bounded on the north by Mullalelish, east by Ahory, west by Ballynahinch and Mullabrack parish and south by Mullabrack. Proprietor Miss Elizabeth Richardson, agent C. Brush Esq. Contains 483 acres 1 rood 1 perch, farms from 3 to 52 acres, rent from 20s to 27s, soil good and well cultivated. Lime principal manure, raw stone obtained in Mullaletra townland at 1d ha'penny per cwt, which merely pays for the quarrying, the proprietor bestowing the use of a kiln at the quarry. It contains a school at the north eastern side, see under head of Schools, likewise a flax mill, see under head of Manufactories. Market Tanderagee, distant 4 miles. Cess from 1s to 1s 3d. Fuel principally obtained from the Montiaghs <Moyntiaghs>, some from Derryhale and Vinecash bogs.

Ballyleany Townland

Ballyleany, pronounced Bally-lay[stressed]-ny, is situated in the barony of Oneiland West and bounded on the north by Drumnahuncheon and Mullaletra, west by Rich Hill, south by Ballynahinch and south west by Maynooth and Annareagh. Proprietors Mr Bacon and Miss E. Richardson, agent C. Brush Esq. Contains 434 acres 3 roods 35 perches, farms from 1 to 53 acres, rent 25s to 34s, soil good and in a high state of cultivation. The new road from Armagh to Belfast passes through this townland. There is likewise a portion of the demesne belonging to the Richardson family in it, and the remains of an old fort. It is equidistant from the market towns of Portadown and Tanderagee <Tandragee> 5 miles.

Ballybreagh Townland

Ballybreagh, pronounced Bally-bray[stressed], is situated in the barony of Oneiland West near the centre of the parish and is bounded on the west by Mulladry and Mullalelish, south by Ballyloughan and Ahory and on the east by Cornerscube and Derryhale. Proprietor Miss Isabella Richardson, agent C. Brush Esq. It contains 455 acres 2 roods 14 perches and is let in perpetuity to different persons, of whom Mr Clendinning of Wheatfield holds the largest share, about 200 acres. The farms let to the under-tenants are from 5 to 20 acres, rent 25s to 30s, soil good and in an excellent state of cultivation. It contains a small flax mill, see under head Manufactories. Nearest market Portadown, 2 and three-quarter miles distant.

Ballylisk Townland

Ballylisk, pronounced Bally-lisk[stressed], is situated in the barony of Oneiland West and is bounded on the west by Drumcree parish, north by Unshinagh and Bracchagh, north east by Mullahead, south west by Ballyknock and Mullavilly and on the east by Ballymore parish. Proprietor Count De Salis of Rockby Hall, county Louth, agent Charles A. Creery Esq. Contains 342 acres 3 roods 39 perches, farms from 1 to 40 acres, let at 25s. Lower classes very poor, general occupation weaving and agriculture. It contains a good house known by the name of Laurel Hill, and a fine commodious school. The master receives 30 pounds per annum, the mistress 22 pounds. The latter teaches English grammar, reading, writing, plain and fancy needlework (see under head of Schools). Cess 1s 1d per acre. Market Tanderagee, 1 mile distant.

Ballyknock Townland

Ballynock, pronounced Bally-nock[stressed], is situated in the barony of Lower Orier and bounded on the north west by Mullavilly, north by Ballylisk, south by Cordrain, west by Tamnavelton and east by Ballymore parish. Proprietor Count De Salis, agent Charles A. Creery Esq. It contains 293 acres 3 roods 7 perches, farms from 1 to 20 acres, rent from 10s to 25s. The Glebe House is situated on the north east side and is at present occupied by the Rev. Maxwell Carpendale, curate of Mullavilly church. There are 2 old forts in this townland, one on the east side, the other on the west. The latter mentioned is planted. Cess 1s 1d, market Tanderagee, distant half a mile.

Ballintaggart Townland

Ballintaggart <Ballintegart>, pronounced Ballinteg[stressed]-art, is situated in the barony of Oneiland West and bounded on the west by Bottlehill, south by Mulladry and on the north and east by Drumcree parish. Proprietor Miss Isabella Richardson, agent C. Brush Esq. Contains 592 acres 1 rood 26 perches, of which 8 and a half are bog and which supplies a few with fuel, and a small demesne with a neat house containing 115 acres, of which [blank] Todd Esq. is proprietor and holder. The remaining farms from 1 to 40 acres, rent 24s 6d to 30s. Lime obtained from Kilmore townland at 1s per barrel of 4 bushels or 1d per load for raw stone. Fuel principally obtained from Montiaghs, houses chiefly mud. It contains a good school, the upper storey for the girls, the under for the boys (for further particulars see Schools); likewise a Presbyterian meeting house capable of accommodating 400. Cess 1s 3d, market Portadown, distant 2 and a half miles.

Bottlehill Townland

Bottlehill, so pronounced, is situated in the barony of Oneiland West and is bounded on the north by the parish of Drumcree, east by Ballintaggart, west by Drumard Primate and Clanroot and south by Mulladry. It is churchland and in possession of the Rev. E. Chichester, agent Mr Scott. Contains 202 acres 1 rood 21 perches, farms from 2 to 30 acres, rent 20s to 25s per acre, soil good and well cultivated. This townland is one continuous hill, the highest and most commanding in the northern part of this parish. The highest point is 205 feet above the sea. Cess 1s 6d. It contains a good schoolhouse, formerly under the Kildare Street Society, see under the head Schools.

Bracchagh Townland

Bracchagh, pronounced Brack[stressed]-ey, is situated in the barony of Lower Orier and is bounded on the east by Mullahead, south by Ballylisk, west by Drumcree parish and north by Seago parish. Proprietor Count De Salis, agent Charles A. Creery <Creerey> Esq. It contains 760 acres 1 rood 9 perches. The largest farm is 100 acres, held by Mr Adams of Bracchagh House, rent 10s. The remaining farms are from 3 to 20 acres, rent 25s. The portion of this townland lying between the canal and River Bann is used as meadow and pasture in summer and is flooded in winter. There are 2 fir plantations containing 32 acres. Lime and soil mixed with that of cattle are the principal manures. The lower orders of the people are extreme[ly] poor. Cess 1s 1d. It likewise contains a good school, see Schools. Market Portadown, 1 and a half miles distant.

Castleraw Townland

Castleraw, so pronounced, is situated in the barony of Oneiland West and bounded on the north by Derryloughan, east by Tullymore, Annahugh and Upper Grange, south by Ballyhagan and west by Kincon townland and Loughgall parish. Proprietor Mrs Cope, agent Mr Hardy. Contains 259 acres 3 roods 1 perch, of which 6 are spent bog. Farms from 5 to 25 acres, rent 20s to 35s, tenure life leases and at will. The ruins of Castle Roe, as it was formerly called, are still visible in this townland. The base is 176 feet above the sea. The inhabitants can give no account of the rise or fall of it, see Antiquities. The nearest market Armagh, distant 5 and a half miles.

Cavan Townland

Cavan, pronounced Cav[stressed]-an, is situated in the barony of Oneiland West and bounded on the north by Mooney, west by Tullygarden, south by Corcreeny and east by Mullaletra. Primate land attached to the see of Armagh, and let in perpetuity to the Rev. France Atkinson of Greenhall. It contains 166 acres 19 perches and is let to undertenants at will in farms of 10 acres, rent 32s, soil good and well cultivated. There are 2 lime quarries in it. It likewise contains about 2 and a half acres of bog. Cess 2s 3d, the prevailing name O'Neill and chief employment labour.

Clonroot Townland

Clonroot, pronounced Clon-root[stressed], is situated in the barony of Oneiland West and bounded on the north by Drumard Primate, east by Bottlehill, west by Annaboe and south by Drumnahuncheon. Proprietor Lord Viscount Dungannon, agent [blank] Jebb Esq. Farms from 2 to 30 [acres], rent 15s to 25s, tenure 1 life or 31 years, cess 1s 3d per acre and contains 404 acres 32 perches. Market Portadown, 3 miles distant.

Cloghan Townland

Cloghan, pronounced Clogh[stressed]-an, is situated in the barony of Oneiland West and bounded on the north and north west by Creenagh, east by Liskeyborough and Tullygarden, south by Suez and west by Loughgall parish. Proprietor General Molyneux, agent [blank] Evans Esq., a magistrate of Armagh. Contains 358 acres 1 rood 10 perches. The largest farm is occupied by Gabriel McClane, with a handsome cottage called Sandymount, 88 acres at 14s per acre. The remaining farms are from 5 to 25 [acres], rent 20s to 26s, soil good and in a high state of cultivation. It contains a small limestone quarry near the west side, also a portion of bog about 3 acres and about three-quarters of an acre of marsh. The new road from Armagh to Belfast runs through this townland. The prevailing name is Hutchison and the chief employment labour. Nearest market Armagh, 3 and a half miles distant.

Cordrain Townland

Cordrain, pronounced Cor-drain[stressed], is situated in the barony of Lower Orier and bounded on the north by Ballyknock townland, east and south by Ballymore and west by Mullabrack parish. Proprietor Count De Salis, agent Charles A. Creery Esq. Contains 303 acres 2 roods 5 perches, rent 25s per acre, farms generally small. Manure lime and soil mixed with that of cattle, weaving the general occupation. The houses generally stone and have a comfortable appearance. There is a steam engine in this townland, used for dressing the yarn for a check factory adjoining it. It belongs to Mr J. Montgomery. Cess 1s 1d, market Tanderagee, one-third of a mile distant.

Cornerscube Townland

Cornerscube, pronounced Cor-ner-scube[stressed], is situated in the barony of Lower Orier and bounded on the north by Derryhale, east by Lissavogue and Tamnamore, west by Ahory and Ballybreagh and south by the parish of Mullabrack. Proprietor Count De Salis, agent Charles A. Creery Esq. Farms from 5 to 50 acres, rent 23s to 25s, it contains 651 acres 3 roods 7 perches. Near the north is a good farmhouse, Cornerscube House, and the fences about it are neatly planted with fir trees. Markets Tanderagee and Portadown, equidistant 2 and a half miles.

Creenagh Townland

Creenagh, pronounced Cree[stressed]-na, is situated in the barony of Oneiland West and bounded on the north by Ballyhagan and Lisheffield, south by Cloghan, west by Loughgall parish and south west by Tullygarden. Proprietor Mrs Cope, agent J. Hardy Esq. It contains 276 acres 1 rood 7 perches, farms from 10 to 32 acres, rent 20s to 35s. There are 2 limestone quarries in it. The prevailing name is Williamson and chief employment labour.

Corcreevy Townland

Corcreevy, pronounced Cor-cree[stressed]-vy, is situated in the barony of Oneiland West and bounded on the north by Cavan, west by Tullygarden, east by Rich Hill and Crewcat and south by Maynooth. Proprietor Mr Bacon, agent C. Brush Esq. Contains 230 acres 2 roods 18 perches, farms from 1 to 37 acres, rent from 22s to 35s, soil good and in a high state of cultivation.

Crewcat Townland

Crewcat, pronounced Crew-cat[stressed], is situated in the barony of Oneiland West and bounded on the north by Mullaletra, north west by Cavan, west to south by Corcreevy and east by Rich Hill and Mullaletra. Proprietor Mr Bacon, agent C. Brush Esq. It contains 107 acres 2 roods 23 perches, farms from 4 to 40 acres, rent 29s 6d to 30s, soil good and well cultivated. Lime principal manure and there is 1 limestone quarry near the west side of townland. Cess 1s 3d per acre, market Armagh, 5 miles [distant].

Drumnahuncheon Townland

Drumnahuncheon, pronounced Drum-na-hunch[stressed]-on, is situated near the centre of parish and barony of Oneiland West. It is bounded on the north by Clonroot, east by Derryhale, west by Mullaletra and south by Mulladry. Proprietor Miss Isabella Richardson, agent C. Brush Esq., middleman Rev. Dean Magennis, who holds 110 acres, agent Mr Evans. It contains 361 acres 1 rood 29 perches, farms from 2 to 38 acres, old leases 15s, new from 22s to 32s, soil good and well cultivated. In the west side of this townland there is a Roman Catholic chapel capable of accommodating 400, and on the north there is 8 and a half acres of marsh. The new road from Armagh to Belfast passes through it. Cess varies from 1s 6d to 1s 3d per acre. Nearest market Portadown, distant 4 miles.

Drumard Jones Townland

Drumard Jones, pronounced Drum[stressed]-ard-jones; this townland formerly belonged to a family called Jones, but the present proprietor [is] Mr Bacon, agent C. Brush Esq. It is situated near the centre of parish, in the barony of Oneiland West and bounded on the north by Annaboe and Clonroot, east by Drumnahuncheon, west by Kilmore and Mullaletra and south by Ballyleany. It contains 221 acres 2 roods 30 perches, farms from 3 to 37 acres, rent 17s 6d to 34s. It is a good soil bearing excellent crops. On the east side is Fieldmount, the residence of the Rev. [blank] Taylor, curate of Kilmore church. Cess from 1s 2d to 1s 4d, market Portadown, distant 3 miles.

Drumard Primate Townland

Drumard Primate, pronounced Drum[stressed]-ard-primate, is situated in the barony of Oneiland West and bounded on the north by Grange, east by Bottlehill, west by Lurgancot and south by Clonroot. Primate land attached to the see of Armagh, agent [blank] Kelly Esq., contains 248 acres 1 rood 8 perches. The whole townland is let to Messrs Joyce and Atkinson at 4s 6d per acre. The former holds the greater share (160 acres) and is sublet by them in farms of from 2 to 20 acres at 40s to 45s. The lease by which Joyce and Atkinson hold this townland is renewable yearly. Cess 2s, market Portadown, 2 and a half miles distant.

Derryhale Townland

Derryhale, pronounced Derry-hail[stressed], is situated in the barony of Oneiland West and is bounded on the east by the parish of Drumcree and townland of Lissavogue, south by Cornerscube and west by Ballybreagh, Ballintaggart and Mulladry. Proprietor Miss Isabella Richardson, agent C. Brush Esq. It contains 834 acres, of which about 63 are bog. [Blank] Cox holds the largest farm, about 98 acres, at 10s per [acre]. The remaining farms are from 1 to 20, rent 20s to 30s. The bog in this townland supplies the surrounding neighbourhood with fuel. Oak and fir trees are found in it. In general the roots are in position as when growing, the trunks apparently broken off by force. It contains a neat schoolhouse, see Schools. Market Portadown, distant 2 and a half miles.

Derryloughan Townland

Derryloughan, pronounced Derry-lough[stressed]-an and Donny-lough[stressed]-an, is situated in the barony of Oneiland West and is bounded on the north by Tartaraghan parish, east by Tullymore and Lower Grange, south by Castleraw and Kincon and west by Loughgall parish. Contains 259 acres 2 roods 35 perches. Proprietor Mrs Cope, agent Mr Hardy. Farms from 5 to 34 [acres], rent 16s to 32s, tenure life leases and at will. There are about 100 looms at work in this townland, but they weave very coarse cloth <cloath>. Lime is the principal manure, which the farmers bring from Annahugh and burn in their own kilns. Market Armagh, distant 6 miles.

Grange Upper and Lower Townlands

Grange Upper and Lower, so pronounced. They both belong to the Lordship of Newry, although in the county Armagh and barony of Oneiland West. Lower Grange is bounded on the north by Tartaraghan parish, east by Drumcree parish, south by Drumard Primate, Lurgancot, Ballytrew and Tullymore and west by Tullymore and Derryloughan townlands. Upper Grange [is bounded on the] north east by Tullymore, south by Annahugh and west by Castleraw. Proprietor Mrs Cope, agent Mr Hardy. Lower Grange contains 903 acres 3 roods 19 perches, Upper Grange 64 acres 2 roods 14 perches, farms from 5 to 40, rent 15s to 30s. Of the former about 100 acres are flooded in winter, and is on[ly ?] 62 feet above the sea. The highest part is called the Diamond hill and is 144 feet above the sea. The Diamond Cross is remarkable for being the seat of the first Orange lodge in Ireland, also for a battle between the Protestants and Catholics in the year 1795 in which some on each side were killed. These 2 townlands are tithe free, but the cess is from 5s to 6s per acre. Lower Grange contains a good school, see Schools. Armagh chief market, 7 miles distant, but they frequent Portadown, 3 and a half miles distant.

Kincon Townland

Kincon, pronounced Kin[stressed]-can(stressed), is situated in the barony of Oneiland West and bounded on the north east by Loughgall parish and Derryloughan townland, east by Castleraw and south west by Loughgall parish. Proprietor Mrs Cope, agent Mr Hardy. It contains 112 acres 3 roods 25 perches, farms 4 to 27 [acres], rent 26s to 34s, tenure life leases and at will. It is good soil and well cultivated, and there is 5 or 6 acres of an orchard to every house, which gives them a very comfortable appearance. Market towns Armagh 6 miles and Portadown 5 [miles] distant. There is a poor kind of limestone in the west of [the] townland.

Kilmore Townland

Kilmore, pronounced Kil-more[stressed], is situated in the barony of Oneiland West and is bounded on the north and east by Annaboe, west by Mooney and south by Mullaletra. Primate land attached to the see of Armagh, and let to Mr Atkinson at 4s 6d per acre, who relets it at 40s. The soil is good and well cultivated. It is famous for its lime quarries and the surrounding townlands are supplied from it at 1d per load for the raw stone and 1s per barrel of 4 bushels for it burned. It contains 86 acres 2 roods 20 perches, the parish church and a school, and for further particulars respecting them see Public Buildings, Schools and Antiquities. Cess 1s 8d, market Portadown, distant 5 miles.

Kilmacanty Townland

Kilmacanty, pronounced Kil-ma-ken[stressed]-ty, is situated in the barony of Oneiland West and is bounded on the north by Annahugh <Annahue>, north west by Ballyhagan, west by Creenagh, south by Tullygarden and east by Mooney. Primate land attached to the see of Armagh, and let to C. Atkinson Esq. of Greenhall and W. Williamson of Springhill at 2s 6d per acre, renewable for ever, and relet by them in farms of from 4 to 8 acres at from 30s to 35s. It contains 125 acres 2 roods 23 perches, soil good and in a high state of cultivation. There is a small lime quarry on the west side, also an old corn mill in ruins and about 3 and a half acres of marsh. Market towns Armagh and Portadown, equidistant 5 and a half miles.

Lissheffield Townland

Lissheffield, pronounced Lis-shef[stressed]-field, is situated in the barony of Oneiland West, bounded on the north and west by the parish of Loughgall and south and east by Creenagh townland. Proprietor Mrs Cope, agent Mr Hardy. Contains 44 acres 35 perches, farms 3 to 10 acres, rent 28s. This townland contains 3 limestone quarries and an old tanyard in ruins. Cess 1s 2d, market Armagh, distant 5 miles.

Lurgancot Townland

Lurgancot, pronounced Lur-gan-cot[stressed], is situated in the barony of Oneiland West, bounded on the north by Grange and east by Drumard Primate. Proprietor Rev. H. Caulfield, agent Mr Pepper. Farms 2 to 30 acres, rent 20s to 25s, contains 218 acres 1 rood 36 perches, soil good and well cultivated. Cess 2s, market Portadown, distant 3 miles.

Lisavogue Townland

Lisavogue, pronounced Lis-a-vogue[stressed], is situated in the barony of Lower Orier and is bounded on the east by Drumcree parish and Tamnavelton townland, west by Derryhale and Cornerscube and south by Tamnamore. Proprietor Count De Salis, agent Charles A. Creery Esq. Contains 336 acres 2 roods 13 perches, of which 22 are bog, farms from 5 to 30 acres, rent 23s to 25s. It contains a neat farmhouse known by the name of the Lodge. The farm itself has a good appearance, the fences being planted with fir and ash trees, likewise a corn mill in good repair (see Manufactories) and a fort in good preservation. Nearest market Tanderagee, 2 and a half miles distant.

Liskeyborough Townland

Liskeyborough, pronounced Lis-key-bor[stressed]-row, is situated in the barony of Oneiland West, bounded on the north by Tullygarden, west by Cloghan, south by Suez and east by Maynooth and Corcreevy. Proprietor Mr Bacon, agent C. Brush Esq. Contains 277 acres 2 roods 27 perches, of which 2 and a half are marsh, farms from 1 to 39 acres, rent 23s to 34s. Soil good and in a high state of cultivation. The new road from Armagh to Belfast runs through this townland. There is likewise an old fort in the south end of it. Market Armagh, 5 miles [distant].

Mooney Townland

Mooney, pronounced Mon[stressed]-ey, is situated in the barony of Oneiland West and is bounded on the north by Annahugh, west by Kilmacanty, south by Cavan, east by Kilmore and Annaboe and south east by Mullaletra. Proprietor Captain Atkinson of Crow Hill. Contains 173 acres 1 rood 32 perches, of which 8 and a half are bog, farms from 3 to 50 acres, rent 30s. Soil good and well cultivated. It contains a limestone quarry. Chief employment labour. Market Armagh, distant 5 and a half miles.

Maynooth Townland

Maynooth, pronounced May-nooth[stressed], is situated in the barony of Oneiland West and is bounded on the north by Rich Hill, north west by Corcreevy, west by Liskeyborough and Suez, south by Rockmacreeny, south east by Annarea and east by Ballyleany. Proprietor Mr Bacon, agent C. Brush Esq. Contains 234 acres 1 rood 22 perches, farms from 1 to 17 acres, rent 20s to 30s. Soil good and well cultivated. [Market] Armagh, 4 and a half miles distant.

Mullaletra Townland

Mullaletra, pronounced Mul-el-eat[stressed]-tra, is situated in the barony of Oneiland West and is bounded on the north by Kilmore, north west by Mooney, west by Cavan, south and west by Crewcat and north by Rich Hill. Proprietor Mr Bacon, agent C. Brush Esq. Contains 221 acres 7 perches, of which 7 and a half are bog, farms from 1 to 43 acres, rent 25s to 30s 6d. Soil good and well cultivated. It contains a limestone quarry. It is 7 miles from Armagh and 5 miles from Portadown [markets].

Mulladry Townland

Mulladry, pronounced Mul-la-dry[stressed], is situated near the centre of parish and in the barony of Oneiland West. It is bounded on the north by Bottlehill, east by Derryhale, west by Ballyleany and south by Mullalelish. Proprietors Misses Isabella and Elizabeth Richardson, agent C. Brush Esq. The former holds 626, the latter 122 acres. It contains 748 acres 35 perches, of which 80 along the east boundary is excellent meadow or pasture called Pulrawer bog, called so on account of its richness. Farms from 2 to 60 acres, the largest of which is occupied by Mr Hewitt, rent 17s to 30s. The road from Armagh to Belfast runs through this townland. It contains a school, see Schools. The soil is of excellent quality, cess 1s 4d. The neatest house is occupied by Mr Hewitt. Market Tanderagee, 4 and a half miles distant.

Mullalelish Townland

Mullalelish, pronounced Mul-la-lay[stressed]-lish, is situated in the barony of Oneiland West and bounded on the north by Mulladry, east by Ballybreagh, west by Ballynahinch and south by Ballyloughan. Proprietor Miss Elizabeth Richardson, agent C. Brush Esq. It contains 620 acres 3 roods 36 perches, farms from 2 to 70 acres, the largest held by J. Greer. Rent 25s to 30s, soil good and well cultivated. On the west side there is a plain neat house called Killynahawagh House. Cess 1s to 1s 3d per acre, nearest market town Tanderagee, from which it is distant 4 and a half miles.

Mullahead Townland

Mullahead, pronounced Mul-ly-head(stresed), is situated in the barony of Lower Orier and is bounded on the north by Seagoe parish, east by Tullylish parish, south by Ballymore parish and west by Ballylisk townland. Proprietor Lord Mandeville, agent Mr Hunt. Contains 864 acres 17 perches, farms from 1 to 40 acres, rent 25s, soil good, lime the principal manure. The road from Tanderagee to Portadown runs through this townland, and the bridge over the old course of River Bann is called the Knock bridge. There are some good houses on this road, and those worthy of notice are Mount Pleasant, Mr Haddock, J. Christy's, Mandeville Hall, Mr Bagbey's, Prospect House, Mr Caple's. There is an old fort in the south west side of townland and a school supported by Lord Mandeville. [Market] Tanderagee, 1 mile distant.

Mullavilly Townland

Mullavilly, pronounced Mul[stressed]-ly-vil[stressed]-ly, situated in the barony of Lower Orier and bounded on the north west by Drumcree parish, north east by Ballylisk, south east by Ballyknock and on the south west by Tamnavelton. Proprietor Count De Salis, agent Charles A. Creery Esq. Mr James Atkinson holds the greater part of it at 10s per acre, the remainder is let at 25s. Mullavilly House is occupied by J. Atkinson. Mullavilly church is situated in the east side of the townland (see Public Buildings). It contains 159 acres 1 rood 34 perches, soil good, cess 1s 1d. Market Tanderagee, distant 1 and a half miles.

Rockmacreeny Townland

Rockmacreeny, pronounced Rock[stressed]-ma-cree[stressed]-ny, is situated in the barony of Oneiland West and bounded on the north by Maynooth, west by Suez, east by Annareagh and south by the parish of Mullabrack. Proprietor Mr Bacon, agent C. Brush Esq. It contains 280 acres 3 roods 13 perches, of which 2 and three-quarters in the north extremity are marsh. Farms from 6 to 64 acres, the largest is occupied by R. Williamson. Rent from 22s to 25s 6d, soil good and in a high state of cultivation. It contains a flax mill, see Manufactories, and 2 old forts. Market Tanderagee, 5 miles distant.

Rich Hill Townland

Rich Hill, pronounced Rich-hill[stressed] and formerly called Legacorry, is situated in the barony of Oneiland West and is bounded on the north by Crewcat, west by Corcreevy, south by Maynooth and east by Ballyleany. Proprietor Miss Elizabeth Richardson, agent C. Brush Esq. Farms from 1 to 40 [acres], rent from 27s 6d to 34s, soil good and in a high state of cultivation. It contains 347 acres 2 roods 24 perches, of which 1 and a half is used as a mill dam in winter and pasture in summer. It likewise contains the town of Rich Hill, with the greater part of the demesne belonging to the Richardson family, a Quaker meeting house, one belonging to the Presbyterians, one to the Methodists and an Evangelical meeting house. For further particulars respecting these see Towns. It likewise contains a corn mill, see Manufactories. The highest part of this townland is the hill on which the town is situated, being 270 feet above the level of the sea. Armagh is the principal market but Portadown and Tanderagee are likewise attended, all nearly equidistant.

Suez Townland

Suez, pronounced Shew[stressed]-is, is situated in the barony of Oneiland West and bounded on the north by Cloughan and Liskeyborough, on the west by Loughgall parish, east by Rockmacreeny and north east by Maynooth. Proprietor Mr Bacon, agent C. Brush Esq. It contains 214 acres 2 roods 34 perches, farms from 1 to 45 acres, rent from 20s to 26s. There are 2 small portions of bog, one containing 4 acres the other 3, and 2 old forts. [Market] Armagh, distant 5 miles.

Tullymore Townland

Tullymore, pronounced Tully-more[stressed], is situated in the barony of Oneiland West and is bounded on the north by Lower Grange, east by Ballytrew, south by Ballywilly and Anahugh and west by Upper Grange, Kincon and Derryloughan townlands. It is churchland in possession of the Rev. E. Chichester. It contains 367 acres 34 perches, of which about 35 are bog, 68 feet above the level of the sea. Farms from 5 to 30 acres, rent from 20s to 34s, tenure yearly. It is well cultivated, and they manufacture some coarse linen cloth. Bloom hill is the best farmhouse in the townland. Market Armagh, 7 miles [distant].

Tamnamore Townland

Tamnamore, pronounced Tam-na-more[stressed], is situated in the barony of Lower Orier and is bounded on the north by Lissavogue, east by Tamnavelton and Cordrain, west by Cornerscube and south by the parish of Mullaghbrack. Proprietor Count De Salis, agent C.A. Creery Esq. It contains 534 acres 3 roods 30 perches, farms from 5 to 30 [acres], rent 23s, tenure life leases. There is a good farmhouse in the west side known by the name of Ashtree hill, likewise a place called [?] Corner's Grave at the meeting of 4 roads on the south west side of the townland, most probably on account of a man called [?] Corner having hung himself near the place at some remote period. It contains an old fort. Tanderagee is the nearest market, 2 and a quarter miles distant.

Tullygarden Townland

Tullygarden, pronounced Tully-gard[stressed]-en, is situated in the barony of Oneiland West and is bounded on the north by Kilmacanty, north west by Creenagh, west by Cloughan, south by Liskeyborough and east by Corcreevy. Primate land attached to the see of Armagh, agent A.J. Kelly Esq. It contains 168 acres 3 roods 21 perches, of which Mr Delap holds 80 acres at 2s 6d renewable for ever, and relets it in farms from 3 to 10 [acres] at 30s. Miss Joyce holds 45 acres and relets it in 1 farm at 31s 6d. C. Atkinson Esq. of Greenhall near Charlemont holds 29 acres and relets it in farms of from 1 to 6 [acres] at 31s 6d, and J. Hutchison holds about 15 at 2s 6d per acre. Soil good and well cultivated. Cess from 2s 3d to 2s 6d. Market Armagh, 4 miles distant.

Tamnavelton Townland

Tamnavelton, pronounced To[stressed]-ny-bal[stressed]-toney, is situated in the barony of Lower Orier and is bounded on the north by Drumcree parish, north east by Mullavilly, east by Ballyknock, south by Tamnamore and west by Lissavogue. It is a manor townland, formerly giving title to Lord Toneybaltoney, which is claimed by the present proprietor, Count De Salis. Agent Charles A. Creery Esq. Contains 378 acres 1 rood 5 perches, let at 25s per acre. Houses generally mud and occupation weaving and agriculture. There is a Roman Catholic chapel on the east side of townland, see Public Buildings, and about an eighth of a mile south of it the priest's house is situated, and in the north end of the townland there is a good nursey, the property of J. Colwell. Market Tanderagee, 1 mile distant.

Unshenagh Townland

Unshenagh, pronounced Un[stressed]-she-na, is situated in the barony of Lower Orier and is bounded on the north east by Bracchagh, north west by Drumcree parish and north by Ballylisk townland. Proprietor Count De Salis, agent Charles A. Creery Esq. Contains 172 acres 12 perches and is let in small farms at 25s per acre. Houses generally mud, occupation weaving, lime principal manure, mixed with that of cattle, cess 1s 1d. Market Tanderagee, 1 and a half miles distant.

Parish of Loughgall, County Armagh

Fair Sheets for Memoir by J. Cumming Innes [and J.R. Ward]

Natural State

Name

The parish is said to derive its name from a small lake situated in it.

Locality

The parish of Loughgall is situated in the west of the county of Armagh and occupies portions of 2 baronies viz. Armagh and Oneilland <Oneiland> West. It is bounded by the following parishes: on the north by Killyman, on the east by Tartaraghan and Kilmore, on the south by Grange and Mullabrack and on the west by Grange, Clonallan and county of Tyrone. It is 8 and a quarter miles long and 4 and a half miles broad. Its content is 10,924 acres 1 rood 24 perches, including 59 acres 2 roods 4 perches of water, of which [blank] are cultivated. It is divided into [blank] townlands and is valued at [blank] pounds to the county cess.

Natural Features

Hills

The surface of the parish consists of innumerable small egg-shaped hills, sometimes running in ridges and at others rising singly out of bogs or flat marshy ground. The highest point is in the townland of Loughgall, 204 feet above the level of the sea. The lowest ground is along the banks of the Callan and Blackwater rivers, 50 feet above the sea. The average height of the hills is 150 feet above the sea, [signed] J.R. Ward.

Rivers

Callan river [runs] through this parish for 2 miles in a north west direction; its average breadth is 24 feet. In summer it is a stream, but in winter it rises considerably. Its source is in the parishes of Lisnadill and Keady, county Armagh. It is usefully situated for water power and drainage. It runs over a sandy bed. [The] banks are well cultivated and the scenery not at all picturesque.

Tall river is the boundary of this parish for 8 miles in a westerly direction. Its average breadth is 15 feet and its depth from 1 to 4. Its source is in the parish of Mullaghbrack, county Armagh. It is usefully situated for drainage and overflows very much in the months of December and January. The parish is well supplied with water from springs and rivulets.

Blackwater river forms the western boundary of the parish for 1 mile and a half. It runs in a north east direction by north. It is 10 feet deep and averages 120 feet in breadth. It rises in the county Tyrone. It is navigable as far as Blackwatertown for boats of 20 tons burthen. It is usefully situated for navigation and drainage, but the fall is not great enough for water power. There are no falls or rapids in this part of the river, the general fall one half a mile an hour. The river is subject to floods in wet seasons, which do not subside until dry weather commences. These floods leave a deposit of sand and mud which are useful to the meadows. The river both impedes and facilitates communication in its natural state, and flows over a sandy bed, [signed] J. Cumming Innes.

Lakes

Loughgall lake occupies portions of the townlands of Loughgall, Ballytyrone, Drumilly and Levalleglish. Its total content is 39 acres 2 roods 7 perches. It is 90 feet above the level of the sea, the depth is not known. There is a small island situated at the east side, covered with plantation.

Productive Economy

Crops

The crops are wheat, oats, barley, potatoes and flax. Wheat is sown in November and December and reaped in August. Oats and barley are sown in April and reaped in September and October. Potatoes are set in April and May and dug in October and November, and flax is sown April and pulled in July.

Natural Features

Bogs

There are small patches of bog interspersed through this parish which are nearly cut out.

Modern Topography

Public Buildings: Chapel

Loughgall chapel, situated in the townland of Eagralougher, is a plain stone building, roughcast, whitewashed and slated, 68 feet long and 20 feet broad, built in 1787, the cost not known. There is accommodation for 500 persons and the general attendance is 400. The interior is very plain. The parish priest is the Rev. [blank] Caten.

Church

Loughgall church, situated at the south west end of Loughgall in the townland of Levalleglish, is a neat stone building, roughcast and slated, with a cut stone front. It is 82 and a half feet long and 36 feet broad, built in 1795.

Charlemont Church

Charlemont church, situated at the south end of Charlemont in the townland of Corr and Dunavally, is a neat stone building, roughcast and slated, corniced with whinstone, having 2 minarets on the porch and a small erection of masonry for a bell, but there is none in it at present. The form and dimensions of the building are represented by the following figure: [ground plan, main dimensions 67 and a half feet by 21 feet, rectangular shape with projection at both ends]. Built in 1831.

Presbyterian Meeting House

Loughgall Presbyterian meeting house, situated in the townland of Cloveneden, is a plain stone building, roughcast, whitewashed and slated, 64 feet long and 38 feet broad. It was built in 1791, the cost not known. There is accommodation for 500 persons and the general attendance is 100. The interior is very plain, having pews, a mud floor and no ceiling. The minister is the Rev. William Henry, who receives 20 pounds stipend and 50 pounds Irish currency of Regium Donum per annum.

Methodist Meeting Houses

Methodist meeting house, situated in the townland of Clonmain, is a mud-wall building, roughcast, whitewashed and thatched, 36 and a half feet long and 19 and a half broad. The interior is plain, having no pews, a mud floor and no ceiling. There is no stationary minister.

Methodist meeting house, situated in the townland of Ballymagerny, is a plain stone building, roughcast, whitewashed and thatched, 42 and a half feet long and 22 and a half feet broad. The interior is very plain, having neither pews or ceiling and a mud floor. There is no stationary minister.

Bridge

Callan bridge, on the road between Charlemont and Loughgall over the Callan river, is 26 feet long and 25 and a half feet broad, built of limestone with parapet walls. It consists of 1 semicircular arch.

Schoolhouses

Summer Island schoolhouse, situated in the townland of Summer Island, is a stone house, roughcast, whitewashed and slated, 40 and a half feet long and 20 and a half feet broad. Neither the date of building or cost known. There were repairs done lately which cost 25 pounds. Part of the house is used as a dwelling for the master.

Clonmain schoolhouse, situated in the townland of Clonmain, is a stone cottage, roughcast, whitewashed and thatched, 29 and a half feet long and 18 feet broad. Built in 1777, the cost not known. There were repairs done in 1823 which cost 60 pounds, and some in 1837 which cost 25 pounds.

Kinnegoe schoolhouse, situated in the townland of Kinnegoe, is a stone cottage, roughcast, whitewashed and thatched, 44 feet long and 18 feet broad. Built in 1816 and cost 80 pounds, which was defrayed by William Parnell Esq., Avondale, county Wicklow.

Loughgall schoolhouse, situated in the townland [of] Levalleglish, is a neat stone house, roughcast, yellow-washed and slated. The form and dimensions are represented by the following figure: [ground plan, main dimensions 47 and a half feet by 34 and a half feet, "L" shape]. It was built in 1811 and cost 300 pounds, defrayed by the trustees of Erasmus Smith. Repairs done in 1837 which cost 10 pounds.

Court House

The court house, situated at the north east end of the town of Loughgall, is a plain stone building, roughcast, whitewashed and slated, 52 feet long and 29 feet broad, built in 1746. The upper part of the building is used as a court house and the under as a market house.

Dispensary

The dispensary, situated at the north end of the town of Loughgall, is a plain stone dwelling house, not built for the purpose of a dispensary. It is rented for its present purpose at 12 pounds per annum.

SOCIAL ECONOMY

Residence of Magistrate

John Hardy Esq. resides at the south end of the town.

Streets

The town consists of 1 street [blank] yards long and averaging 30 feet broad. The houses are straggling and irregular: they consist of 18 of 1, 27 of 2, and 4 of 3-storeys; of these 33 are thatched and the remainder slated. The town is neither lighted, paved or watched. There are no new houses building.

Habits and Occupations

The people are mostly employed in retail dealing, farming, weaving and labouring. They have no scientific or literary institutions, no libraries, reading rooms or societies for the encouragement of useful arts or inventions! [Table of occupations]: boot and shoemaker 1, grocer and spirit store 2, lodging and entertainments 1, saddler <sadler> 1, public house 1, blacksmith 1, doctor 1, surgeon 1. There are no banks, branch banks or savings banks. Markets are held every Friday, fairs every month. There are no tolls or customs levied.

Public Conveyance

The Dungannon and Belfast coach passes through the town every Monday and Wednesday and Friday at 5.30 a.m. on its route to Belfast, and on its return at 6.30 p.m. every Tuesday, Thursday and Saturday.

Dispensary

There is a dispensary in the town which has had some good effects on the comforts and health of the poor classes. For further particulars see Benevolence table. There is no other provision for the poor, aged and infirm.

Local Government

John Hardy Esq., residing in the town of Loughgall, is the only magistrate in the parish. He is firm and much respected by the people. There is 1 sergeant and 3 privates of the constabulary police stationed in the town of Loughgall. A court baron is held every month and a court leet every year in the town of Loughgall.

Schools

The introduction of schools has been of great service to the inhabitants and has led to a perceptible improvement in their moral habits. There are several schools.

Poor

There is no provision for the poor, aged or infirm. Subscriptions are raised in the several places of worship, which are divided by the different clergymen or churchwardens.

Habits and Occupations of the People

The cottages are generally of 1-storey, thatched, having glass windows and containing 2 rooms. There is not much attention paid to cleanliness. The people have no amusements except in attending the fairs and markets in the neighbourhood.

Education

[Table of schools contains the following headings: name, situation and description, when established, income and expenditure, physical, intellectual and moral instruction, number of pupils, subdivided by age, sex and religion, name and religion of master or mistress, date on which visited].

Summer Island, a neat house in the townland of Summer Island, established 1831; income: from Hibernian Society 4 pounds 10s, from Mrs William Verner 7 pounds 10s, 5 pounds from pupils; intellectual instruction: Hibernian Society books; moral instruction: visited by the Reverend Silver Oliver, rector of the parish, and the Reverend James Disney, Protestant curate of Charlemont, Authorised Version of Scriptures read; number of pupils: males, 14 under 10 years of age, 22 from 10 to 15, 4 above 15, a total of 40; females, 12 under 10 years of age, 16 from 10 to 15, 2 over 15, a total of 30; total number of pupils 70, 43 Established Church, 10 Presbyterians, 17 Roman Catholics; master Thomas Jackson, Established Church, visited 8th December 1837.

Clonmain, a cottage in the townland of Clonmain, established 1821; income: from the Hibernian Society 5 pounds, 14 pounds from pupils; intellectual instruction: Hibernian Society books; moral instruction: visited by the Reverend Silver Oliver and the Reverend James Disney, Authorised Version of Scriptures read; number of pupils: males, 11 under 10 years of age, 15 from 10 to 15, 5 above 15, a total of 31; females, 9 under 10 years of age, 14 from 10 to 15, 9 above 15, a total of 32; total number of pupils 63, 51 Established Church,

7 Presbyterians, 5 Roman Catholics; master James Murphy, Established Church, visited 8th December 1837.

Kinnegoe, a cottage in the townland of Kinnegoe, established 1816; income: from William Parnell Esquire 20 pounds, 5 pounds from pupils; moral instruction: visited by the Reverend Silver Oliver and the Reverend James Disney, Authorised Version of Scriptures read, catechisms taught on Saturday; number of pupils: males, 26 under 10 years of age, 26 from 10 to 15, a total of 52; females, 6 under 10 years of age, 20 from 10 to 15, 1 above 15, a total of 27; total number of pupils 79, 26 Established church, 11 Roman Catholics; master John Barry, Established Church, visited 14th December 1837.

Loughgall male school, a neat house in the townland of Deralleglish, established 1811; income: from Eramus Smith 30 pounds, 5 pounds from pupils; intellectual instruction: Kildare Place books; moral instruction: visited by the Reverend Silver Oliver and the Reverend Hugh Hamilton Madden, Protestant curate of Loughgall, catechism of the Established Church taught on Saturday, Authorised Version of Scriptures read; number of pupils: 55 under 10 years of age, 30 from 10 to 15, 15 above 15, a total of 100, 64 Established Church, 36 Roman Catholics; master Thomas Hughes, Established Church, visited 20th January 1838.

Loughgall female school, a room in the male schoolhouse, established 1811; income: from Reverend Silver Oliver 4 pounds, Miss Madden 6 pounds, Mrs Hardy 2 pounds; intellectual instruction: Kildare Place books; moral instruction: visited by the Reverend Silver Oliver and the Reverend Hugh Hamilton Madden, Protestant curate of Loughgall, catechism of the Established Church taught on Saturday, Authorised Version of Scriptures read; number of pupils: 38 under 10 years of age, 20 from 10 to 15, a total of 58, 38 Established Church, 6 Presbyterians, 14 Roman Catholics; mistress Anna Buchanan, Established Church, visited 20th January 1838.

Productive Economy

Table of Mills

[Table gives townland, proprietor, tenant, date of erection, diameter, breadth and type of wheel, fall of water, type of machinery, number of pairs of stones or sets of scutches, remarks].

Clonmain, proprietor [blank] Thompson Esq., tenant Charles Atkinson, erected 1817, wheel 15 feet by 3 feet 9 inches, breast, fall 3 feet, machinery wood and iron, 1 double engine, 1 wash mill and rubbing board, a good slated house.

Ballygasey, proprietor Arthur Cope Esq., tenan William Jackson, erected 1825, wheel 18 feet by feet 9 inches, overshot, fall 2 feet, machinery woo and iron, 3 pair of stones, a good slated house [signed] J.C. Innes.

Statistical Report by Lieut C. Bailey, 1 Ma 1835

Natural State

Name

The name is spelt thus: Loughgall in *Carlisle' Topographical dictionary*, in the *Irish ecclesiastical register*, in Beaufort's *Ecclesiastical memoir* in the House of Commons' *Report on the population of Ireland* and in various other documents; th emphasis being laid upon the last syllable, Loughgall[stressed]. There is a lake close to the village o Loughgall from which the name of the parish ma have been derived, as in the Irish language lough signifies "lake" and, I believe, geal "white", o Loughgeal "the white lake".

Locality

It is situated in the county of Armagh and baronie of Armagh and Oneilland <O'neiland> West bounded on the north and north west by the parish of Clonfeacle <Clonfeckle>, east by the parishe of Tartaraghan and Kilmore, south by the parish o Mullaghbrack and on the west by Armagh parish Extreme length 9 miles, extreme breadth 4 and half miles, containing 10,924 statute acres, o which 5,584 are under cultivation, 5,200 uncultivated and 140 water. The average rate of count cess is about 1s 6d per acre half yearly.

Natural Features

Hills

There are no hills of any consequence. The whol parish is composed of gently undulating ground The highest points above the level of the sea ar Rathdrumgranna Fort 463 feet, Castle Dillo obelisk (ground) 260 feet, Loughgall hill 204 fee Ligar hill 140 feet and Ardress House 140 fee decreasing in altitude from south to north.

Lakes

There are only 2 lakes, one close to the village o

Loughgall 91 feet above the sea. It contains about 40 acres. The bottom is of sand, marl and gravel. There is a small island in the lake. The other is situated close to Castle Dillon, 155 feet above the sea, containing 52 acres, of which 20 are in Loughgall parish and 32 in the parish of Armagh.

Rivers

The Blackwater river, which flows from the north west boundary of the parish dividing the counties of Tyrone and Armagh, flows north and empties itself into Lough Neagh. Average breadth 100 feet and depth from 6 to 8 feet, and is navigable for barges as high as Blackwatertown. It is a very sluggish river in the summer, but during the winter is subject to rapid floods, owing to the waters of Lough Neagh not running off sufficiently quick. They are backed up and inundate the whole of the low country in the valley of the Blackwater.

The Callan <Callen> is a small river about 30 feet broad, flows north dividing the parishes of Armagh and Loughgall for about 1 and a half miles, passes for a distance of 2 and a half miles through Loughgall parish where it is joined by the River Tall, and becomes the boundary between the parishes of Clonfeacle and Loughgall for 1 and a half miles and falls into the Blackwater river at about a mile below Charlemont bridge. It is very subject to floods.

The Tall is another small river about 20 feet broad, flows west forming the boundary between the parishes of Loughgall and Tartaraghan for about 1 and a quarter miles [and] passes for a distance of 2 miles through the northern extremity of the parish. It then becomes for about 2 and a half miles the boundary between the parishes of Loughgall and Clonfeacle when it joins the Callan river at Fairlawn bridge. It is very subject indeed to floods, in fact the meadows all along its course are inundated during a great part of the winter.

Bogs

There is a large tract of bog in the northern extremity of the parish in the townlands of Derrycoosh, Annaghmore and Ardress, and a considerable quantity on the western side in the townlands of Runaghan, Aghinlig and Kinnego. Fir and oak timber is found imbedded in the bog. The fir timber is met with at about 6 feet deep in the bog, broken off at the same height, the roots and stumps remaining upright. The oak timber is attached to its roots and is found under the fir timber, lying on the clay at the bottom of the bog. The depth of the bogs in the centre is not known, but near the edges it is about 10 feet deep. It is very light and spongy for about 4 feet, the next 3 feet are closer and then hard black turf to the clay. There are several insulated hills or islands rising through the bogs in the north extremity of the parish, evidently of diluvial formation, consisting of loose tumbling stones embedded in clay. Pieces of wood, partly silicified and having in some cases the appearance of having been burnt, are found 30 or 40 feet under the surface. One of the hills has received the name of the Burnt Island from the quantity of this wood found in it.

Woods

There is a natural wood containing about 20 acres called Derrycree wood, situated on an insulated hill in the townland of Derrycoosh. It consists of oak, hazel, birch and holly. The whole of this hill was covered with wood a few years ago, but is now cleared and brought into cultivation. From the great number of roots and stumps of trees found in all parts of this parish, it must originally have been one mass of wood, which opinion is strengthened by general report.

Modern Topography

Loughgall Village

The village of Loughgall is in the county of Armagh, barony of Oneilland West and about the centre of the parish, in a very rich and highly productive part of the country. The demesnes of Loughgall and Drumilly, with rather an extensive lake, are situated close to the village and add much to beauty of the scenery. The church is situated at the western extremity of the village, built in the year 1795 when Dr Bissett, the late Bishop of Raphoe, was rector of the parish. It will accommodate 400 persons. [Crossed out: the western gable of the old church is still standing and the burial ground made use of]. There is a court house in the centre of the village and a schoolhouse close to the church. The principal private residences are those of the Rev. Dr Oliver, rector of the parish, and of Mr Hardy, agent to the Loughgall estate. Most of the houses are bad and much out of repair. A few comfortable cottages have been lately built by Mr Hardy adjoining his own house, and a large brick house is now building in the centre of the village.

Productive Economy

Trade in Loughgall

The village of Loughgall is not remarkable for any

particular trade. There are 3 large shops which carry on an extensive business in cloth, groceries, spirits and general merchandize. There are no markets nor fairs. Grazing for cattle is procured in Loughgall demesne at 2 pounds 8s per head for the summer season and 1 pound per head during the winter. Land in the neighbourhood is let at 1 pound 10s per acre statute, leasehold for 1 life or 21 years. Lime is procured at the Ballygawsey kilns about half a mile distant. Timber, slates and iron for building are brought from Blackwatertown, Moy and Portadown.

ANTIQUITY

History of Charlemont

Charlemont is a small town, situated in the county of Armagh and north west corner of Loughgall parish, on the southern side of the Blackwater river and connected with the town of Moy by a stone bridge across the river. The erection of Charlemont Fort to defend the passage of the Blackwater must have led to the first establishment of the town. It has been greatly distinguished in history, and was considered a place of much consequence during the civil wars of Ireland. In Leland's *History of Ireland* volume 2 p406 it is stated that Charlemont Fort was erected by Lord Mountjoy to assist him in carrying on active operations against the Earl of Tyrone; in another place, that Sir Phelim O'Neill <O'Nial> seized and ransacked the castle of Charlemont on the 22nd October 1641 and made the governor Lord Caulfeild and all his family prisoners. Again in volume 3 p557 he mentions that James II was sensibly afflicted by the loss of Charlemont. This fort was esteemed so strong and so well provided that Schomberg in his progress did not venture to attack it.

MODERN TOPOGRAPHY

Town of Charlemont

There is [a] neat church built in 1831 and situated at the extremity of the town, on the road to Armagh in the townland of Corr and Dunavally. It will accommodate 270 persons. The fort with the stable yard and ordnance storekeeper's department forms the greater part of the town. According to the census taken in the year 1831, Charlemont is stated to contain 77 houses and 370 inhabitants. The houses are built with stones or bricks. There are 2 fairs in the year, held on the 12th of May and 12th November, for the sale of cattle, provisions and yarn, but they are badly attended in consequence of the town being close to Moy, in which a very large monthly fair is held. There is a school in the town, supported principally by the Association fo Discountenancing Vice. The Earl of Charlemon derives his title from this town.

Public Buildings

The only public buildings in the parish are the places of worship, viz. the parish church, situatec in the village of Loughgall, the new church a Charlemont, in the townland of Corr and Duna vally. The Roman Catholic chapel in the townlan of Eganalurghan is a plain commodious building capable of containing 2,000 persons. The congre gation at present consists of about 800. The Pres byterian meeting house in the townland of Clon neden will contain 300 people. It was built by the parishioners in 1791 and is now much out of repair There are 2 Methodist meeting houses, one i Ballymagerney, the other in Clonmain, which wil contain from 100 to 150 persons each.

Gentlemen's Seats

The principal gentlemen's seats are Castle Dillon the residence of Lieutenant-General Sir Thoma Molyneux, situated partly in the parish of Loughgal and partly in the parish of Armagh. The hous stands in the centre of an extensive demesne con taining a great deal of wood and ornamental plan tation, with a large and picturesque lake whicl adds much to the beauty of the place.

Hockley Lodge, the residence of the Honorabl H. Caulfeild, is a modern house built in the cottag style, standing in a small demesne with a goo walled garden and pleasure grounds close to th house.

Drumilly House, the residence of Mrs Cope, a excellent house and offices, with an extensive de mesne including part of Loughgall lake and con taining a considerable quantity of ornamental woo and plantation.

Ardress House, the residence of George Inve Esq., and Summer Island, belonging to Colone Verner but at present unoccupied.

Bleach Greens, Manufactories and Mills

The only bleach green in the parish is in th townland of Clonmain, but like many other estab lishments of the same kind it is not doing mucl business at present. There are potteries in th townlands of Corr and Dunavally, Ardress Wes and Derrycrew, at which large crocks, pitchers an other coarse earthen vessels are manufacturec Bricks are made in many parts of the parish. Ther is a corn mill in Ballygawsey called Gregg's mill, worked by an overshot water wheel whose diameter is 17 feet and breadth 3 feet 9 inches. There is also a windmill in Clonmain. It has not been used for the last year or two and is out of repair.

Communications

The mail coach road from Armagh to Dungannon passes for a distance of 2 miles through the western part of the parish. The other principal roads are from Loughgall to Armagh, to Charlemont, Blackwatertown, Portadown and to Verner's bridge. They are repaired with broken stone or gravel and are kept in tolerably good order at the expense of the county. The Ulster Canal (now forming) passes for a distance of about 1 and a half miles through the parish and close to the village of Charlemont. It will open a communication between Lough Neagh and Lough Erne, traversing a highly productive country. The boats will convey coals, iron and timber into the interior and will return laden with corn, flour and other agricultural produce.

Ancient Topography

Forts and Antiquity

There are several small forts or raths within the parish, but none very remarkable.

In Sir John Temple's *History of the rebellion of 1641* p111, it is stated that above 200 persons were drowned in the lough near Loughgall village.

Modern Topography

General Appearance and Scenery

The northern part of the parish contains a large tract of bog with small hills or elevated spots of ground rising through it, and has a cold, bleak appearance. The western part, in the vicinity of Charlemont, is also flat and uninteresting, but in the neighbourhood of Loughgall the country is rich and well cultivated, containing wood, gentlemen's seats and many homes of respectable persons. The cottages are tolerably clean and comfortable, with in many cases a good orchard or garden attached, which very much improve the scenery and general appearance of the country.

Social Economy

Local Government

Charlemont Fort is a military station consisting of 1 company of the Royal Artillery. There is a small police force in the neighbourhood of Loughgall. A manor court is held in Loughgall for the manors of Loughgall and Drumilly.

Schools

The introduction of schools has decidedly led to a perceptible improvement in the moral habits of the people, who are anxious to procure information and knowledge: see table. [Table gives name of townland, number of Protestants and Roman Catholics, males and females, how supported, when established].

Lisleglish: Protestants 161, Roman Catholics 50, males 117, females 94, total 211. Free school, supported by the Erasmus Smith's charity, established 1811.

Ballytyrone: Protestants 101, Roman Catholics 47, males 88, females 60, total 148. Supported by Mrs Cope of Drumilly, established 1798.

Annaghmore: Protestants 38, Roman Catholics 25, males 46, females 17, total 63. Mrs Cope pays the master 10 pounds per annum, the children pay from 1d to 2d ha'penny per week, established 1833.

Kinego: Protestants 60, Roman Catholics 5, males 42, females 23, total 65. Supported by J. Parnell Esq. for the use of his tenantry, established 1816.

Annasamory: Protestants 38, Roman Catholics 10, males 30, females 18, total 48. London Hibernian Society free school. Col [name blank] gives 7 pounds 10s per annum, established 1831.

Drumain: Protestants 54, Roman Catholics 12, males 38, females 28, total 66. London Hibernian Society free school, established 1820.

Altaturk: Protestants 66, Roman Catholics 3, males 37, females 34, total 71. Parish school, supported by subscription, established 1828.

Charlemont: Protestants 38, Roman Catholics 10, males 28, females 20, total 48. Master paid 8 pounds per annum by the Association for Discountenancing Vice, the children pay 1d each per week.

Mullinavillin or Hockley: Protestants 104, Roman Catholics 41, males 84, females 61, total 145. Supported by Sir Thomas Molyneux and the Rev. Dr Oliver, rector, established 1809.

Ardress East: no information obtained.

Poor

There is no permanent provision for the poor and infirm.

Religion

The greater part of the inhabitants are Protestants.

Habits of the People

The cottages throughout the parish generally are of mud, thatched, 1-storey high and divided into 2 or 3 bays or rooms. There is a great want of comfort and cleanliness about them, except in the neighbourhood of Loughgall village, where the houses are of a better description. The usual articles of food are meal prepared in various ways, butter, milk, potatoes and occasionally meat.

Emigration

But few persons emigrate from this part of the country.

Productive Economy

Manufacturing or Commercial

Most of the families are engaged more or less in manufacturing very coarse narrow linen or coarse 900 cambric. A weaver at the present time will earn from 3s to 4s per week. Hand spinning is very little resorted to as a profitable employment: the yarn can be purchased much cheaper than it could be manufactured. A spinner can earn only from 1s to 1s 3d per week, and work hard for that. Very few of the inhabitants depend solely on the profits of the loom for their support, but are occupied through the greater part of the year in agricultural pursuits and weave a web or two during the winter. Now that so little is to be earned by spinning, the females and children are usually employed in weaving, the wheel furnishing occupation only to those advanced in years. A great deal of yarn is brought from the county Fermanagh.

Fairs and Markets

There are not any fairs or markets in the parish. Those usually attended are Armagh, Dungannon, Portadown, Moy and Blackwatertown. The coarse linens are sold at 2d or 2d ha'penny and the cambrics at from 8d to 9d per yard.

Rural Economy

The principal proprietors are the Earl of Charlemont, Sir Thomas Molyneux, Arthur Cope Esq., John Parnell Esq. and Mrs Cope of Drumilly. The farms contain from 6 to 30 statute acres, generally held under leases of 1 life or 21 years, at the yearly rent of 1 pound to 1 pound 10s per acre. There is no land let in conacre. The farmers are chiefly respectable yeomen who appear to farm for subsistence only. The fields are small and enclosed with banks of earth. In the vicinity of Loughgall hedges are more common. The farm buildings are small and are kept in order by the tenants.

The soil in the north and western portions of the parish is clay, sand and gravel with a great quantity of bog. The centre is a rich loam resting upon limestone. The southern portion is a sharp stony soil with rocks of [author's alternatives] (greywacke? or greenstone?) slate very near the surface. Lime is procured at the Ballygawsey kilns and at several other places in the neighbourhood at from 10d to 1s per barrel, and is much used as manure. Carts and wheel cars are in general use. Oxen are not much used in agriculture. 1 horse is employed in a cart or car and 2 in a plough. 1 cwt of wheat and from 5 to 7 bushels of oats are generally sown upon a statute acre, which produces from 10 to 16 cwt of wheat, from 40 to 50 bushels of oats [and] from 200 to 300 bushels of potatoes. Flax yields from 4 to 5 stone to the peck of seed. Farm servants hired by the day get on an average 10d, those hired by the half year get about 30s 6d and their diet.

Cattle

The common breeds of cows, horses and pigs are usually kept. Green feeding is only practised by a few of the principal inhabitants.

Uses made of the Bogs

The bogs are used wholly as fuel: a great quantity of turf is carried into Armagh and disposed of there at 2s or 2s 6d per cart. The bog timber is much used for roofing. The stumps and roots are cut up for fuel. Very nice furniture (such as tables) is frequently made of the black bog oak. Occasionally small blocks of yew are found imbedded in the bogs, from which small articles of drawing-room furniture such as ink-stands and book-stands are made. It takes a beautiful polish and is much sought after by cabinet makers.

Planting

There are no tracts of waste land planted and brought into profit. Planting is almost entirely confined to demesnes and pleasure grounds.

General Remarks

Cultivation is carried over the whole parish, with the exception of the bogs, which are situated so low that it might be found difficult to drain them sufficiently for cultivation; besides which they are very valuable as affording an almost inexhaustible supply of fuel. The southern extremity of this parish about Rathdrumgrand and Altaturk is much exposed to violent winds which are often very injurious to the crops. Lime is much used for manure and is easily procured. The land is much better adapted for tillage than to any other purpose. There are no farms kept exclusively for grazing.

Parish of Loughgilly, Co Armagh

Notes on Balleek (Loughgilly) by John Heather, 16 March 1838

MODERN TOPOGRAPHY AND SOCIAL ECONOMY

Town of Balleek

The town of Balleek, situated in the parish of the same name, lies on the side of a valley halfways between Newry and Newtownhamilton, on the leading road between the above mentioned towns. It is small, there being 15 2-storied houses and 2 thatched 1-storied [houses], 4 public <publick> houses, 1 carpenter, 1 smith, 1 shoemaker and 1 nailor. There is no public house of worship in it. The town may be said to be composed of 1 street, if it can be called so. The houses are principally clean and almost all on one side of the street. There are 3 police, forming a detached station from Newtownhamilton.

Boys' and Girls' School

They have 1 school in the town, boys' and girls', which are under the same roof. In the boys' apartments of the school there are 50, 25 of whom are Protestants; in the girls' school, there are 30, 20 of whom are Catholics <Catholicks>. The girls' school is under the Ladies' Hibernian Society and the mistress receives 9 pounds per annum, together with 1d per week from each pupil. The boys' school is under the London Hibernian Society and receives 4 pounds per annum, with 1d per week from each pupil. I could not ascertain [at] what time this was established nor by whom or the costs, [signed] John Heather, Carrickmacross, 16 March 1838.

Statistical Return by Corporal W. Tozer

TOWNLAND DIVISIONS

List of Townlands

[Table gives townland, proprietor's and agent's name, size of holding, length of leases, rent per acre, valuation of county cess, remarks].

Killycairn Upper, Mr Cope, Loughgall, Mr Hardy, Loughgall, 5 to 30 acres size, 1 life or 21 years lease, 22s to 25s rent, 13 pounds 17s 3d ha'penny county cess, extraordinary for the growth of flax, land good quality.

Killycairn Lower, Mr Cope, Loughgall, Mr Hardy, Loughgall, 13 to 22 acres size, 1 life or 21 years lease, 22s to 25s rent, 10 pounds 6s ha'penny county cess, extraordinary for the growth of flax, land good quality.

Corenure, Mr Cope, Loughgall, Mr Hardy, Loughall, 2 to 18 acres size, 1 life or 21 years lease, 22s to 25s rent, 5 pounds 7s ha'penny county cess.

Drumero, Mr Cope, Loughgall, Mr Hardy, Loughgall, 2 to 33 acres size, 1 life or 21 years, 22s to 25s rent, 8 pounds 2s 4d county cess.

Maytone, Mr Cope, Loughall, Mr Hardy, Loughgall, 2 to 33 acres size, 1 life or 21 years lease, 22s to 25s rent, 10 pounds 10s 1d county cess.

Ballygorman, Mr Cope, Loughgall, Mr Hardy, Loughgall, 3 to 28 acres size, 1 life or 21 years lease, 22s to 25s rent, 11 pounds 5s 8d county cess, good quality of land.

Lisnalee, Reverend Dr Stewart, rector of the parish, himself agent, 4 to 12 acres size, statute measure, no leases given, 25s rent, 10 pounds 1s 11d county cess, middling quality of land; crops: oats, potatoes; manure: lime and soil.

Lisnalee in Forkhill parish, Reverend Dr Campbell, rector of Forkhill parish, himself agent, 1 holding, glebe land, no leases, middling quality, contains bog.

Crankey, Lord Mandeville <Manderville>, Captain Lofty, Tanderagee, 4 to 15 acres size, 3 lives or 31 years, 15s rent, middling quality, the tythe paid by the landlord.

Lush, Councillor MacCartney, [blank] Murphy, Rathfriland, 4 to 15 acres size, 25s to 30s rent, middling quality.

Ballydogherty, Mr Dunbar, Donaghadee, Mr McCartney, Dublin, proprietors, [blank] Murphy, Rathfriland, agent, 4 to 15 acres size, 25s to 30s rent, middling quality.

Drumitt, Reverend Dr Stewart, rectory, proprietor of half, Captain Fulton, Lisburn, Mr Woodhouse, agent, Markethill rectory, 122 acres size, 8 pounds 10s 6d county cess.

Drummond, Reverend Dr Stewart, himself agent, half the glebe of Loughgilly, 5 pounds 7s ha'penny county cess.

Crugans Upper and Lower, Lord Gosford, Mr Blackard, 3 to 20 acres size, 21 years or 1 life lease, 20s to 25s rent, 14 pounds 16s 10d county cess, good quality of land, bears wheat and good crops of flax.

Derlitt, Lord Gosford, Mr Blackard, 4 to 20 acres size, 21 years or 1 life lease, 24s rent, 8 pounds 9s, middling quality of land, crops chiefly oats and potatoes.

Lisdrumwhorr Lower, Lord Gosford, Mr Blackard, 4 to 20 acres size, Captain Atkinson is the chief occupier, 21 years or 1 life lease, 24s rent, 4 pounds 4s 4d county cess, good land, bears wheat, oats, potatoes and flax.

Lisdrumwhorr Upper, Lord Gosford, Mr Blackard, 4 to 35 acres size, 1 life or 21 years lease, 18s to 20s Irish acre rent, 4 pounds 4s 4d county cess, good quality.

Counaght, Lord Gosford, Mr Blackard, 3 to 36 acres, 1 life or 21 years lease, 20s to 25s rent, 8 pounds 9s county cess, this sum is charged to Upper and Lower Counaght.

Lurgaross, Lord Gosford, Mr Blacker, 3 to 25 acres size, 1 life or 21 years lease, 20s to 25s rent, 16 pounds 17s county cess, middling quality, potatoes and oats.

Drumgain, Lord Gosford, Mr Blackard, 3 to 27 acres size, 1 life or 21 years lease, 20s to 25s rent, 7 pounds 8s county cess, good quality.

Balleenan, Robert Hardy Esquire, [?] Clare, 20 acres size, a quarter of this townland is called Ballymore, good quality.

Coreniar, Colonel Close, Drumbanagher, Mr Blackard, Armagh, 20 acres size, 25s to 30s rent, good quality.

Lisnisk, Colonel Close, Mr Blackard, Armagh, 14 to 20 acres size, 25s to 30s rent, good quality of land.

Carron, Colonel Close, Mr Blackard, Armagh, 14 to 20 acres size, good quality of land.

Brackagh, Colonel Close, Mr Blackard, Armagh, 14 to 20 acres size, good quality of land.

Rathconwell, [blank].

Kilcon, half to Mr Cope, Loughgall, the other half belongs to the school lands, 5 to 20 acres size, 20s rent, good quality of land.

Half Kilcon Bolton, Cornagrally, Mullaghamore, Ballyvalley, Moymawhillen: under the Board of Education, rents appropriate to the support of Armagh College and other places of instruction and are called the school lands; Mr Evans, Armagh, secretary of the grand jury of the county, agent, 5 to 20 acres size, no leases, 20s rent, 3 pounds 11s 3d county cess.

Keadybeg, Mr Cope, Loughgall, Mr Hardy, Loughgall, 2 to 20 acres size, 21 years or 1 life lease, 20s to 28s rent, 10 pounds 17s 10d ha'penny county cess, good quality.

Keadymore, Mr Cope, Loughgall, Mr Hardy, Loughgall, 2 to 20 acres size, 21 years or 1 life lease, 20s to 28s rent, 11 pounds 5s 8d county cess, good quality.

Tullyherron, Mr Cope, Loughgall, Mr Hardy, Loughgall, 3 to 21 acres size, 21 years or 1 life lease, 20s to 28s rent, 10 pounds 13s 4d county cess, good quality.

Balleek, Lord Gosford, Mr Blackard, Armagh, 21 years or 1 life lease, 20s to 28s rent, 11 pounds 19s 11d county cess, bad quality.

Carrowmannon, Lord Gosford, Mr Blackard, Armagh, 15 pounds 4s 2d county cess, bad quality.

Carrickgalloghy, Lord Gosford, Mr Blackard, Armagh, 7 pounds 1s 10d county cess, middling quality.

Carrickananny, Lord Gosford, Mr Blackard, Armagh, 4 pounds 8s 5d county cess, middling quality.

Drumnahuncheon, Lord Gosford, Mr Blackard, Armagh, 5 pounds 19s 11d county cess, middling quality.

Drumnahoney, Lord Gosford, Mr Blackard, Armagh, 8 pounds 13s 7d county cess, middling quality.

Greyhillan, Lord Gosford, Mr Blackard, Armagh, 7 pounds 11s 5d county cess, middling quality.

Tullya, Mr Whaley, Mr White, resident, agent, 4 to 20 acres size, 20s to 25s rent, land middling quality.

Tullywinney, Lord Charlemont, Captain Algeo, Armagh, 4 to 20 acres size, 15s 6d rent, land middling quality.

Drumherriff, half Lord Charlemont, half trustees of late Newry Bank, Mr Boyd, Newry, 16s rent, 19 pounds 3d 4d county cess, charged to Upper and Lower Drumhirriff.

Lisadian, half Lord Charlemont, half trustees of late Newry Bank, Mr Boyd, Newry, 15 acres size, 3 lives or 31 years lease, 20s to 23s rent, 21 pounds 18s 10d county cess.

Rathcarbery, Colonel Hogsham, Mr White, 10 to 20 acres size, 3 lives or 31 years lease, 15s 6d county cess.

The last 12 townlands form the parish of Balleek, a perpetual cure in the endowment of the rector of Loughgilly, the whole of which pays cess to the church in Carrickananny townland called Balleek church, but the following 4 townlands continue to pay tythe to Loughgilly parish: Lisadian, Rathcarbery, Drumherriff, Tullya.

Modern Topography

Table of Mills

[Table with headings: townland, occupier, nature

of wheel, breadth and diameter, nature of mill, name of river].

Carnure, Loughlin Toner, breast wheel, 3 feet 7 inches breadth, 15 feet 2 inches diameter, flax mill, Creggans river.

Keadybeg, Robert Geary, [1st mill] overshot wheel, 3 feet 1 inch breadth, 15 feet diameter, flax mill, Tullaghaggy water; [2nd mill] breast wheel, 3 feet breadth, 14 feet 8 inches diameter, flax mill, Tullaghaggy water.

Lisnalee, Michael Boal, breast wheel, 2 feet 9 inches breadth, 15 feet diameter, flax mill, Tullaghaggy water.

Carnbeg, Robert McBride, [1st mill] breast wheel, 3 feet breadth, 15 feet 8 inches diameter, corn mill, Tullaghaggy water; [2nd mill] breast wheel, 2 feet 8 inches breadth, 12 feet 2 inches diameter, flax mill, Tullaghaggy water.

Mullaghmore, William Douglass, [1st mill] breast wheel, 4 feet breadth, 18 feet diameter, corn mill, [on a] stream; [2nd mill] overshot wheel, 2 feet 11 inches breadth, 13 feet 4 inches diameter, flax mill, [on a] stream.

Killeyhern, David Douglass, undershot wheel, 4 feet 9 inches breadth, 14 feet 8 inches diameter, flax mill, River Cusher <Cuser>.

Mountownlandorris, Captain Atkinson, breast wheel, 6 feet breadth, 26 feet 2 inches diameter, beetling engine, [stream and lough ? Shaw's lough ?].

Tullyallen, Capt. Atkinson, breast wheel, 4 feet 8 inches breadth, 30 feet diameter, beetling engine, [stream and lough ? Shaw's lough ?].

Lisdrumher, Capt. Atkinson, [1st] breast wheel, 3 feet breadth, 29 feet diameter, spinning machine; [2nd] breast wheel, 4 feet breadth, 24 feet diameter, weaving machine; [3rd] breast wheel, 3 feet 8 inches breadth, 20 feet diameter, spinning machine, [stream and lough ? Shaw's lough ?].

Mountownlandorris, William Byers, overshot wheel, 3 feet 4 inches breadth, 18 feet diameter, flax mill, [stream and lough ? Shaw's lough ?].

Lisdrumhorr, Joseph Mathers, overshot wheel, 3 feet 10 inches breadth, 16 feet diameter, flax mill, [stream and lough ? Shaw's lough ?].

Creggan, Alexander Scott, breast wheel, 2 feet 5 inches breadth, 14 feet diameter, corn mill, Creggan river.

Creggan, Alexander Scott, breast wheel, 3 feet breadth, 16 feet diameter, flax mill, Creggan river.

Ballydogherty, John Hanna, [1st mill] overshot wheel, 3 feet breadth, 16 feet diameter, flax mill, stream; [2nd mill] overshot wheel, 3 feet breadth, 15 feet diameter, flax mill, stream.

Mowhan, William Byers, breast wheel, 3 feet breadth, 16 feet diameter, flax mill, Clady.

Mowhan, [blank] Armstrong, [1st mill] breast wheel, 3 feet 6 inches breadth, 18 feet diameter, flax mill, Clady; [2nd mill] breast wheel, 3 feet breadth, 14 feet diameter, flax mill, Clady.

Kingsmills, Dennis Boylease, [1st mill] breast wheel, 4 feet breadth, 15 feet diameter, flax mill, Blackwater; [2nd mill] overshot wheel, 2 feet 6 inches breadth, 15 feet diameter, corn mill, stream.

Keadybeg, Robert Kiliwell, breast wheel, 3 feet 6 inches breadth, 13 feet diameter, flax mill, Blackwater.

Carrickgallogley, Michael Markey, overshot wheel, 2 feet 8 inches breadth, 14 feet diameter, flax mill, stream.

Carrickananny, Sarah Patten, [1st mill] breast wheel, 2 feet 6 inches breadth, 14 feet diameter, flax mill, stream; [2nd mill] breast wheel, 3 feet breadth, 13 feet diameter, corn mill, stream.

SOCIAL AND PRODUCTIVE ECONOMY

Places of Divine Worship

[Table with headings: townland, persuasion, clergyman, average number of attendants].

Loughgilly, Protestants, Reverend Dr Stewart, curates [bracketed together] Viscoile, Riggs, 116.

Balleek, Protestants, Reverend Miller, 71.

Mountnorris, Presbyterians, [blank] McGowan, 550.

Ballainen, Covenanters, [blank] Boggs, 200. Tullyallen, Seceders, [blank] Porter, 500.

Lisadian or Kingsmills, Seceders, [blank] Henry, 325, total 1762.

Tullyherran, Roman Catholics, Reverend Conly P.P., 478.

Carneckananny, Roman Catholics, Reverend O'Toole C.C., 700.

Ballymoyrent, Roman Catholics, 600; half the number 600 only belong to Loughgilly parish; total 1778 [minus] 300 [=] 1478.

Schools

[Table with headings: townland, males, females, Protestants, Protestant Dissenters, Presbyterians, Roman Catholics, remarks].

Loughgilly, males 66, females 56, Protestants 30, Protestant Dissenters 52, Presbyterians 20, Roman Catholics 20, total 122; 30 pounds per annum from the Board of E. [Erasmus] Smith and 1d per week from the children.

Lisdrumwhorr, males 50, females 32, Protestants 24, Protestant Dissenters 11, 33 Presbyterians, Roman Catholics 14, total 82; 20 pounds per annum contributions and 1d per week from the children.

Tullyherran, males 26, females 27, Protestants 6, Protestant Dissenters 4, Presbyterians 14, Roman Catholics 29, total 53; 10 pounds per annum from the National Board, 7 pounds from the children.

Carrickgallogley, males 20, females 10, Protestants 12, Protestant Dissenters 8, Presbyterians 11, Roman Catholics 10, total 30; 2 pounds from Reverend Mr Miller, 1d from the children weekly.

Balleek, males 45, females 34, Protestants 11, Protestant Dissenters 18, Presbyterians 8, Roman Catholics 42, total 79; 8 pounds from the Society for Discountenancing Vice, 1d per week from the scholars.

Cotton Manufactory

In Lisdrumwhorr there is a cotton manufactory, the property of Mr Atkinson. About 250 persons are employed in it. The men earn from 6s to 10s per week, women earn from 2s to 3s 6d per week, children earn from 2s to 2s 6d.

Medicine and Dispensary

There is no public dispensary. There are 4 medical practitioners: Mr Ingram, Mountnorris, Mr Torrentine, Derlitt, Mr McCormaik, Derlitt, Mr McGowan, Keadybeg. No particular disorder is prevalent in this district. The inhabitants are healthful and longevity is not unfrequent.

Notes by John Heather

Modern Topography

Loughgilly Mills

Corn mill, the wheel in diameter is 12 and a half feet, across the buckets 2 and a quarter feet. It has 10 feet fall of water.

This mill, which is flax, is situated on the same stream as the above mill. The wheel is 15 feet in diameter, 3 feet across the buckets and 6 feet fall of water.

Flax mill, situated on the same stream as the previous mill, has 15 feet fall of water, 3 feet across the buckets and 5 feet fall of water.

Church

This church is a chapel of ease, is neat and has a little plantation adjoining, which adds greatly to its appearance. It has no gallery. There are 24 seats in the aisle <isle>. It is capable of accommodating about 150, but there are only 60 of a congregation. It was built in 1827 and cost 900 pounds, which sum was [a] grant from the Board of First Fruits.

Social Economy

School

This school is quite close to the church and was built in about the same time as the church and cost 60 pounds, which sum was raised by subscription. It is under [the] Kildare Place Society. There are 60 children, 4 of whom are Catholics. The master receives 1d per week from the pupils, has nothing from the board or subscription, [signed] John Heather, Carrickmanny, 16 March 1838.

Modern Topography

Loughgilly Mills

This mill, which is a corn one, the wheel is 16 and a half feet in diameter, 3 feet across the buckets and 20 feet fall of water. There is also a flax mill belonging to the same person which has 10 feet fall of water. The wheel is 16 feet in diameter, 2 and a half feet across the buckets. They are both overshot wheels.

Corn mill, wheel is 15 feet in diameter, 2 feet across the buckets and 4 feet fall of water.

Flax mill, its wheel is 14 feet in diameter, 3 feet across the buckets and 4 feet fall of water.

Notes by George Scott on Mills

Mills in Drumharif

Corn mill, in the townland of Drumharif, belongs to Dennis Boyle, diameter of wheel 12 feet, breadth 1 foot 6 inches, fall of water 4 feet, breast wheel.

Flax mill, in the same townland, belongs to same person, diameter of wheel 16 feet, breadth 3 feet, fall of water 4 feet, breast wheel.

Mills in Lisdrumcore

In the townland of Lisdrumcore, belongs to William Atkinson, diameter of wheel 30 feet, breadth 4 feet, fall of water 4 feet, overshot wheel.

Bleach mill, in the same townland, belongs to the same person, diameter of wheel 23 feet, breadth 4 feet, fall of water 24 feet, overshot wheel.

A second bleach mill, belongs to same person, in the same townland, diameter of wheel 30 feet, breadth 4 feet, fall of water 20 feet, overshot wheel.

Mill in Lurgygross

Bleach mill, in the townland of Lurgygross, diameter 16 feet, breadth 4 feet, fall of water 16 feet, overshot wheel.

Parish of Montiaghs, County Armagh

Fair Sheets by Thomas McIlroy, 20 December 1837

NATURAL STATE

Locality

The parish of Montiaghs is situated in the northern part of the county of Armagh. It is in the barony of Oneilland West and is bounded on the north by Lough Neagh, on the east by the parish of Seagoe, on the west by the parishes of Tartaraghan and Drumcree and on the south by the parishes of Seagoe and Drumcree. Its extreme length is 6 and a half miles and extreme breadth 4 miles. Its content is 18,098 acres 1 rood 15 perches including [blank] of water, [blank] of which are uncultivated. It contains or is divided into [blank] townlands and is valued at [blank] to the county cess.

NATURAL FEATURES

Hills

The hills in this parish are in general islands surrounded with bog. The highest point is in the townland of Derrytrasna, 83 feet above the sea and the lowest ground along the shore of Lough Neagh, 50 feet above the level of the sea. The average height of the hills is 50 feet above the sea. They are not highly cultivated.

Lakes

Part of Lough Neagh forms the northern part of the parish, the content of which is 12,178 acres 2 roods 36 perches. It is very shallow but deepens gradually. The greater part of the shore is covered with fine white sand, petrified wood, holly and deal, and the Lough Neagh pebble or species of cornelian are sometimes found in this parish. The following islands are in this part of the lake. Rathlin Island is situated in Lough Neagh in the eastern side of this parish. It is connected with the mainland by a ridge of sand and pebbles which is impassable in winter. Its content is 5 acres 1 rood 32 perches. It is thickly planted with oak, alder and fir. There are the remains of the entrenchments of a fort in it. Rath-lin signifies "a fort in a pool".

Scawdy Island, little: Scawdy Island is situated three-quarters of a mile north of Rathlin. It is 1 chain broad and 1 and a half chains long.

Lough Gullion is situated nearly in the centre of this parish. It is 49 feet above the level of the sea, its extreme length is 1 and a half miles and extreme breadth half a mile in the summer. It is 10 feet deep in the centre. Its content is 358 acres 1 rood 13 perches. There are no other lakes in this parish.

Rivers

The River Bann forms the south western boundary line of this parish for 6 miles, for description of which see the parish of Drumcree. The Close river forms the west boundary. [Insert query: which river forms the east boundary?].

Bogs

The greater part of this parish is bog. The highest point in the bog is [blank] feet above the level of the sea and [blank] feet above the River Bann. Timber is found embedded, principally oak and fir. It is made use of by the people as firewood and in building.

Shore of Lough Neagh

Ardmore Point is a headland running out into Lough Neagh, the eastern side of which is precipitous and nearly perpendicular. The western side falls off more gently into the lake and a very extensive tract of bog. The remaining part of the shore of this parish is flat and uninteresting.

General Appearance and Scenery

The appearance of the country is wild and dreary. The immense tracts of bog which extend along the shore of Lough Neagh down to high water mark, with only a few islands far distant from each other, give the country a dreary and lonely aspect.

MODERN TOPOGRAPHY

Church

Ardmore church, situated in the townland of Derryadd, is a plain stone building supposed to have been erected in 1797, not known what cost or how defrayed. The form and dimensions are shown by the following figure: [ground plan, main dimensions 53 and 29 feet, rectangular shape with projection at one end]. At the east end is a tower on which is a wooden spire. In the tower is a belfry containing one bell. The accommodation is for 200 persons and the general attendance is 200. The interior is very plain, the windows are rectangular. The present rector is the Reverend D.W. McMullan.

The old parish church was situated in the townland of Ardmore, from whence the present takes its name.

Glebe House

The Glebe House, situated in the townland of Derryadd, is an old plain stone building, roughcast and whitewashed. It is 2-storeys high and is about 3 perches from the shore of Lough Neagh.

Ardmore Schoolhouse

Ardmore schoolhouse, situated in the townland of Derryadd, is a small stone cottage, whitewashed and thatched, 19 feet 6 inches long and 22 feet broad. Not known when built, what cost or how defrayed.

Towns

There are no towns in this parish except the village of Charlestown, built by the Honourable Charles Brownlow from whom it takes its name. It consists of 21 houses built of brick, slated, 2-storeys high, to which are attached neat little yards and office houses. The greater number of the houses are unoccupied. It forms 1 street overgrown with grass. It has a deserted appearance and seems to be fast sinking into ruin.

Social Economy

Amusements

The people have no amusements except dancing, of which they are very fond.

School

[Table contains the following headings: name, situation and description, when established, income and expenditure, physical, intellectual and moral instruction, number of pupils subdivided by age, sex and religion, name and religion of master or mistress, date on which visited].

Ardmore, a cottage adjoining Ardmore church; income: from the rector of the parish 3 pounds per annum, 8 pounds from pupils; intellectual instruction: Hibernian Society books; moral instruction: visited by the Reverend D.W. McMullan, Authorised Version of Scriptures read daily, catechism taught by the master, assisted by the Reverend D.W. McMullan; number of pupils: males, 35 under 10 years of age, 2 from 10 to 15, a total of 37; females, 37 under 10 years of age, a total of 37; total number of pupils 74, 65 Established Church, 9 Roman Catholics; master Samuel McClelland, Established Church, visited 14th November 1837, [signed] T.C. McIlroy.

Statistical Memoir by Lieut G.A. Bennett, 2 June 1835

Natural State

Name

In Armstrong's map of the county, published by the authority of the grand jury, we find this parish spelt Moyntaghs and in Sir Charles Coote's *Statistical survey of the county* it is Muntuaghs alias Mointaghs. Its usual pronunciation is Mun-ches and is derived from the Irish Moin-tagh which signifies a "bog". According to Colonel Blacker in his *History of the parish of Seagoe*, it was formerly a part of that parish. [Insert marginal note: Moinmore is the "great bog"].

Locality

It is situated in the north east extremity of the county Armagh and in the barony of Oneiland East, and is bounded on the north by Lough Neagh, on the west by the River Bann dividing it from the barony of Oneiland West, on the south by the parish of Seagoe and on the east by Lough Neagh and part of the parish of Seagoe. Its greatest length is from where the road from Lurgan to Bannsfoot ferry enters the parish at the south east to the Bannsfoot, which is at the north west extremity of the parish: this is 5 miles. Its greatest breadth is from Rush's ferry on the River Bann to Ardmore Point, 2 and a half miles, but its breadth from the River Bann across Derrytrasna townland to Lough Neagh is scarcely a mile. Its total content is [blank], of which 2,670 acres are actual cut bog, 316 acres are in a lake called Lough Gullen and 80 acres are the half of the River Bann which forms its western boundary.

Natural Features

Hills and Lakes

The whole of the parish may be considered as a flat, no part rises more than 35 feet above Lough Neagh. Taking this lake as 48 feet above the sea, which is the summer low water level, the highest ground in the parish is in the townlands of Derryinver, Derrytrasna and Derryvicafoe, all 82 feet above the sea. The bogs vary from 76 to 60 feet (being a mean of 68 feet) above the sea and 20 above the lake.

Lough Neagh has been mentioned as forming the northern boundary of this parish. No part of it, however, is in the parish, though the island of Rathlin or Raughlin, which is separated by a bank of sand in summer and water in winter, belongs to the townland of Derryvicafoe. The fish found in this lake are said to be salmon, trout of a very large description, roach, tench, perch, pike, eel and pullin. The last, a fish peculiar to this lake, are taken in great quantities and are sold through the country to the poorer inhabitants. They are a cheap food, being sold when in the harvest season from 30 to 40 for 1s. Various petrified woods are found along the shores as oak, ash and holly. The latter is much esteemed as forming hones or sharping stones. Pebbles of a transparent appearance and taking a fine polish are picked up on the shore. These are manufactured into bracelets, seals and other ornaments and are capable of being finely engraved. Roots of trees are seen projecting from the sand for a considerable distance in the lake.

Lough Gullen, situated between Lough Neagh and the Bann river and nearly in the middle of Derryetta townland, contains 315 acres 3 roods 24 perches. It is 1 and a quarter miles in length and nearly half a mile in breadth and only a few feet in depth. It contains pike, eel and bream. Mr Brownlow, the proprietor, succeeded in draining this lake and bringing a large portion of it under cultivation, but in a severe storm in December 1833 the River Bann, into which the drainage ran, burst the embankment made to protect it and again laid the lake under water. The drainage was effected by means of a 4 horse power steam engine erected on the banks which raised the water 2 feet and sent it on in a drain to the River Bann. The nearest distance from Lough Gullen to the Bann is three-eighths of a mile, but at the place where the drain ran it is a little more. The level of the lake and river are the same viz. 48 feet.

Bogs

The whole parish, as its name imports, is boglands. Nearly half is reclaimed but there still exists 267 acres of bog. They vary in altitudes from 76 to 60 feet. The mean height may be taken as 68 feet for the whole, now Lough Neagh being 48 feet. There exists a surface 2,670 acres with an average depth of 20 feet, making a content of 86,152,000 cubic yards of turf.

The parish supplies fuel to all the surrounding parishes, both in the counties of Down and Armagh. Vast numbers of bargeloads are sent to Portadown and by the Newry Canal to Madden bridge, Scarva and Poyntzpass, from whence it is distributed to the neighbouring towns of Gilford, Banbridge and Loughbrickland and the parishes of Aghaderg, Seapatrick and Tullylish.

The parishes and towns of Magheralin and Moira also draw their fuel from this parish and give in exchange their limestone. The timber found embedded in the bogs is principally oak with roots in their natural position and the trunk generally attached and in a horizontal position. There are also fir trees in the eastern end of this parish. The greater part of the bog has as yet been untouched and is covered with heath. Grouse, snipe, hares are found throughout.

River Bann

The River Bann runs from the south east to the north west and forms the southern boundary of the parish for 6 miles and empties itself into Lough Neagh at its northwestern extremity and in Derryinver townland, where there is the ferry of Bannsfoot. The current is extremely slow, there being only a fall of 1 foot from the Newry Canal 1 mile above Portadown to where it enters Lough Neagh. From this cause, when the heavy rains sets in, the rivers soon outtops its banks and overflows the meadow and lowlands on each side. Its general and average breadth is from 200 to 250 feet and depth generally about 30 feet and is not fordable in any place. It is used for navigation of barges with turf from Lough Neagh and this parish to the Newry Canal.

The bed of the river appears to be of a boggy nature and its scenery is flat and insipid. There are few springs in the parish and the inhabitants have to sink from 20 to 30 feet before meeting with water. In order to prevent the river from overflowing Derrytrasna and Derryetta townlands and to drain Lough Gullen, Mr Brownlow erected a sod embankment along the side of the river. It is 1 and a half miles long, 10 feet long, 15 feet at the base and 7 feet at the top, and a windmill was erected at the north west extremity of the embankment to carry off the water collected in the drains. This, as has already been stated, was broken down in the winter of '33, but is now under repair.

Woods

That the whole of this parish was formerly covered with forest trees there can be little doubt, as the roots are found in every part of the parish and even stretching into the Loughs Neagh and Gullen in the upright position they occupied whilst growing. Now, however, scarcely a tree can be found to vary the heavy appearance of the immense bog tracts. A few large trees round the Glebe House and some young firs round Mr Forde's of Raughlin are all that now exist.

Coast

Lough Neagh forms a sandy coast to the west and north west extremities of the parish. Trowagh bay and Derryadde bay are much used for the nets, as indeed is the whole of the northern coast of this parish. The fish taken have already been mentioned.

Modern Topography

Buildings

About a dozen houses called Charlestown were built about 5 years since by Mr Brownlow in the north western extremity of the parish, in Derryinver townland. They are of brick and slated, but throughout the remainder of the parish the houses are few and generally built of mud and thatched.

The parish church, Ardmore, is a plain building situated in the townland of Derryadd, nearly in the centre of the parish. There is no Roman Catholic chapel in the parish but the inhabitants, the majority of whom are Catholic, resort to Derrymacash chapel in Seagoe, about half a mile to the east of this parish.

Gentlemen's Seats

Mr Forde's of Raughlin or Rathlin is the only resident gentleman in the parish. His house is situated on a point on the lake between Derryadd and Raughlin bays. The Glebe House is a plain building near the church, surrounded by a few trees.

Mills

There is a windmill for grinding corn and a drying kiln in Derryadde townland near the lough shore, the property of Mr Forde. This is the only mill in the parish nor is there any manufacture except linen, which is carried on in the houses of the individual.

Communications

The principal roads are from Lurgan to Bannsfoot ferry running north of Lough Gullen, and from Portadown to the same place, running south of Lough Gullen and nearly parallel to the River Bann. The latter road communicates with the parish of Drumcree across the River Bann by means of a ferry called Robb's ferry, about half a mile below where the river enters the parish. A little more than a mile lower down is Rush's ferry, which does not communicate with the roads and is only used for foot passengers. The next ferry is that at the mouth of the river called Bannsfoot ferry and is communication with Tartaraghan parish. This latter ferry is for horses, carts; a foot passenger pays 1d ha'penny, a horse and cart 10d. There is no bridge lower than Portadown and it has for some years been in contemplation to throw one across at the Bannfoot in lieu of the ferry. This is, however, opposed by the Canal Company and the ferry still remains.

Social and Productive Economy

Newry Canal

The canal from Newry to Lough Neagh may be considered as benefitting this parish so far as affording an export for their turf into the parishes on each side of the canal into the counties of Down and Armagh.

Markets for Export

From the poverty of the soil they grow but little corn, which is sold in the market of Portadown where corn-factors readily purchase and forward [it] by means of the canal to England. Lurgan is the market for the linen trade and yarn. Portadown is nearly 9 miles from the north west end of the parish and about 3 from the south east; Lurgan is nearly the same.

Poor, Dispensaries and Schools

The people are poor and almost universally occupy thatched mud cottages where a few of them carry on weaving of linen whilst the women and children spin. This and farming their land and along the coast fishing constitutes the employment of the people. There is no dispensary nor any provision for the poor in the parish and but 1 school, which is in Derryadd townland and near the church. It is under the Hibernian Society from whom the master gets 6 pounds per annum, 3 pounds from the Reverend Mr McMullen, rector, and a trifle from the scholars. The average attendance is about 30 males and 30 females.

Landlords

The principal and head landlord is Charles Brownlow Esquire, who resides at Lurgan, as well as his agent, W. Handcock Esquire. The farms are generally held direct from him and vary in size from 5 to 20 acres and 3 or 4 of 100. They are principally tenants at will at an average rent of 24s to 28s per acre. Where bog is set for pasture it is about 10s per acre and when set for cutting for sale at 30s per acre. The manure is lime which is generally brought as rock from <Maralin> Magheralin and burnt in this parish.

TOWNLAND DIVISIONS

Ardmore Townland

The only divisions known is that of townland of which there are 9 viz. Ard-more[stress], so pronounced. Proprietor Charles Brownlow Esquire, agent William J. Hancock Esquire, both residents of Lurgan. It contains [blank] acres, of which 147 acres are bog on the west side and 8 acres of the south east side. Distance from Lurgan 5 miles and 7 from Portadown. Land is held direct from the landlord and [they] are tenants at will. Rent about 26s per English acre. Bog for pasture at 10s per acre and bog for cutting for sale 30s per acre.

Ballynery Townland

Bally-ne[stress]ry, contains [blank], of which 287 acres are bog and 15 acres of the River Bann. Distance from Lurgan 3 and a half miles and from Portadown 4 miles. Rent the same as Ardmore townland.

Derryadd Townland

Derry-add[stress], so pronounced, contains [blank], of which 395 acres are bog on the west side and 8 acres in the north east corner. In the northern end of this townland is the parish church (built in 1799) and a schoolhouse. Half a mile south east of the church is the glebe (13 acres) and Glebe House. Distance from Lurgan 4 miles and from Portadown 6 miles. Rent the same as above [Ardmore].

Derrycorr Townland

Derry-corr[stress], so pronounced, contains [blank], of which 100 acres are bog. Distance from Lurgan 4 and a half and from Portadown 6 and a half miles. Rent the same as the last [Derryadd].

Derryinver Townland

Derry-in[stress]ver, so pronounced, contains [blank], of which 430 acres are bog. Distant from Lurgan 8 miles and from Portadown 9 miles. Rent the same as Ardmore townland.

Derryetta Townland

Derry-ett[stress]a, so pronounced, contains [blank], of which 206 acres are bog in the north and 95 and a half in the south end, 21 acres of the River Bann and 315 acres 3 roods 26 perches of Lough Gullen. Rent the same as above [Ardmore]. 5 miles from Lurgan and Portadown.

Derrylost Townland

Derrylost, pronounced Derry-lust[stress], contains [blank acres], of which 162 are of the bog joining Derryinver and 2 other smaller pieces in the south of the townland; one contains 45 and a half acres, the other 22 acres, 26 acres are of the River Bann. Rent the same as the above [Ardmore]. From Lurgan 6 and a half miles and 7 miles from Portadown.

Derryvicasse Townland

Derryvicasse, pronounced Derryma-cash[stress], contains [blank], of which 317 acres are bog. In the northern end of this townland is the residence of Mr Forde. Distance from Lurgan 12 and a half miles and from Portadown 4 and a half miles. Rent the same as above [Ardmore].

Derrytrasne [Derrytrasna] Townland

Derry-tras[stress]ne, so pronounced, contains [blank], of which 401 are bog and about 47 acres are bog at the west side and 9 and a half acres of the River Bann. Distance from Lurgan 5 and a half miles and from Portadown 6 and a half miles. Rent the same as the above townland [Ardmore], [signed] George Bennett, 2nd June 1835.

Parish of Mullaghbrack, County Armagh

Part of Memoir by J. Hill Williams, 1837 to January 1838

NATURAL STATE

Locality

The parish of Mullaghbrack is situated nearly in the centre of the county of Armagh, partly in the baronies of Oneilland West and Lower Fews, bounded in the north and south by the parish of Kilmore, to the south by the parish of Kilclooney, to the east by the parish of Ballymore and to the west by the parish of Armagh, its extreme length from east to west being 5 and three-quarter miles and extreme breadth from north to south 4 and a half miles. It contains 11,557 acres 6 perches, which are divided between the 2 baronies as follows: in Oneilland West 3,656 acres 8 perches, including water 53 acres 19 perches; in Lower Fews 7,900 acres 3 roods 38 perches including water 40 acres 2 roods 20 perches. Total water contained in parish 92 acres 2 roods 39 perches.

NATURAL FEATURES

Lakes

The lakes in this parish are Moyrourkan lough, situated in the eastern part of the parish 2 miles north east of Markethill, divided between 4 townlands and elevated to the height of 254 feet above the level of the sea, is three-quarters of a mile long from the north east to the south west and 220 yards broad from north west to south east.

Marlacoo lake, situated in the north eastern part of the parish 3 and a half miles south east of the town of Richhill, is situated 230 feet above the sea. Length from north east to south west 600 yards. Breadth from north west to south east 230 yards. It is partly in the townland of Marlacoomore and partly in Marlacoobeg.

Ballynewry lake, situated nearly three-quarters of a mile south west of Marlacoo lake, is elevated 252 feet above the sea, length from north east to south west 285 yards, breadth from north west to south east 200 yards. It is situated partly in the townland of Cornacrew and partly in the townland of Ballynewry.

MODERN TOPOGRAPHY

Markethill

The town of Markethill is situated in the diocese of Armagh, province of Ulster, county of Armagh, parish of Mullaghbrack, townland of Coolmillish and north east circuit of assize, on the mail coach road between Armagh and Newry, at the distance of nearly 5 and a half miles from the former and 11 and a half miles from the latter. Distance from Dublin 59 and a half Irish miles. Latitude [blank] north, longitude [blank] west. The following are its distances (in statute miles from the neighbouring towns): south east of Armagh 5 and a half miles, north west of Newry 11 and a half miles, south west of Tanderagee 6 miles, south by east of Richhill 5 miles, north east of Keady 8 and a half miles.

Streets

The town consists of 1 principal street with an obtuse angle in the middle of its length, the upper half being in a direction north by west, the lower half lying south by west. At the obtuse angle above mentioned there is a row of houses on the Keady road which is sometimes called Keady Street, and at the lower of the southernmost extremity of the main street a short street lets off to the eastward (consisting principally of new houses) and its being the Newry road has given it the name of Newry Street (parish of Kilclooney). The breadth of the streets vary, it averages 60 feet and their lengths are as follows: Main Street 550 yards, Newry Street 285 yards, Keady Street 143 yards. Also Gray's Lane, a narrow lane also in the parish of Kilclooney, runs in a south easterly direction from the lower extremity of the main street for the distance of 176 yards.

Public Buildings and Houses

The principal public buildings in the town are a Presbyterian meeting house, 2 Methodist chapels, a court house, a police station.

The greater number of the houses in Markethill are in tolerable order. The following is their number: 3-storey houses none, 2-storey houses 262, cabins and 1-storey 5, total 267. They are all built of unhewn stone and roughcast. The most respectable houses and shops are in the northern half of the main street. From the circumstance of the number of houses of unhewn stone not being roughcast and the rest for the greater part not cleanly whitewashed, the town presents upon the whole a ruinous and comfortless appearance.

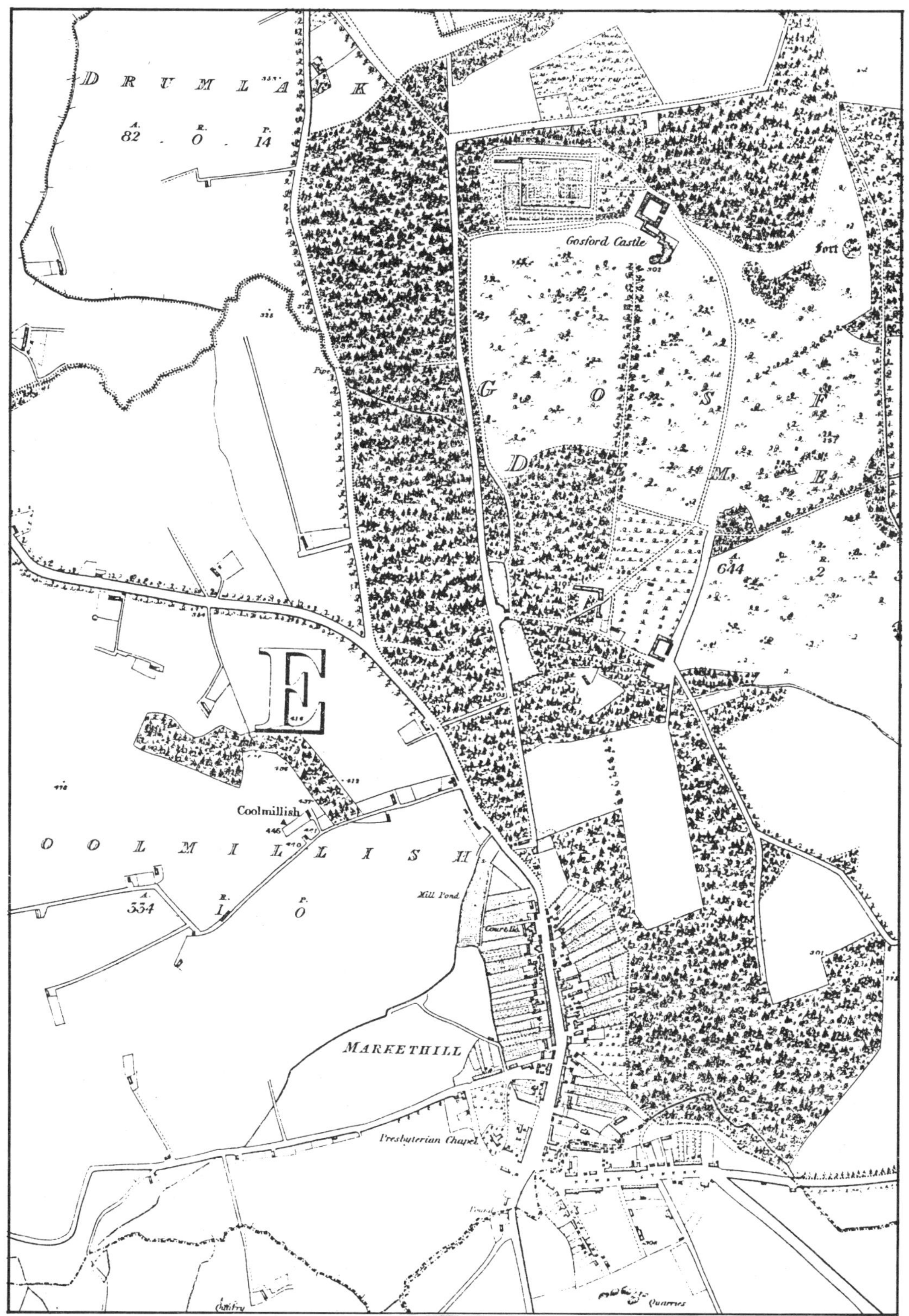

Map of Markethill from the first 6" O.S. maps, 1830s

Presbyterian Meeting House

The Presbyterian meeting house of Markethill, situated on the western side of the lower extremity of the main street, is a plain slated rectangular building in good repair (the inside being unfinished, unceiled and unflagged) of the following form and dimensions: [ground plan, main dimensions 76 and 55 feet, rectangular shape with projection at north west and sessions house attached to north east]. It is surrounded by a number of fine ash trees.

Roads

The principal roads which pass through this parish are the mail coach road from Armagh to Dublin through Markethill, Newry, entering this parish at its south western extremity, runs nearly along the boundary to the end of Newry Street (Markethill) where it enters the parish of Kilclooney, its length being for that distance 2 miles and average breadth 32 feet clear of drains and fences. It is macadamised and kept in good repair at the expense of the county.

The road from Richhill to Newry, which joins the mail coach road from Armagh at the distance of a quarter of a mile to the north north west of Markethill, enters the parish of Mullaghbrack near its northern extremity and crosses it in a south south easterly direction to its junction with the Armagh mail coach road, its length being 3 and a half miles and average breadth being 22 feet. It is macadamised and kept in good repair.

The road from Markethill to Tanderagee crosses the eastern portion of the parish in a north easterly direction for the distance of 3 and three-quarter miles, its average breadth being 21 feet clear of drains and fences. It is macadamised and kept in good order.

The road from Armagh and Markethill through Pointzpass and Banbridge branches off in an easterly direction from the Markethill and Tanderagee road at the distance of 1 mile from Markethill, its length being from that point 1 and a quarter miles and average breadth 24 feet. It is macadamised and kept in good order.

The road from Armagh to Tanderagee traverses the northern portion of the parish in a direction nearly east and west for the distance of nearly 5 and three-quarter miles, its average breadth being 24 feet. It is macadamised and kept in good order.

Also, half a mile of the road from Markethill to Keady in an east south east direction, average breadth being 21 feet, macadamised and in good order.

Productive Economy

Trades and Occupations

Trades and occupations in Markethill: surgeons 2, grocers 8, haberdashers 4, spirit dealers 22, painters and glaziers 1, watchmakers 1, bakers 2, jailors 1, shoemakers 3, hardware shops 1, nailors 1, wheelwright 1, smiths 2, pawnbrokers 1, hotels 2, ironmonger 1, chandler 1, delf shops 2, gunpowder dealer 1, butchers 2, reed makers 1.

Modern Topography

Roman Catholic Chapel

The Roman Catholic chapel, situated in the townland of Drumlack near the road between Markethill and Richhill at a distance of nearly a mile and a quarter from the former, is a plain slated rectangular whitewashed building in good repair, built in the form of a cross of which the extreme length is 66 feet and the extreme breadth 58 feet. The Reverend [blank] Tyrrell.

Methodist Chapel

The Markethill Methodist chapel, situated near the western extremity of the town on the Keady road, is a plain rectangular building of unhewn stone, slated and in good order, built in 1833. Length 49 feet, breadth 24 and a half feet.

Social Economy

Education

[Table contains the following headings: name, situation and description, when established, income and expenditure, physical, intellectual and moral instruction, number of pupils subdivided by age, sex and religion, name and religion of master or mistress, date on which visited].

Gosford school (male and female), a pretty ornamented cottage surrounded by flower pots, situated in the Gosford demesne, Markethill, established June 1815; income: from Lady Gosford 40 pounds per annum; expenditure: salary of master and mistress 40 pounds per annum; intellectual instruction: Scriptures, reading, writing and arithmetic, girls are taught needlework; number of pupils: males, 35 under 10 years of age, 27 from 10 to 15, 13 above 15, a total of 75; females, 20 under 10 years of age, 28 from 10 to 15, 17 above 15, a total of 65; total number of pupils 140, 59 Established Church, 52 Presbyterians, 29 Roman Catholics, 1 other denomination; master and mistress: John Woodhouse and Mary Woodhouse, Established Church, visited 21st August 1837, [signed] J.H. Williams.

Notes for Memoir by J. Heming Tait, January 1838

MODERN TOPOGRAPHY

Mills in Marlacoo

Flax mill, situated in the townland of Marlacoo, is the property of Robert Boyd. The wheel is 10 feet in diameter and 3 feet in breadth. It is a breast wheel and machinery of wood, built 1837.

Flax mill, situated in the townland of Marlacoo a short distance west of the above and belongs also to Robert Boyd. The wheel is 16 feet in diameter and 3 feet in breadth, the machinery of wood.

Corn mill, situated in the townland of Marlacoo, the property of Arthur Quin. The wheel is 16 feet in diameter and 4 feet in breadth. It is a breast wheel.

PRODUCTIVE AND SOCIAL ECONOMY

Hamiltonsbawn Village

Hamiltonsbawn village, situated on the road between Richhill and Markethill at the distance of 2 miles from the former and 3 miles from the latter. It has 2 fairs in the year viz. on the 26th May and on the 26th November. It contains 38 cabins and 23 2-storey houses. The trades are 6 grocers and publicans, 2 carpenters, 3 shoemakers and 1 smith. There is no place of worship nor police force nor magistrate.

Education

[Table contains the following headings: name, situation and description, when established, income and expenditure, physical, intellectual and moral education, number of pupils subdivided by age, sex and religion, name and religion of master or mistress, date on which visited].

Bally Newry school, townland of Bally Newry; income: a small salary from the London Hibernian Society, voluntary contribution from pupils; expenditure: none; physical instruction: none; intellectual and moral instruction: Bible only used; number of pupils: males, 45 under 10 years of age, 14 from 10 to 15, a total of 59; females, 37 under 10 years of age, 16 from 10 to 15, a total of 53; total number of pupils 112, 49 Established Church, 44 Presbyterians, 16 Roman Catholics, 3 other denominations; master James McClelland, Wesleyan Methodist, visited July 1837.

Parish of Newtownhamilton, County Armagh

Fair Sheets by John Heather, 16 March 1838

MODERN TOPOGRAPHY AND SOCIAL ECONOMY

Newtonhamilton: Houses and Occupations

There are 34 thatched 1-storied houses, 6 thatched 2-storied houses, 189 2-storied slated houses and 10 3-storied houses. There are 2 saddlers, 4 blacksmiths, 8 woollen drapers, 6 coopers, 10 shoemakers, 7 brogue makers, 9 carpenters, 2 pawnbrokers, 1 hardware shop, 1 cabinet maker, 2 wheelwrights, 5 flaxdressers, 5 nailors, 5 tailors, 2 reedmakers, 36 spirit shops, 3 hotels, 4 [surgeons ?]. There are 9 police foot and 1 horseman, with a chief constable.

Fairs

There is a fair held in the town on the last Saturday of every month which is pretty well attended, but the largest fair is on the last Saturday of the month of November and on the last Saturday in May which are termed "hiring fairs" where hire servants are engaged till next fair. The town on those days is crowded to excess and for some market days after it, for when the servants who are hired on fair days, when on going to their place they find it not so agreeable as they expected, they then come the following market day to look out for another master.

Court House

There is a court house lately built by Councillor Hamilton, but I could not ascertain the cost. It is a small building and could not have cost more than 300 pounds.

Boys' and Girls' School

This school, which is rather a spacious building, is at the commencement of the town of Newtownhamilton as you enter it from Newry. It is a good commodious house and capable of containing much more pupils. The girls' and boys' school is under the same roof. In the boys' apartments there are 72, 27 of whom are Catholics. In the girls' there are 33, 19 of whom are Catholics. The house was built in the year 1817 by Councillor Hamilton, he who owns the town, and cost 800 pounds. It is under the Board of Erasmus Smith, which board gives to the master 30 pounds per annum, but the present master has to give 16 pounds per annum allowance to the late master. The present master receives from each pupil 1d per week. The mistress is under the same board and receives 12 pounds per annum, but is subject to give 6 pounds per annum to the late mistress. The mistress receives 1d per week from each pupil.

Church

The church is about 1 and a quarter of a mile from the town of Newtownhamilton. It is in the same parish. It was built in the year 1775, the cost nor how that sum was raised I could not ascertain. It is capable of containing 240 persons. There are upwards of 1300 parishioners.

Schools

There is a small school adjoining, of young children. There are 14 girls, all of whom are Catholic. There are 9 boys, almost all of whom are Catholics. It is under no board of education. It is principally kept up by the rector of the parish who lives quite close to it. The master receives 1d per week from each pupil.

This school, which is a private one, is in the town and is composed of both boys and girls. In the boys' apartments there are 30, in the girls' 10, all of whom are Protestant. The school is under no board of education nor yet receives any private or public contributions. The master receives 2s 6d a quarter from each pupil.

Dispensary

There is a dispensary in town and a great number attend in the days of [blank].

General Appearance

The town is situated on the side of a valley on the road between Newry and Castleblayney. From the former place it is 8 miles and about 9 from Armagh. The houses are pretty clean and generally kept whitewashed, but the streets are narrow and dirty. The market house is in the middle of town and is in a dilapidated state, which adds greatly to its dirty appearance, and if it was removed there would be a small square found in its stead and would be a great improvement. The town is improving gradually. The regular market days are held on Saturday and generally well supplied with all kinds of meat and wearables. There is no linen market held here. The poorer class of people are

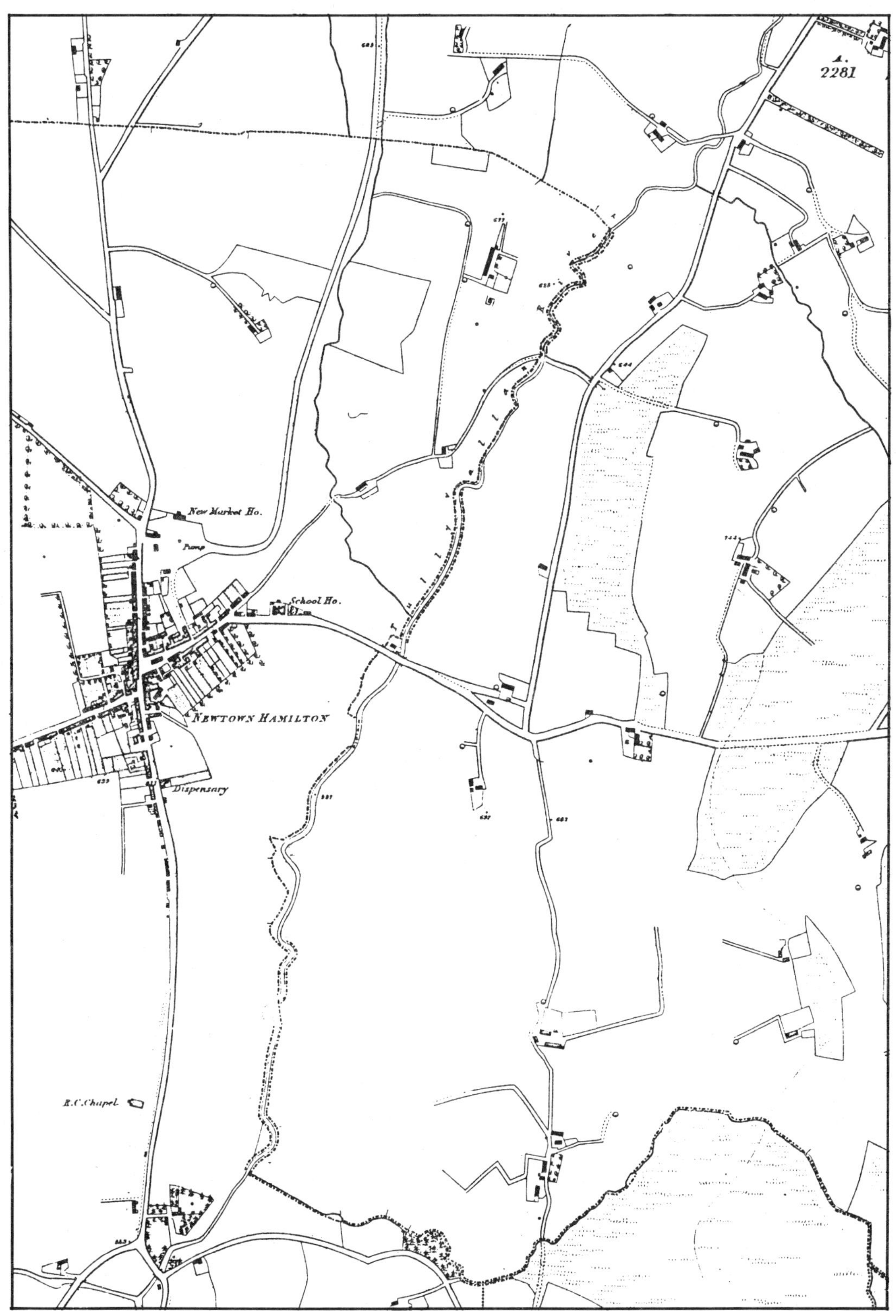

Map of Newtownhamilton from the first 6" O.S. maps, 1830s

principally occupied in farming in place of manufacture.

Conveyances

There is a kind of caravan drawn by 4 horses passes through on its way from Monaghan to Newry. It also carries the mail. This is the only conveyance leaves or passes through the town. It arrives here from Monaghan at 8 in the morning and in the evening from Newry at 6 o'clock p.m.

Presbyterian Meeting House

Presbyterian meeting house is situated at the end of the town. It was built in 1821. It would hold 600. The number of parishioners are 1,050. The exact cost of the meeting house could not be ascertained, for those meeting houses are built by the congregation and totally at their expense, so the prime cost is never ascertained. Perhaps one draws the timber with his horses, another will quarry and draw the stones.

School

This school is about a mile from the town of Newtownhamilton. It was built by J. Reid Esquire in the year 1831 and cost 250 pounds. There are both boys and girls. There are 36 girls, 12 of whom are Protestants; there are 46 boys, 26 of which are Protestants. The master receives 2d per week from each pupil. The school is under no board of education nor receives any sum from private contributions.

Seceding Meeting House

Seceding meeting house, situated in the townland of Corlamlall. It was built in 1738, holds 600 people and the number of parishioners are 1000. It cost 400 pounds, but this sum was given by the parishioners.

Presbyterian Meeting House

Presbyterian meeting house in the townland of Altnamuckan. It was built in 1796. It would hold 500, there are 320 parishioners. I could not ascertain the exact cost nor how the sum was raised.

Schoolhouse

Schoolhouse, situated in the same townland as the above meeting house [Altnamuckan] and is quite close to it. It was built in 1832 by B. Magbagh Esquire for his tenants' children. At present there is no school held in it. Cost 300 pounds.

Flax Mill

Flax mill, the size of which is 13 feet in diameter, 3 feet across the buckets, 6 feet fall of water, undershot wheel.

Boys' and Girls' School

This school, which is a private one, is in the town and is composed of boys and girls. In the boys' apartment there are 30, in the girls' 10, all of which are Protestants. The school is under no board nor yet receives no contribution. The master receives 2s 6d per week from each pupil.

Corn Mill

The size of the wheel is 8 feet in diameter, 4 feet across the buckets, 15 feet fall of water, breast wheel. [Signed] John Heather, Carrickmacross, 16 March 1838.

Parish of Seagoe, County Armagh

Fair Sheets by Thomas McIlroy, 10 November 1837

Natural State

Locality

The parish of Seagoe is situated in the north east corner of the county of Armagh. It is in the barony of Oneilland East and is bounded on the north by the parish of Montiaghs and Lough Neagh, on the east by the parish of Shankill <Shankhill> and the county Down, on the west by the parish of Drumcree and on the south by the parish of Kilmore. Its extreme length is 6 and a half English miles and extreme breadth 3 and a half miles. Its content is 10,982 acres 39 perches including 1,286 acres 1 perch of water, [blank] of which are uncultivated. It contains or is divided into [blank] townlands and is valued at [blank] to the county cess.

Natural Features

Hills

The highest point in the parish is in the townland of Drumgask, 200 feet above the level of the sea and the lowest ground is along the River Bann, 50 feet above the sea. The average height of the hills is 100 feet above the sea. They are well cultivated and fertile. They fall gradually northward toward Lough Neagh.

Lakes and Rivers

[Lakes]: none in the parish. The River Bann forms the western boundary line of this parish for 4 miles, for description of which see the parish of Drumcree.

Bogs

There is a bog situated in the north west corner of this parish in the townland of Ballynacor, the extreme length of which is three-quarters of a mile and extreme breadth is half a mile. The highest point in the bog is 72 feet above the level of the sea and 20 feet above the River Bann. Timber is found embedded, principally fir, along the parish boundary line where the bog is highest. The depth is not known. The bog stuff is very light at the surface but becomes heavier as you descend.

Woods

None in this parish.

Climate and Crops

Same as the parish of Shankill.

Modern Topography

Gentlemen's Seats

Carrick House, the seat of William Blacker Esquire, is situated in the townland of Carrick adjoining the River Bann. It is a plain and antiquated looking house, 3-storeys high, roughcast and whitewashed. The situation is pretty as it overlooks the wide and extensive flats on each side of the River Bann. The demesne and ornamental grounds are not extensive.

Communications

The main road from Armagh to Belfast passes through this parish in a north easterly direction for 3 miles. Its average breadth is 35 feet. It is a well laid out road and is kept in good repair by the commissioners of the turnpike. There are several by-roads also, which are kept in good repair by the county.

General Appearance and Scenery

This parish is very fertile and well cultivated. It is thickly inhabited and the cottages are neat and in general have a pleasing appearance.

Church

The parish church, situated north east of Portadown in the townland of Upper Seagoe. It is a neat country church built of stone, roughcast and whitewashed. It is 77 feet long and 37 feet 6 inches broad. At the north west end is a tower decorated with 4 minarets, which is 17 feet 6 inches long and 17 feet 6 inches broad. In the tower is a belfry containing one bell on which is the following inscription: "Parish of Seagoe <Sego>, AD 1781." The church was built in 1814, not known what cost or how defrayed. The interior is neat, the general attendance is 400 persons and the accommodation is 400. The windows are Gothic and there is a gallery at the north west end.

Monuments in the Church

On the wall in the interior are 2 monuments of

white marble; the one to the left is oval with the following inscription on it: "Sacred to the memory of the Reverend Richard Buckley, who departed this life January 18 1796, aged 72 years. Late vicar of the parish of Seagoe 33 years, a sincere friend to the family, drops a tear of sorrow for the departure of the above worthy and honourable character."

To the right is a neat square one on which is the following inscription: "Dedicated to the memory of the Reverend George Blacker, late vicar of this parish, eminently distinguished by private worth and public spirit, but more particularly by his ardent zeal and unwearied exertions in the sacred cause of Christianity and the Protestant religion to which this church owes its foundation. He lived sincerely beloved and died deeply lamented, May 1st 1810, aged 46 years." The present rector of the parish is the Very Reverend James Saurin.

Glebe House

The Glebe House is situated in the townland of Seagoe Lower. It is a large and antiquated looking house, 2-storeys high, whitewashed and slated. It is situated on the top a hill and is rather conspicuous from the opposite side of the River Bann. It is at present occupied by the Reverend James Saurin.

Bridge

Joyce's bridge, over the River Bann on the boundary line which divides the townlands of Hacknahay and Ballydonaghy. It consists of 1 arch and is built of whinstone. It is 41 feet long and 30 feet broad.

Roman Catholic Chapel

There is a Roman Catholic chapel situated in the townland of Lyle. It is a rectangular building, whitewashed, 40 feet long and 25 feet broad. It was erected in 1814 and cost 350 pounds, defrayed by subscriptions. The accommodation is for 310 persons and the general attendance is 300. The interior of the chapel is plain. It is not ceiled and there are no seats but forms. The floor is not boarded.

Modern Topography and Social Economy

Salary of Priest

The parish priest is the Reverend Laurence Morgan. His salary is 100 pounds per annum.

Schoolhouses

Aghacommon schoolhouse, situated in the townland of Aghacommon, is a stone cottage, slated and whitewashed. It is 28 and a half feet long and 20 feet broad. Date of building or cost not known.

Lisnamintry schoolhouse, situated in the townland of Lisnamintry, is a neat stone cottage patronised by Lady Mandeville. [Insert footnote: refused information by the schoolmaster Jonathan Webb, said he was directed to give none by the Reverend James Saurin].

Aghacommon schoolhouse, situated in the townland of Aghacommon adjacent to Derrymacash Roman Catholic chapel, is a neat stone cottage, slated. It is 28 and a half feet long and 28 feet broad, not known when built or what cost.

Balteagh schoolhouse is situated in the townland of Balteagh. It is a very handsome cottage. Information refused by the master, said he was directed to give none by Henry John Porter, moral agent to Lady Mandeville.

Hacknahay schoolhouse, situated in the townland of Hacknahay, is a very neat stone cottage, slated. It is 31 feet long and 18 feet broad, not known when built or what cost.

Lavery's schoolhouse is situated in the townland of Levaghery. It is a neat stone cottage 32 feet long and 16 feet broad. It was built in 1816 by William Blacker Esquire and cost 50 pounds. Repairs done in 1820 which cost 30 pounds, defrayed also by William Blacker.

Meeting House

There is a Presbyterian meeting house situated on the east side of Portadown, in the townland of Edenderry. It is a plain stone building, roughcast and whitewashed. It is [blank] feet long and [blank] feet broad. It was built in 1822 and cost 400 pounds, raised by subscription. There is accommodation for 400 persons and the general attendance is 100. The present minister is the Reverend William Dowlan, who receives 50 pounds of Regium Donum and 40 pounds per annum of stipend. The interior is plain.

Schoolhouse

Carrick female schoolhouse is situated in the townland of Levaghary. It is a mud cottage, thatched, 68 feet 6 inches long and is 16 feet 6 inches broad. It was built in 1831, cost not known.

Amusements

The people have no amusements except in attending the fairs and markets held in Lurgan and

Portadown, some on business but the greater number for amusement.

Towns

There are no towns in this parish except a small part of Portadown, which is connected by a stone bridge and contains 6 houses of 3-storeys, 12 of 2, and 5 of 1, of which there are 3 thatched and the rest slated.

Schools

[Table of schools contains the following headings: name, situation and description, when established, income and expenditure, physical, intellectual and moral education, number of pupils subdivided by age, sex and religion, name and religion of master or mistress, date on which visited].

Aghacomman, a cottage in the townland of Aghacomman, established 1797; income: 26 pounds per annum paid by a committee, including a contribution of 3 pounds from the Reverend James Saurin, archdeacon; intellectual education: a few of the Kildare Place books; moral education: Authorised Version of Scriptures; number of pupils: males, 10 under 10 years of age, 10 from 10 to 15, a total of 20; females, 13 under 10 years of age, 4 from 10 to 15, 1 above 15, a total of 18; total number of pupils 38, 29 Protestants, 8 Presbyterians, 1 Roman Catholic; master Richard Wilson, Protestant, visited 26th September 1837.

Aghacomman, a cottage in the townland of Aghacomman; income from pupils 12 pounds; intellectual education: *Universal spelling book*; moral education: Reverend Morgan, parish priest; number of pupils: males, 24 under 10 years of age, 12 from 10 to 15, 2 above 15, a total of 38; females, 25 under 10 years of age, 1 from 10 to 15, a total of 26; total number of pupils 64, 8 Protestants, 57 Roman Catholics; master Hugh Caulfield, Roman Catholic, visited 20th September 1837, [signed] J.C. Innes.

Hacknahey, a very neat cottage in the townland of Hacknahey, established 1827; income: from the London Hibernian Society 3 pounds, from the Reverend William Blacker Esquire 2 pounds, from the Reverend James [Saurin ?] 2 pounds, 8 pounds from pupils; intellectual education: London Hibernian Society books; moral education: visited by the Reverend James Saurin, archdeacon, and the Reverend Simon Foote, Authorised Version of Scriptures read daily; number of pupils: males, 35 under 10 years of age, 10 from 10 to 15, a total of 45; females, 25 under 10 years of age, 5 from 10 to 15, a total of 30; total number of pupils 75, 69 Protestants, 6 Presbyterians; master George Edbrooke, Established Church, visited 22nd September 1837, [signed] T.C. McIlroy.

Lavarys, a neat cottage in the townland of [blank], established 1816; income from pupils 4 pounds; intellectual education: London Hibernian Society's books; moral education: visited by the Reverend West and the Reverend Simon Foote, catechism taught by the master, Authorised Version of Scriptures read daily; number of pupils: males, 40 under 10 years of age, 4 from 10 to 15, a total of 44; females, 6 under 10 years of age, a total of 6; total number of pupils 50, 44 Protestants, 3 Presbyterians, 3 Roman Catholics; master James Forsyth, Established Church, visited 18th September 1837.

Lisnamintry, a neat cottage in the townland of Lisnamintry; [author's note] refused information by the master Johnathan Webb, visited 12th September 1837.

Balteagh, a very neat cottage in the townland of Balteagh; [author's note] refused information by the master Reid Booth, visited 9th October 1837.

Carrick female school, a mud cottage in the townland of Lemaghery; income: from the Hibernian Society 4 pounds per annum, 5 pounds from pupils; intellectual education: Hibernian Society's books; moral education: visited by the Reverend Thomas Leslie, Authorised Version of Scriptures read daily; number of pupils: 41 under 10 years of age, 18 from 10 to 15, a total of 59, 52 Protestants, 1 Presbyterian, 6 Roman Catholics; mistress Anne Burrel, Established Church, visited 28th November 1837.

Mills

[Table gives name of townland, proprietor, tenant, date of erection, type of water wheel, fall of water, material of machinery, number of pairs of stones or sets of scutches, remarks].

Ballynaghey, William Blacker Esquire, Thomas Joyce, 1835, 18 feet diameter, 3 feet 6 inches breadth, overshot wheel, [blank] fall of water, wood and iron machinery, 6 stocks and 1 pair of rollers, a good stone building, slated.

Ballynaghey, William Blacker Esquire, Thomas Joyce, 1835, 14 feet diameter, 3 feet 6 inches breadth, overshot wheel, [blank] fall of water, wood and iron machinery, 1 pair of stones, a stone building, thatched.

Knockramer, Honourable Charles Brownlow, Joseph Mairs, 1834, 15 feet 6 inches diameter, 4 feet breadth, breast wheel, 1 foot fall of water, wood and iron machinery, 4 sets of scutches, 1 set of rollers, a stone building, slated.

Memoir by Lieut G.A. Bennett, 2 June 1835

Natural State

Name

This parish in Armstrong's *Survey of the county* is spelt Seagoe and in Blacker's *History of the parish* it is spelt the same. It is sometimes spelt Seago. According to Colonel Blacker, it derives its appellation from a family of the name of Smith (in the Irish tongue Gabha or as it is pronounced Gabh-wa or Gawa) who, as tradition says, emigrated from a neighbouring district about 2 centuries back and settled themselves here, whence the name Seagabh was softened or corrupted into Seagoe signifying literally "the seat of the smiths."

Locality and Extent

It is situated in the north east end of the county Armagh and in the barony of Oneilland East, and is bounded on the north by Lough Neagh, on the east by the parish of Shankill in Armagh and by the parish of Donaghclony in county Down. On the south east it is bounded by the parish of Tullylish, county Down, on the south west and west the River Bann is its boundary between the parishes of Kilmore and Drumcree and on the north west it is bounded by the Montiaghs.

Its greatest length is from its extreme southern point where the River Bann enters the parish to its north east extremity where it meets the parish of Shankill and Lough Neagh, 6 and five-eighth miles. Its greatest breadth is from its junction with Shankill and Donaghcloney parishes on its eastern boundary to the River Bann on the west, rather more than 3 miles. It contains 9,745 acres 3 roods 18 perches divided into 47 townlands. Of these 498 acres are bog, 45 are water of the River Bann. It is divided into 3 manorial districts viz. Carrowbrack, Kerdnan, Derry or it is called from the proprietor, Brownlow's Derry. It is a rectory and vicarage in the diocese of Dromore, the archdeacon having the rectorial tithe. It is in the gift of the bishop and at present held by his son, the Reverend James Saurin. Besides the tithe there is a large glebe belonging to the rector, consisting of the townlands of Lower Seagoe and Kilvergan.

Natural Features

Hills

The highest ground lies in the triangle formed by Drumgask townland (201 feet) going east to Killycomain (200 feet) and Ballygargin (204 feet), including Crossnamucklagh (198 feet). From this the ground falls towards Lough Neagh and the River Bann. These hills command a good view of nearly the whole parish.

Rivers

There is no lake in the parish. The River Bann enters it at its extreme south point quarter of a mile above the old Knock bridge, and after running nearly west for a quarter of a mile it meets the Cusher water and forms the western boundary of the parish for 6 miles, where it becomes the boundary between the parishes of Drumcree and Montiaghs <Montaghs> to its junction with the waters of Lough Neagh. A mile and a half below its meeting with the Cusher it joins the Newry Canal, from whence its average depth may be taken as 30 feet and its breadth 150 feet. Lower than the canal the Bann is not fordable and there is but 1 bridge viz. at Portadown, but above the canal it is fordable in summer, nearly at the junction with the Cusher, and there are bridges over the Bann and the Cusher called the Knock bridges, by which name the bridge over the canal is also known. These 3 bridges are about 200 yards apart, the canal running nearly parallel to the River Bann.

In this parish the river is nearly, if not perfectly, flat, not having a fall of more than 3 or 4 inches. Its summer level is 48 feet. In winter it rises much higher and with a strong north wind which blows back the waters from Lough Neagh, it overflows its banks and inundates the adjoining meadows, giving the low grounds the appearance of a large lake. The fish taken are pike, eels, pullen and dolahan, the 2 latter peculiar to Lough Neagh and this river, but fishing is not followed as an employment, the supply not affording a sufficient remuneration. There is a quay belonging to Mr Overand in the part of the town of Portadown situated on the east side of the river, where coals, both English and Irish, are kept for the supply of this and the adjoining parishes. The produce exported by the Newry Canal Navigation, already mentioned in the Statistical Memoir on Drumcree parish, is, of course, common to this parish. Turf is supplied to the southern townlands of this parish by bargeloads brought up the river from the Montiaghs.

The Cusher water enters at the middle Knock bridge and after running north quarter of a mile, it joins the Bann. It is about 40 feet in breadth.

The Closet river is a small narrow stream separating this parish from the Montiaghs for about 1 and a half miles before it enters Lough Neagh. For the last half mile it becomes broader, varying from

30 to 100 feet. An embankment has been thrown across it at the junction of Analoist and Knockramer, thus preventing the back floods from Lough Neagh, and the stream itself has lately been turned by another course through the Montiaghs parish.

Bogs

There are only 498 acres of bog in this parish, the greatest part of which is in the north end. The largest is in Ballynacor townland, containing 108 acres. The height of this bog is 63 feet above the sea and 15 feet above the River Bann. The highest ground in the same townland is 123 feet. Analoist bog in that townland contains about 80 acres and is only 5 feet above Lough Neagh. There are 50 acres in Kynego and 45 in Derryvore. In the south end the Brown bog in Crossmahilly townland contains 44 acres and is 151 feet above the sea. Dynes hill above it in the same townland is 198 feet. Oak is the principal wood found in the bog in the south, and Colonel Blacker informed me that he has seen in a bog near his place, Carrick, a part in which 2 layers of trunks of trees appear superseded by about 6 feet of turf. Oak are found in the bogs in the north end. There is no general arrangement of the trunks, which are found in every position.

Woods

The country is very bare of timber. In Carrick demesne there is some fine old oak of about 140 years standing and some young planting laid out with taste and which has a picturesque effect on the river. Mr Robinson, about half a mile south of Portadown, has a few acres of planting round his house, as well as Mr Cuppage of Silverwood near Lurgan, but the numerous orchards throughout the parish give it, in summer, the appearance of a well wooded country.

Coast

Lough Neagh bounds the northern portion of this parish for about 2 and a half miles, reckoning the curves of the headlands. Kynigo Gut, nearly in the middle, is a small inlet and is resorted to as a harbour for fishing boats and a place where lighters disembark coals and timber for the consumption of the neighbourhood.

Climate

The climate is generally good, though the damp occasioned by the flooded ground adjoining the Bann is supposed to be prejudicial in pulmonary cases.

Natural History

Geology

Near the boundary of Kilvergan and Balteagh townlands in the north west end of the parish, a hard white limestone makes its appearance and was for some time quarried in for the kiln. It is now covered with water, being difficult to drain. The only other rock which projects above the surface is greywacke and a flinty or siliceous slate.

Modern Topography

Towns

A portion of the town of Portadown has extended over the river into this parish. A description of the town will be found in the Drumcree memoir.

Public Buildings

The parish church is about a mile from Portadown. It is a plain building that would accommodate 500. The first stone was laid in the year 1814 near the site of the old church, which was found too small for the congregation. In Aghacommon townland there is a Roman Catholic chapel that would hold 1000 and there is a smaller one in Lyle townland.

Gentlemen's Seats

The only gentlemen's seats are Carrick, belonging to and inhabited by Colonel Blacker. A large edifice originally built in 1692 as appears by a stone in the wall, but has been much improved and enlarged. It is surrounded by extensive planting and a number of old oak and beech, and commands a beautiful view of the River Bann.

Silverwood House, the residence of Mr Cuppage, is a neat built edifice surrounded by a few slips of planting, and the Glebe is also a good plain building.

Mills

There is but one corn mill in the parish. This arises from the want of fall in the rivers and streams. There is a windmill in Turmoyra townland which was erected by Mr Brownlow for the purpose of draining the meadow. It was not, however, found effectual and subsequently the direction of the stream was changed and the ground is now good meadow.

Communications

The high road from Portadown by Lurgan to Belfast runs nearly east and west through the parish. From this by-roads dis.. [descend ?] to Waringstown and Banbridge and Lough Neagh.

The road from Banbridge to Portadown enters the parish at the south and runs in a direction nearly parallel to the River Bann to the high road already mentioned, whence another road still keeping a parallel course with the river and continues till it enters the Montiaghs parish. This last road leads to Bannsfoot ferry and runs north and south.

The River Bann is crossed at Portadown by a bridge. It consists of 7 arches, the centre arch being sufficiently wide to admit the passage of the sloops which trade on the river and canal. The old bridge was swept away in 1751 and the present one was built on dry land and the course of the river turns into it.

Ancient Topography

Remains of Antiquity

There is no building of any antiquity or anything deserving of record except for what the military call quitee, which Colonel Blacker states in his *History of the parish* to have found. He says, "A few years ago, 3 swords and a spear of cast brass were found in a morass adjoining Carrick demesne, where tradition says a battle had been fought about the year 380 between 2 chieftains and their septs whose names are lost." These are now in the possession of Colonel Blacker.

Social Economy

Local Government and Dispensary

The petty sessions are held in Lurgan and Portadown. There is a dispensary in both places. In Portadown it is supported by Lord Mandeville and solely for the use of his own tenantry.

Schools

There are 5 schools in the parish viz. 2 in Edenderry townland, a male school supported by the scholars and a female school supported by Mrs Blacker. In Hacknahay townland a school with an attendance of 50 and another in Lisnamintry, supported by the Society for Discountenancing Vice. The other is in Balteagh townland, supported by Lord Mandeville, attendance 100.

Religion

The people are divided in religion, about half are Roman Catholics, the remainder are Episcopalians, Presbyterians, Quakers and Methodists. The three latter attend at Lurgan or Portadown as they have no place of worship in this parish.

Habits of the People

The cottages in the northern end of the parish are mud, in the centre and southern are partly mud and partly stone. They are usually on the ground floor, divided into 2 apartments. The food and dress is the same as in the adjoining parishes. Turf is used for fuel in the northern townlands, found on the spot and brought up the river to those in the southern.

Productive Economy

Occupations

Handspinning occupies the women and children in every cottage and weaving is the almost universal occupation joined in the necessary attendance on their small patches of ground, which are usually under 5 acres. The fairs and markets are Lurgan and Portadown, mentioned under the head of those towns.

Proprietors and Farms

The principal landlords are Lord Mandeville who holds 14 townlands, Colonel Blacker who holds 7, Mr Brownlow who holds 9. The remainder are held by various persons which will be seen in the annexed list of townlands. The general rent is 21s per acre but varies from 20s to 27s. The farms are from 3 to 30 acres but generally below 12.

Townland Divisions

Annaloist Townland

This parish is divided into 47 townlands viz. Annaloist, the property of Mr Burges, lets from 10s to 20s per acre, farms 10 to 80 acres. The west half lies so low as to be covered with water every winter. Contains about 80 acres of bog. It is 2 miles north west of Lurgan. Area 285 acres 2 perches.

Aghacommon Townland

Aghacommon, proprietor Charles Brownlow Esquire. Farms about 10 acres at 20s per acre. It is a flat good soil. In the east end is Mark Roaney's pub[lic] ho[use] and a large Roman Catholic chapel. The old road from Portadown to Lurgan runs through the south end. From the latter it is 2 miles. Area 222 acres 19 perches.

Ballynacor Townland

Ballynacor, proprietor Lord Mandeville of Tanderagee. Farms about 15 acres, from 15s to 22s per acre. About 108 acres are bog. The surface of the bog is of a spongy nature. There is small patches of ground covered with shrubs which appear never to have been laboured, about 2 and a half miles west of Lurgan. Area 320 acres 21 perches.

Ballynemony Townland

Ballynemony, proprietor C. Brownlow Esquire, Lurgan. Farms about 12 acres at 17s per acre and leases of 3 lives. The new line of road from Armagh to Belfast touches the south east point of this townland at a quarry. It is about 1 and a half miles west of Lurgan. Area 467 acres 2 roods 22 perches.

Ballygargin Townland

Ballygargin, the property of Mrs Cope of Loughgall. It is let from 1 pound 1s to 1 pound 5s per acre in leases of 1 life and 21 years. The farms vary from 3 to 18 acres. It is about 3 miles from Portadown. Area 304 acres 2 roods 12 perches.

Ballydonaghy Townland

Ballydonaghy, the property of Mrs Cope of Loughgall. The farms vary from 3 to 30 acres. It is let from 21s to 30s per acre in leases of 3 lives and 31 years. Portadown about 2 and three-quarter miles from the north end. Area 122 acres 1 rood 8 perches.

Ballyhannen Townland

Ballyhannen, Colonel Blacker of Carrick House is the proprietor. The farms are from 10 to 20 acres at about 21s per acre. The houses in general have a comfortable appearance with orchards of 1 or 2 acres attached. Portadown about 1 and three-quarter miles distant. Area 275 acres 3 roods 14 perches.

Breagh Townland

Breagh, the property of Colonel Blacker. The farms vary from 10 to 20 acres and let at 21s per acre. 22 acres are cut bog, 3 and a half acres are covered with water and a portion of meadow along the Bann are flooded in winter. Portadown 1 and a half miles distant. Area 257 acres 1 rood 30 perches.

Ballymacrandle Townland

Ballymacrandle, the property of Colonel Blacker and let in farms from 10 to 30 acres at 21s per acre. Nearly every house has an orchard attached, distant from Portadown about 1 and a half miles. Area 169 acres 2 roods 3 perches.

Ballynaghy Townland

Ballynaghy, the property of Colonel Blacker, who let it in farms of 10 to 25 acres at 1 pound 1s per acre. In the west end is a corn mill. The houses are all of stone with an orchard attached. Distant from Portadown 2 and three-quarter miles. Area 83 acres 3 roods 26 perches.

Boconnell Townland

Boconnell, the property of Charles Brownlow, who lets it from 15s to 20s per English acre. County cess 2s 6d per acre. 15 acres are bog at the north end, which is generally flooded in winter. This townland lies 1 and a quarter miles north west of Lurgan. Area 175 acres 21 perches.

Bocombra Townland

Bocombra, proprietor Mr Richardson of Lisburn, who lets it from 21s to 26s per acre. Tolerable good farm houses and orchards. The west end of the townland is 1 and a quarter miles from Portadown. Area 103 acres 2 roods 22 perches.

Balteagh Townland

Balteagh, proprietor Lord Mandeville of Tanderagee, his agent Mr Hunt, who generally lets it at 21s per acre. Near the centre is a school supported by Lord Mandeville, generally 100 in attendance. Situated about half way from Lurgan and Portadown viz. 2 and a half miles. Area 239 acres 1 rood 1 perch.

Carrick Townland

Carrick is the property and seat of Colonel Blacker. It is well wooded. The west boundary is the River Bann, of which 5 acres are in this townland and a portion of meadow subject to floods in winter. Portadown is 2 and a quarter miles distant. Area 167 acres 18 perches.

Clanrole Townland

Clanrole, the property of Lord Mandeville. County cess 2s 6d per acre. The north west end of the townland from Portadown is 2 and a half miles. Area 132 acres 1 rood 37 perches.

Crossmacahilly Townland

Crossmacahilly, the property of Lord Mandeville. About 44 acres of bog are on the east side, county cess 2s 6d per acre. About 2 and a half miles from Portadown. Area 221 acres 3 roods 39 perches.

Drumgask Townland

Drumgask, the property of Lord Dungannon, who lets it at 21s per acre. County cess 2s 6d per acre. The north end is 1 and a half miles from Lurgan. Area 171 acres 10 perches.

Drumnacanveny Townland

Drumnacaveny, the property of Colonel Blacker, who lets it at 21s per acre in farms from 10 to 30 acres. The houses have a comfortable appearance. The nearest market town is Portadown, 2 and a half miles distant. Area 111 acres 2 roods 37 perches.

Drumlisnagrilly Townland

Drumlisnagrilly, the property of Colonel Blacker, who lets it at 25s per acre in farms of from 8 to 20 acres. Portadown is 2 and a quarter miles distant. Area 70 acres 1 perch.

Drumnakelly Townland

Drumnakelly, proprietor C. Brownlow Esquire, who lets it at about 24s per acre. County cess 2s 6d per acre. Mr Rutherford occupies a handsome farmhouse in the south end of this townland, which is about 1 mile from Lurgan. Area 199 acres 2 roods 11 perches.

Derryvore Townland

Derryvore, proprietor Mrs Cope of Loughgall, who lets it at about 21s per acre. 45 acres are bog and 10 and three-quarters water. Portadown is 2 and a quarter miles distant. Area 177 acres 3 roods 15 perches.

Drumnagoon Townland

Drumnagoon, proprietor Lord Mandeville, who lets it at 21s per acre. County cess 2s 6d per acre. Near the centre of this townland is Mr Donahoe's handsome farmhouse. From the south end of this townland Portadown is 2 miles distant. Area 254 acres 2 roods 22 perches.

Drumgor Townland

Drumgor, proprietors Lord Mandeville and Mr Richardson. The latter holds rather more than the half. It is generally let at 21s per acre. Distant from Lurgan 2 miles and Portadown 2 and a half miles. Area 328 acres 3 roods 5 perches.

Edenderry Townland

Edenderry, the property of Miss Hogshaw of Lisburn. Farms vary from 10 to 20 acres and the rent is from 20s to 40s per acre. Leases 3 lives or 31 years. It contains a portion of Portadown, in which is a Seceding meeting house. About 12 and a quarter acres of water is in this townland. Area 247 acres 1 rood 19 perches.

Hacknahay Townland

Hacknahay, the property of Mrs Cope of Loughgall, who lets it from 21s to 30s per acre in farms from 3 to 30 acres and leases of 3 lives or 31 years. It contains about 2 roods of water. In the north end is a school under the patronage of the Society for Discountenancing Vice. About 50 children in attendance, the greater part of whom are Protestants. Portadown about 3 miles [distant]. Area 100 acres 2 roods 7 perches.

Knockramer Townland

Knockramer, the property of C. Brownlow Esquire. Farms generally about 12 acres and let about 21s per acre. About 1 mile from Lurgan and 4 from Portadown. Area 157 acres 3 rood 13 perches.

Knocklamuckly Townland

Knocknamuckly, the property of Mr Carleton and Mr Fivey. The former lives at Portadown and the latter at Union Lodge near Poyntzpass. It is let from 25s to 28s per acre in farms from 3 to 15 acres in leases of 3 lives and 41 years. Portadown is about 3 and a quarter miles distant. Area 254 acres 1 rood 39 perches.

Kilvergan Townland

Kilvergan, it is glebe land and at present held by the rector, the Reverend James Saurin, who lets it to tenants at will at 20s per acre. About 9 acres are bog at the northern point. About 2 and three-quarter miles from Lurgan. Area 218 acres 26 perches.

Killycomain Townland

Killycomain, the property of Mr Fivey. Farms vary from 10 to 20 acres and rent from 20s to 40s per acre. Portadown about three-quarters of a mile distant. Area 195 acres 24 perches.

Knock Townland

Knock, the property of Lord Mandeville, who lets it from 21s to 25s per acre in leases of 1 life or 21 years. There is near 2 acres of water in this townland. Portadown is 2 and a half miles distant. Area 105 acres 2 roods 22 perches.

Kynigo Townland

Kynigo, the property of C. Brownlow Esquire. County cess 2s 6d per acre. About 50 acres of bog. Let from 10s to 27s per acre. The middle ground rises 30 feet above Lough Neagh, but the boundary all round is nearly level with the lough. It is about 2 miles north of Lurgan. Area 387 acres 3 roods 15 perches.

Karn Townland

Karn, the property of J. Thompson Esquire of Dublin. County cess about 2s 6d per acre. About 2 acres are bog at the north east end. Also the farmhouse of Mr W. Irwin. Distant from Portadown 2 miles. Area 193 acres 1 rood 37 perches.

Kernan Townland

Kernan, the property of Messrs Moore and McNeight, who let it from 25s to 30s per acre. County cess 2s 6d per acre. Mr Buckbee's farmhouse is in the west end. [Insert marginal note: acreage required].

Knockmenagh Townland

Knockmenagh, the property of Lord Mandeville, who lets at about 21s per acre. County cess 2s 6d per acre. Portadown is 2 miles distant. Area 107 acres 2 roods.

Levaghry Townland

Levaghry, the property of Miss Hogshaw of Lisburn, but there are middlemen, of which Mr Robinson (a resident) is one. The length of leases are 3 lives and 31 years and the rent from 20s to 40s per acre. There are a male and female school in this townland. The latter is patronised by Mrs Blacker. There is 35 acres of worn out bog and about 6 and three-quarter acres of the River Bann. Portadown is half a mile distant. Area 286 acres 2 roods 39 perches.

Lower Seagoe Townland

Lower Seagoe, this is glebe land. The resident incumbent is the Reverend James Saurin, who lets it from 25s to 30s per acre. There is a neat glebe house and the remains of the old church. There is 16 acres of bog and 7 and a third acres of water. It is 1 and a quarter miles from Portadown. Area 290 acres 2 roods 22 perches.

Lisniskey Townland

Lisniskey, proprietor Lord Mandeville, who lets it at 21s per acre. County cess 2s 6d per acre. Area 184 acres 2 roods 9 perches.

Lyle Townland

Lyle, the proprietor a resident, Mr Robinson. The county cess is 2s 6d per acre. In the south end is a small Roman Catholic chapel. Portadown is 2 miles distant. Area 117 acres 13 perches.

Lisnamintry Townland

Lisnamintry, proprietor Lord Mandeville, who lets it 21s per acre. There is a schoolhouse built 1823, patronised by the Society for Discountenancing Vice, number of scholars about 128. From Portadown about 2 miles distant. There is about 29 acres of bog in this townland. Area 173 acres 3 roods 18 perches.

Moyraverty Townland

Moyraverty, proprietors Lord Dungannon, Messrs Atkinson, Overnan and Pedon and Lord Mandeville hold about 8 acres of unreclaimed bog. County cess 2s 6d per acre. North west of the road from Lurgan to Portadown is a Quakers' burying ground and in the north east end of the townland is Mr T. Lutton's farmhouse. Portadown is 2 and a half miles distant. Area 374 acres 3 roods 27 perches.

Silverwood Townland

Silverwood, the property of C. Brownlow Esquire. Middlemen Messrs Cuppage, Fulton and Turner, who have it let at 20s per acre. Silverwood House is near the centre. The town of Lurgan is three-quarters of a mile west by north of this townland. Area 198 acres 3 roods 25 perches.

Tannaghmore West Townland

Tannaghmore West, the property of C. Brownlow Esquire, who let it at 20s per acre. Fairview, the residence of Mr Thomas Uprichard, is at the north end. Lurgan is 2 miles south west of this townland. Area 209 acres 2 roods 14 perches).

Turmoyra Townland

Turmoyra, property of C. Brownlow Esquire, who lets it from 15s to 27s per acre. About 30 acres are bog. Kynigo Gut is in the north east extremity of this townland, a place where boats, lighters and craft load and unload, but very dirty and inconvenient. The only quay is the earth banks of an old drain. There is a good road to it from Lurgan, which is only 2 miles north west. Area 287 acres 1 rood 13 perches.

Tareen Townland

Tareen, the proprietor Lord Mandeville. County cess 2s 6d per acre. About 13 acres are bog, 2 and a half acres are water and the part along the Bann is subject to floods in winter but excellent meadow in summer. Area 203 acres 2 roods.

Tamnaficarbet Townland

Tamnaficarbet, proprietor Lord Mandeville, who lets it at 21s per acre. County cess 2s 6d per acre. Mr Ronay's farmhouse is in the south east end. Portadown is about 2 and a half miles distant. Area 122 acres 3 roods 3 perches.

Tamnafiglassin Townland

Tamnafiglassin, proprietor Lord Mandeville, who lets it at 21s per acre. County cess 2s 6d per acre. The south end is 2 and a quarter miles from Portadown. Area 178 acres 3 roods 18 perches.

Upper Seagoe Townland

Upper Seagoe, proprietor Lord Mandeville, his agent Mr Hunt near Gilford, who lets it at 21s per acre. County cess 2s 6d per acre. In the north end is the parish church, built 1814, would accommodate about 500. Portadown is half a mile distant. Area 130 acres 1 rood 22 perches. [Signed] George A. Bennett, 2 June 1835.

Parish of Shankill, County Armagh

Fair Sheets for Memoir by Thomas McIlroy, 11 October 1837

Natural State

Locality

The parish of Shankill <Shankhill> is situated in the north west corner of the county of Armagh, in the barony of Oneilland East. It is bounded on the north by the county of Down and part of Lough Neagh, on the west by the parishes of Montiaghs and Seagoe, on the south by the county of Down and the parish of Seagoe and on the east by the county of Down. Its extreme length is 4 and a quarter miles and extreme breadth 3 miles. Its content is 4931 acres 2 roods 25 perches including 289 acres and 32 perches of water, and it is valued at [blank] to the county cess. The parish is divided into [blank] townlands.

Natural Features

Hills

The hills are well cultivated and fertile. The highest point in the parish is in the townland of Knocknashane (221 feet above the level of the sea), from which there is a gradual fall in a north westerly direction towards Lough Neagh. The lowest ground is along the shore of the lake, 50 feet above the sea.

Lake

A very small part of Lough Neagh is in this parish, for description of which see parish of Montiaghs. Its content is 223 acres 3 roods 36 perches. There are no other natural lakes in the parish.

Rivers, Bogs and Woods

Rivers: none of any consequence, bogs none, no natural woods in this parish.

Climate and Crops

See journal of weather [cf. end of Memoir] while the party were stationed in Lurgan for 5 weeks (plus 4 days) from the 6th September to the 16th October 1837.

Wheat is sown in the month of November and reaped in the month of August. Barley and oats are sown in March and reaped in July and August. Flax is sown in April and pulled in July. Potatoes are planted in April and dug in November.

Natural State

Town of Lurgan: Locality

The town of Lurgan is situated in the southern part of the parish of Shankill. It is 75 Irish miles from Dublin and 17 from Belfast. It is in [blank] latitude and in [blank] longitude, in the diocese of Dromore, the province of Ulster, the county of Armagh and the parish of Shankill. The main road from Armagh to Belfast runs through it. The town is 1440 yards long and its greatest breadth is 280 yards. The surrounding country is well cultivated and has a fertile appearance.

History

General History of Lurgan

The Brownlow family settled here in 1660. They brought 40 English families with them, to whom they gave grants of land. The descendants of some of those families are still extant. The aboriginal proprietors of the soil were the McCanns, some of the descendants of whom are still in the neighbourhood of the town.

Modern Topography

Streets

The town consists of 1 principal street, 832 yards long and the extreme breadth of which is 44 yards. There are a few lanes branching off from the principal street, and at the north west end is a small street which runs at nearly right angles to the main street.

Houses

The greater number of the houses are old. They consist of 120 of 1, 224 of 2, 92 of 3 and 2 of 4-storeys, in all 438; 242 of these are slated, 2 shingled with bog oak and the remainder thatched. There has been many new houses built at the south east end within the last few years. They are mostly of brick, slated. There are 2 very fine houses at present building by the Messrs Cuppage at the south east end. They are of brick, stuccoed in imitation of Portland stone.

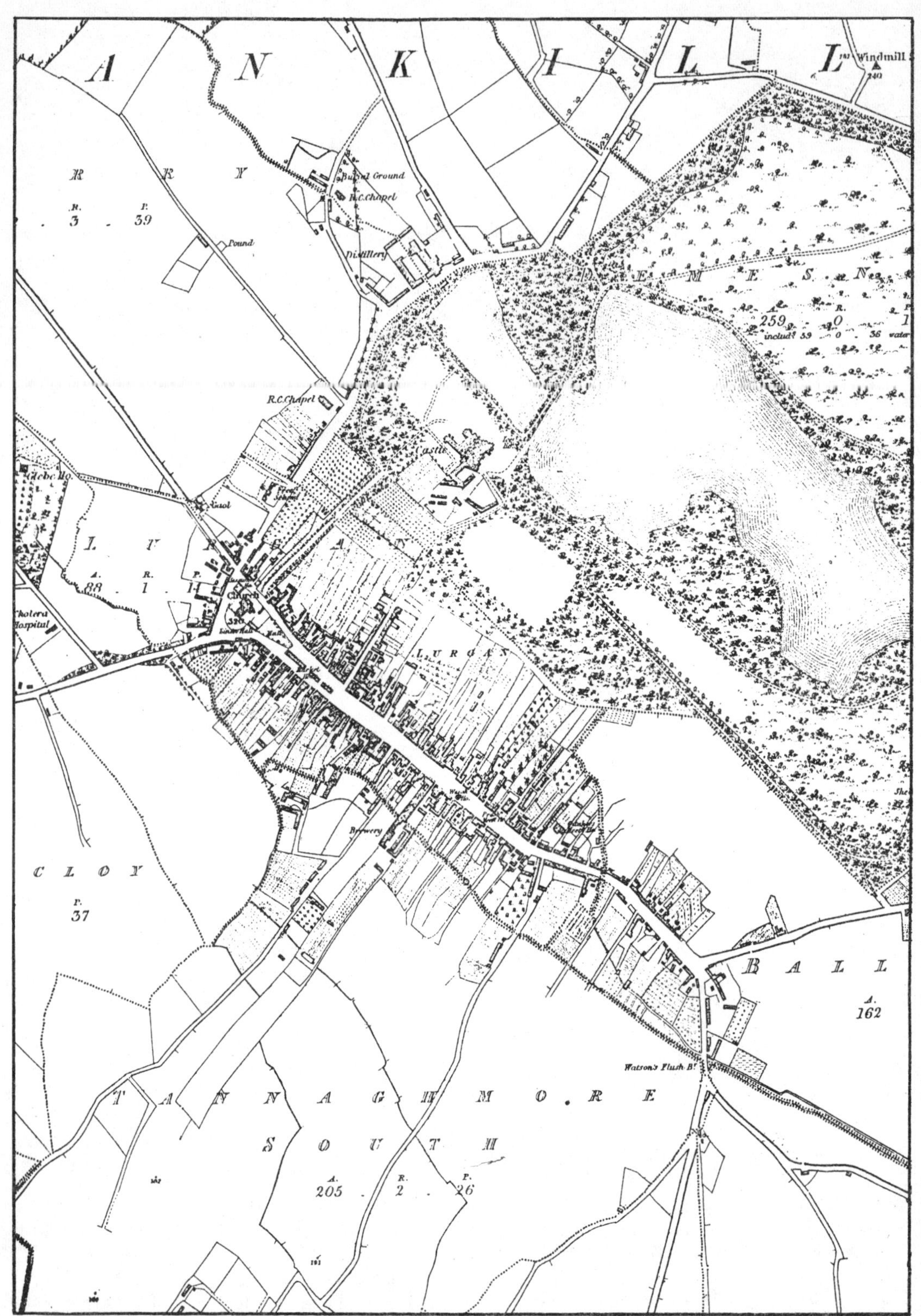

Map of Lurgan from the first 6" O.S. maps, 1830s

Social and Productive Economy

Habits of the People

The people have no amusements except in attending the fairs and markets held in Lurgan.

Newsroom

The newsroom is situated over the market house. It is managed by a committee of 9 persons, 5 to be a quorum, appointed annually. Subscription 1 guinea per quarter. It is open from 7 a.m. in the summer and 8 a.m. in the winter and closed at 10 p.m. Subscribers admitted by ballot. The papers taken up are the *London Times*, *Courier*, *Literary Gazette*, *Dublin Evening Mail*, *Ulster Times*, *Newry Commercial Telegraph*, *Belfast Chronicle*, *Dublin Evening Post*, *Newry Examiner*, *Northern Whig*, *Guardian*, *Spectator*, *Belfast Mercantile Register*, *Blackwood's*, *Tate's* and new monthly magazines.

Table of Occupations

Linen merchants [blank], surgeons 4, grocers 6, grocer and hardware dealer 2, grocer and spirit shop 7, milliner 2, woollen draper 7, watchmaker 2, spirit dealers 34, baker and grocer 1, bookbinders and printer 2, cabinet makers 1, clothiers 3, chandlers and grocers 4, saddlers 5, chandler 1, doctors 2, linen drapers 2, bakers 2, general merchants 3, butchers 2, tailors 5, boot and shoe makers 4, lodging and entertainment 13, smiths 2, painter and glazier 2, pawnbrokers 2, hosier 1, reedmakers 1, huxters 13, watchmaker and spirit dealer 1, leather shops 2, weavers about 200.

Branch Banks

There are 4 branch banks in Lurgan: the Provincial, established in 1834, the Ulster in 1837, the Belfast in 1836 and the Northern in 1835.

Fairs and Markets

There are 2 fairs held in the year in Lurgan, each of which lasts for 2 days. One is held on the 5th and 6th of August, the other on the 22nd and 23rd November. There is also a good weekly market held on Fridays, which is well attended by the country people. The commodities sold are fruit, fish, flesh meat, vegetables, black cattle, pigs, earthenware, haberdashery, old clothes and tinware.

Distillery

The distillery is situated north of the town, 25 perches distant. It is a large and extensive stone building. The greater part of it was burnt on the night of the 13th of October 1837. The amount of property consumed was estimated at 10,000 pounds.

Modern Topography

Gentlemen's Seats

The seat of the Honourable Charles Brownlow, situated on the north side of Lurgan. The house is at present building. It is in the Elizabethan style and will be very beautiful when finished. The content of the demesne and ornamental ground is 259 acres 1 perch, including 59 acres 36 perches of water. The grounds are well laid out. The garden is small and has a bad aspect. There are 2 artificial lakes in the demesne, the banks of which are wooded. They are the resort of immense numbers of wildfowl, mostly ducks. The family library was sold by auction some years since.

Communications

The main road leading from Armagh to Belfast runs through this parish in a north east direction for 2 miles. It passes through the town of Lurgan and its average breadth is 35 feet. It is a well laid out road and is kept in good repair at the expense of the county. There are also several by-roads which are kept in good repair at the expense of the county.

The main road from Tanderagee <Tandragee> to Lurgan runs through this parish on a north east direction for 2 miles. Its average breadth is 30 feet. It is not a well laid out road.

There is a new road from Lurgan to Tanderagee which runs through this parish in a south westerly direction for three-quarters of a mile. It is a well laid out road and a much more direct line of way than the old one. It is not at present open to the public.

General Appearance and Scenery

The country is highly cultivated. It is watered by many rivulets and there is a good deal of wood around the houses of the gentry and farmers. It has a fertile and pleasing appearance. Part of Lough Neagh and Rathlin Island is seen to much advantage from the north west side of Lurgan.

Church

The parish church, situated in the town of Lurgan at the north west end, is a large whinstone building, corniced with cut stone. The south west gable end (in which is the principal entrance) is handsome and entirely composed of cut stone. The church was built in 1725 not known what it cost. Repairs done in 1831 cost 1000 pounds, 700 pounds of which sum was borrowed from the Board of First Fruits. The remainder was raised by subscriptions. Repairs yet to be finished will cost, 'tis supposed, 140 pounds. 75 pounds has been borrowed from the Board of First Fruits. The remainder will be defrayed by subscription. The following figure shows the form and dimensions of the building: [ground plan, main dimensions 95 feet 3 inches and 49 feet, cruciform]. The accommodation is for 800 persons and the general attendance is 400. The interior of the church is rather plain. The ceiling is corniced with oak. There is a small gallery in the south west end. The pulpit is neatly carved. The windows are Gothic. The church has a small organ and choir. At the south west end of the church is a tower on which is a wooden spire, coppered, the total height of which is 320 feet above the level of the sea. In the tower is a belfry in which is one bell with the following inscription on it: "I to the church the living call and to the grave do summon all. Reverend W. Stinton, rector, John Ruddell fecit, 1794." The old shingled spire was burnt in 1792 and the present one was erected at the expense of the church. The present rector is the Reverend Holt Waring of Waringstown.

Glebe House

The Glebe House is situated in the townland of Aghnacloy. It is an old and plain stone building, 3-storeys high, roughcast and whitewashed. It is at present occupied by the Reverend Edward Kent, curate.

Roman Catholic Chapel

The Roman Catholic chapel is situated at the north side of Lurgan in the townland of Derry. It is a very handsome building, decorated with minarets. It is 80 feet long and 40 feet broad. It was built in 1833 and cost 1500 pounds, defrayed by subscription. The accommodation is for 1500 persons and the general attendance is 800. The interior is unfinished. It is supposed 300 pounds will do it. The gallery is large and handsomely finished. The windows are Gothic. The clergyman's salary of the above chapel is 100 pounds per annum. The present clergyman is the Reverend William O'Brien.

Wesleyan Methodist Meeting House

The Wesleyan Methodist meeting house is situated in Castle Lane. It is a neat stone building, 49 feet 6 inches long and 27 feet 6 inches broad. It was built in 1825 and cost 250 pounds, defrayed by subscriptions. The interior is very plain. It is unceiled. The windows are Gothic. The accommodation is for 400 persons and the general attendance is 250. The minister's salary of the above meeting house is 14 pounds per annum.

Gaol

The gaol is situated in the north west end of Lurgan, about 8 perches from the town. It is a small neat building of whinstone, corniced with cut stone. It was built in 1831 and cost 820 pounds, defrayed by assessments on the county. It is 71 feet long and 17 feet 3 inches broad. The cells only accommodate 7 prisoners.

Court House

The court house is situated close to the church. It is a neat stone building (49 feet long and 48 feet broad) with Gothic windows and was erected in 1802. It was since repaired and enlarged and has cost altogether 1,663 pounds, which was defrayed by the county. The old bridewell underneath the courthouse is not at present made use of.

Market House

The market house is situated in the middle of the street near the north west end of the town, a stone building, roughcast. It is 65 feet long and 27 feet 6 inches broad. The cost of building and date of erection are not known.

Linen Hall

The linen hall is a plain building adjoining the church. It is 78 feet long and 31 feet 6 inches broad. The entrance is from the church grounds. When built and what cost not known.

Circulating Library

There is a small circulating library kept by Mr John Reilly, bookseller and stationer. It consists of 200 volumes, mostly novels. It is not very well supported. The average number of subscribers is 12 per week. The charge for the reading of the works is 6d per week.

Presbyterian Meeting House

There is a Presbyterian meeting house nearly in the centre of the town of Lurgan. It is a large stone building. It is 63 feet 6 inches long and 47 feet 6 inches broad. It was built in 1828 and cost 2200 pounds, defrayed by subscriptions. The inside is handsomely fitted up. The gallery is large, in front of which there is a good clock. There is a handsome lustre suspended from the centre of the ceiling. The accommodation for 1000 persons, the general attendance is 500.

Salary of Presbyterian Minister

The salary of the minister of the above meeting house is 75 pounds Irish currency of Regium Donum and 82 pounds Irish of stipend per annum. The congregation is 3000. It has increased treble since the appointment of the present minister, the Reverend Hamilton Dobbin, in 1801.

Methodist Chapel

There is a Methodist chapel in the centre of the town. It is a neat stone building, 40 feet long and 36 feet broad. It was built in 1825 and cost 700 pounds, defrayed by subscriptions. Repairs done in 1835 cost 15 pounds, defrayed also by subscription. The accommodation is for 500 persons. The general attendance is 300. The present ministers are the Reverends John Nelson and William Armstrong. The former has 60 pounds, the latter 48 pounds per annum from the congregation, [signed] T.C. McIlroy, October 11th 1837.

SOCIAL ECONOMY

Schools

Tullygally schoolhouse, situated in the townland of Tullygally, is a neat stone cottage, whitewashed and slated, 35 feet long and 18 and a half feet broad. Built in 1818, the cost not known. 28 September 1837.

Lurgan free schoolhouse is a very neat house, situated at the north east corner of the town of Lurgan. It was built in 1812 and cost 850 pounds, raised by subscriptions. Repairs done in 1834 which cost 100 pounds, defrayed by the Erasmus Smith Board. The school is managed by a committee to whom the pupils pay 20 pounds, which is expended in clothing for them. The form and dimensions of the school house are represented by the following figure: [ground plan, main dimensions 113 feet and 27 feet 3 inches, rectangular shape with projections at various parts]. 5th October 1837.

Tannaghmore national schoolhouse is a neat slated schoolhouse, situated in the townland of Tannaghmore North. It was built in 1827 and cost 120 pounds per annum by subscription. The Kildare Place Society gave 12 pounds and the Honourable Charles Brownlow 25 pounds. Repairs done 1834 which cost 16 pounds, of which William John Hancock gave 6 pounds and the National Board 10 pounds. The length of the schoolhouse is 41 and a half feet and breadth 21 feet. [Signed] J. Cumming Innes, 12 October 1837.

Local Government

Mr William Hancock, agent for the Honourable Charles Brownlow, is magistrate. He resides in [blank]. There is a force of constabulary police consisting of a sergeant and 4 privates stationed in the town of Lurgan. Special sessions are held twice in the year in the court house, town of Lurgan.

Schools

There are 3 schools in this part of the parish of Shankill for particulars see table. [Table of schools contains the following headings: name, situation and description, when established, income and expenditure, physical, intellectual and moral education, number of pupils subdivided by age, sex and religion, name and religion of master or mistress, date on which visited].

Tullygally, a neat cottage in the towland of Tullygally, established 1818; income: from Hibernian Society 4 pounds, 8 pounds from pupils; intellectual instruction: Hibernian Society books; moral instruction: visited by the Reverend Edward Kent, Protestant curate of Lurgan, Authorised Version of Scriptures read, no catechisms taught; number of pupils: males, 30 under 10 years of age, 20 from 10 to 15, 1 over 15, a total of 51; females, 17 under 10 years of age, 8 from 10 to 15, a total of 25; total number of pupils 76, 50 Established Church, 22 Presbyterians, 4 Roman Catholics; master John Mehaffy, Protestant, visited 28th December 1837.

Lurgan male free school, a common room in the free schoolhouse, Lurgan, established 1812; income: from Erasmus Smith 30 pounds, from pupils 10 pounds paid to the committee; intellectual instruction: Kildare Place Society books; moral instruction: visited by the Reverend Holt Waring, Protestant rector of Lurgan, and the Reverend Edward Kent, Established Church catechisms taught on Wednesday and Saturday, Authorised Version of Scriptures read every day except Saturday; number of pupils: 90 under 10 years of age, 22 from 10 to 15, a total of 112, 60 Established Church, 10 Presbyterians, 42 Roman Catholics; master Patrick Carroll, Protestant, visited 5 October 1837.

Lurgan female free school, a common room in

the free schoolhouse, Lurgan, established 1812; income: from Erasmus Smith 20 pounds per annum, 10 pounds from pupils paid to the committee; intellectual instruction: Kildare Place Society books; moral instruction: visited by the Reverend Holt Waring, Protestant rector of Lurgan, and the Reverend Edward Kent, Established Church catechisms taught on Wednesdays and Saturdays, Authorised Version of Scriptures read every day except Saturday; number of pupils: 60 under 10 years of age, 72 from 10 to 15, a total of 132, 90 Established Church, 13 Presbyterians, 29 Roman Catholics; mistress Anne Anderson, Protestant, visited 5th October 1837.

Tannaghmore North national school, a neat cottage in the townland of Tannaghmore North, established 1827; income: from the National Board 8 pounds per annum, 8 pounds from pupils; intellectual instruction: National Board books; number of pupils: males, 18 under 10 years of age, 24 from 10 to 15, a total of 42; females, 12 under 10 years of age, 20 from 10 to 15, a total of 32; total number of pupils 74, 20 Established Church, 49 Presbyterians, 5 Roman Catholics; master Joseph Hewitt, Presbyterian, visited 12th October 1837, [signed] J. Cumming Innes.

Natural Features

Weather Journal

[Table for September and October 1837, with state of weather each morning, noon and afternoon, and wind direction]

September: 6th, fine, fine, fine, north west wind; 7th, wet, wet, fair, changeable; 8th, fine, fine, fine, north; 9th, fine, fine, fine, west; 10th, fine, fine, fine, west; 11th, showery, showery, fine, south west; 12th, fine, fine, wet, south west; 13th, wet, wet, fine, north east; 14th, showery, showery, showery, north; 15th, fine, showery, showery, changeable; 16th, wet, wet, wet, changeable; 17th, wet, fine, fine, south west; 18th, fine, fine, fine, south west; 19th, fine, wet, showery, south west; 20th fine, fine, fine, south west; 21st, fine, fine, fine, south; 22nd, fine, fine, fine, south; 23rd, fine, fine, fine, south; 24th, fine, fine, fine, south; 25th, fine, fine, fine, south; 26th, fine, fine, fine, south; 27th, fine, fine, fine, south; 28th, fine, fine, fine, south; 29th, fine, fine, fine, south; 30th, fine, fine, wet, south.

October 1st, fine, fine, fine, south wind; 2nd, fine, fine, fine, south; 3rd, fine, fine, fine, south; 4th, fine, fine, fine, south; 6th, fine, fine, fine, south; 6th, fine, fine, wet, south; 7th, fine, showery, fine, south; 8th, fine, showery, fine, changeable; 9th, fine, showery, fine, changeable; 10th, fine, showery, fine, west; 11th, fine, wet, wet, south west; 12th, fine, fine, fine, west; 13th, fine, fine, fine, west; 14th, fine, wet, wet, south west; 15th, fine, fine, fine, south west.

Parish of Tartaraghan, County Armagh

Fair Sheets for Memoir by Thomas McIlroy, 15 December 1837

NATURAL STATE

Locality

The parish of Tartaraghan is situated in the northern part of the county of Armagh and in the barony of Oneilland West. It is bounded on the north by Lough Neagh, on the east by the parishes of Montiaghs and Drumcree, on the west by the parishes of Killyman and Loughgall and on the south by part of the parish of Newry and the parish of Kilmore. Its extreme length is 6 miles and extreme breadth 5 and a half miles. Its content is 11,612 acres 35 perches, including 222 acres 2 roods 15 perches of water, [blank] of which are uncultivated. It is valued at [?] 16 pounds to the county cess.

NATURAL FEATURES

Hills

The hills in this parish are well cultivated. The highest point is Cockhill in the townland of Drumanphy, 157 feet above the level of the sea. The lowest ground is along the shore of Lough Neagh, 50 feet above the sea. The average height of the hills is 100 feet above the sea.

Lakes

Annagarriff lake occupies a portion of the townland of Derrylee in this parish, for further particulars see Memoir for the parish of Killyman, county Armagh. Part of Lough Neagh is in this parish. It is 48 feet above the level of the sea. Its content is 1,917 acres 2 roods 34 perches. The following island is in this part of the lake: Coney Island derives its name from the number of rabbits which at one time inhabited it, some of which are still extant. There are a few shrubs and low trees on it. Its content is 2 acres 1 rood 4 perches. It is half a mile distant from the mainland.

Rivers

The River Bann forms the north eastern boundary line of this parish, for description of which see Memoir of the parish of Drumcree, county Armagh. The River Blackwater forms the north western boundary line of this parish for 1 mile, for description of which see Memoir of the parish of Loughgall, county Armagh. The Tall river forms the southern boundary line for 1 mile, for further particulars see the Memoir for the parish of Kilmore.

Bogs

The greater portion of the northern part of this parish is bog. Its extreme length is 2 and a half miles and extreme breadth is 2 miles. The highest point in the bog is 79 feet above the level of the sea and 29 feet above the River Bann. Timber is found embedded, oak and fir. The roots and stumps remain upright. The timber is scattered indiscriminately through the bog. The depth is not known in the central parts, but it becomes shallower as it approaches the islands which are scattered over the surface of the bog.

Woods

There is a small grove of birch trees situated nearly in the centre of this parish, in the townland of Ballynarry on the main road from Dungannon to Portadown. It is said to be the remains of a natural wood, extent of which not known.

Shore of Lough Neagh

The shore of Lough Neagh is one and a quarter miles long. It is interesting and picturesque and is much frequented by pleasure parties during the summer.

Climate and Crops

Same as those in the parish of Drumcree.

MODERN TOPOGRAPHY

Towns and Village

Towns: none in this parish. Maghery is situated in the northern part of this parish in the townland of Maghery, close to the shore of Lough Neagh. It consists of 16 houses of 1-storey, thatched. The houses are rather scattered and the greater number of the inhabitants support themselves by fishing.

Public Buildings: Schoolhouses

Teagy schoolhouse is situated in the townland of Teagy. It is a very neat stone cottage with a projecting roof. It is roughcast and slated. It is 44 feet long and 19 feet 6 inches broad. It was built in 1826. It cost 80 pounds, raised by subscription.

Teagy female school is kept in a room in the west end of the above schoolhouse.

Parish Church

The parish church is situated in the townland of Breagh. It is a neat country church, roughcast and whitewashed. It was built in 1816 and cost 1300 pounds, defrayed by the Board of First Fruits. The form and dimensions of the church are shown by the following figure: [ground plan, main dimensions 76 and 30 feet, rectangular shape with projection at east end]. The interior is neat, the pews are large and commodious. There is a gallery at the east end. The accommodation is for 550 persons and the general attendance is 500. At the east end of the church is a tower, in which is a belfry containing one bell with the date 1779 on it.

Schoolhouse

Derrylard schoolhouse, situated in the townland of Derrylard, is a good stone cottage, slated, 30 feet long and 19 feet broad. It was built in 1826 and cost 14 pounds 8s, defrayed by subscription. There is an apartment in the north end occupied by the master as a dwelling.

Roman Catholic Chapel

St John's chapel, situated in the townland of Eglish, is a neat rectangular stone building, roughcast and slated. It is 69 feet long and 31 feet broad. It was erected in 1837 and cost 500 pounds, defrayed by subscriptions. In the north west gable end is a plate with the following inscription: "Adore ye the Lord in his holy court. Psalm 95 verse 9." The interior of the above chapel is neat. The windows are Gothic. It is unceiled and there is a gallery at the east end. The accommodation is for 600 persons and the general attendance is 500.

Monument in Roman Catholic Chapel

On the wall to the left of the altar is a monument with the following inscription on it: "Erected by his grateful parishioners, to the memory of John Morton, P.P., who departed this life AD 1833, aged 44 years, after having contributed by his unwearied exertions to raise this temple to the glory of God. Requiescat in pace."

Methodist Meeting House

There is a Methodist meeting house situated in the northern part of this parish, in the townland of Derrylee. It is a rectangular stone building, slated, 40 feet long and 20 feet broad, not known when built or what cost. The interior is very plain. The windows are rectangular. The accommodation is for 150 persons. There is no minister connected with the above meeting house as there has not been worship performed in it for some years.

Presbyterian Meeting House

There is a Presbyterian meeting house situated in the townland of Ballynarry. It is a rectangular stone building, whitewashed and slated, 55 feet long and 32 feet broad, expense of building or when erected not known. The interior is commodious. It is fitted up with pews. It is unceiled. The accommodation is for 500 persons and the general attendance is 200. The minister of the above meeting house is the Reverend James Shaw.

Communications

The main road leading from Dungannon to Portadown runs through this parish for 1 mile in a westerly direction. Its average breadth is 40 feet. It is a well laid out road and kept in good repair at the expense of the county. There are several by-roads also, which are kept in good repair at the expense of the county.

General Appearance and Scenery

The southern part of this parish is picturesque and well cultivated. The northern portion consists principally of extensive tracts of bog covered with heath, which (excepting the islands in it) has a wild and barren appearance.

SOCIAL ECONOMY

Religion

The proportions which the numbers of the different persuasions bear to each other are as follows: Established Church 540, Presbyterians 380, Roman Catholic 2000.

Habits and Occupations of People

The general style of the cottages is good. They are mostly built of stone, 1-storey, thatched. The fuel made use of is turf and bog wood. In the northern portion of the parish they are very fond of dancing. In the southern part they are very fond of following on foot the hounds which are kept by Thomas Atkinson of Crowehill, and which meet 3 days in every week during the season.

Schools

[Table of schools contains the following headings: name, situation and description, when established, income and expenditure, physical, intellectual and moral instruction, number of pupils subdivided by age, sex and religion, name and religion of master or mistress, date on which visited].

Teagy, a very neat cottage in the townland of Teagy, established 1826; income: from Thomas Atkinson Esquire, Crowehill, 2 pounds per annum, from pupils 12 pounds; intellectual instruction: Kildare Society books; moral instruction: visited by the Reverend David Donaldson, catechisms taught on Saturdays by the master, Authorised Version of Scriptures read daily; number of pupils: males, 30 under 10 years of age, 25 from 10 to 15, 4 above 15, a total of 59; females, 15 under 10 years of age, 12 from 10 to 15, 2 above 15, a total of 29; total number of pupils 88, 71 Established Church, 9 Presbyterians, 8 Roman Catholics; master Robert McDowell, Established Church, visited 19th November 1837.

Teagy female school, a room in the above cottage, established 1826; income: from Mrs Atkinson, Crowehill, 5 pounds per annum, 5 pounds from pupils; intellectual instruction: Kildare Society books; moral instruction: visited by the Reverend David Donaldson, catechisms taught on Saturdays by the master, Authorised Version of Scriptures read daily; number of pupils: 7 under 10 years of age, 12 from 10 to 15, a total of 19, 16 Established Church, 3 Roman Catholics; mistress Elizabeth Obre, Established Church, visited 19th November 1837.

Derrylard, a neat cottage in the townland of Derrylard, established 1826; income: from the Earl of Charlemont 5 pounds per annum, 5 pounds from pupils; intellectual instruction: Kildare Society books; moral instruction: visited by the Reverend David Donaldson, Authorised Version of Scriptures read daily, catechisms taught on Saturdays by the master, assisted by the Reverend David Donaldson; number of pupils: males, 34 under 10 years of age, 13 from 10 to 15, a total of 47; females, 18 under 10 years of age, 5 from 10 to 15, a total of 23; total number of pupils 70, 62 Established Church, 4 Presbyterians, 4 Roman Catholics; master William Moffat, Established Church, visited 20th November 1837, [signed] Thomas C. McIlroy.

Statistical Report by Lieut C. Bailey, 4 May 1835

NATURAL STATE

Name

The customary way of spelling the name of the parish is Tartaraghan.

Locality

It is situated in the county of Armagh and barony of Oneilland West, bounded on the north by the Blackwater river (which divides the counties of Armagh and Tyrone) and by Lough Neagh, on the east by the River Bann, separating it from the parish of Montiaghs <Moyntaghs> and by the parish of Drumcree, on the south by the Tall <Tell> river and on the west by the parishes of Loughgall and Killyman. Extreme length 6 miles, extreme breadth 5 and a half miles, divided into 31 townlands, containing [blank] acres, [blank] of which are cultivated, 3,315 uncultivated and [blank] of water. [Insert marginal note in Bailey's hand: perhaps these quantities could be supplied in Dublin from documents]. Valuation to the county cess about 1s 6d per acre half yearly. Coney Island, situated in Lough Neagh about half a mile from the shore, belongs to the parish of Tartaraghan but is not included in any townland. It contains 4 acres.

NATURAL FEATURES

Hills

There are no hills of any consequence. The highest are Cockhill, 161 feet above the level of the sea, Cranegill 140 feet, Clantilew 138 feet, Derrycorr 143 feet, Clancarish 133 feet, Mount Hall 133 feet, Derrylard 144 feet, Church 119 feet.

Lakes

Lough Neagh (46 feet above the level of the sea) forms the northern boundary of the parish. Coney Island, which is situated in the lake, is used for grazing during the summer. It was formerly cultivated, but the crops were entirely consumed by rats. The island is connected with the mainland at Derryaugh Point by a kind of causeway or ridge, which in the summer is not more than 2 feet under the water and can be easily traced. Part of it was cleared away to enable the barges to sail over it on their passage from the Bann to the Blackwater river.

There are 2 lakes of considerable size on the east side of the townland of Dengene, but including parts of the adjoining townlands. The northern one contains 66 acres and the southern one 54 acres.

Annagarriff lake, situated in the southern extremity of the townland of Derrylee, is partly in the parish of Tartaraghan and partly in Killyman parish. It contains 86 acres, 36 of which belong to Derrylee townland. There are 2 very small islands in this lake.

Rivers

The Blackwater river, which forms the north west boundary of the parish, flows north and empties itself into Lough Neagh. Breadth 120 feet and depth from 8 to 10 feet. Navigable for barges of 40 or 50 tons burden. Its mouth is obstructed by a deposit of sand and gravel which in the summer time impedes the navigation.

The River Bann forms the north east boundary of the parish, dividing it from the parish of Montiaghs. It flows north and empties itself into Lough Neagh. Its breadth is about 250 feet and navigable for barges of about 50 tons burden. Its mouth is obstructed by a deposit of sand and gravel which was partially removed about 2 years ago by the Newry Navigation Company. The barges were frequently obliged to be lightened of part of their burden before they could be got over the bar.

The Upper Taclough is a small river dividing the parishes of Tartaraghan and Drumcree and empties itself into the Bann, and is navigable for large boats which convey turf from the townlands of Derrinraw and Derrylard to Portadown and other places in the neighbourhood.

The Tall is a small river bounding the southern extremity of the parish, about 20 feet broad and 5 or 6 feet deep, flows west and empties itself into the Blackwater. It is very subject to floods.

Bogs

The northern part of the parish may be said to be almost one continued tract of bog, from 50 to 80 feet above the sea, with insulated hills called islands rising through it. Fir and oak timber and occasionally small pieces of yew are found embedded in the bog, but principally oak. The bogs round the edges are 8 or 10 feet deep. In the centre the depth is not known. The substratum is clay.

Woods

The indigenous wood is birch and hazel. The only appearance of natural woods still remaining is at a place called the the Birches in the townland of Ballynary, on [the] side of road from Verner's bridge to Portadown. There are a few patches of brushwood consisting of stunted hazel and sallow. In the townland of Derrinraw between Green Island and the River Bann there is a large extent of meadow filled with oak stumps still standing, broken off at about 2 feet above the ground. It is stated by the inhabitants that all the insulated hills rising through the bogs were originally covered with wood. Derrylileagh Island is still designated "the Wood." At low water in Lough Neagh stumps of oak trees may be seen extending from Columbkiln to a considerable distance into the lough.

Modern Topography

Public Buildings: Places of Worship

There are no public buildings except the places of worship. The parish church, situated on a commanding hill in the townland of Breagh, was built in the year 1816 at an expense of 1400 pounds and will accommodate 400 persons. The old church stood nearly on the same spot.

The Roman Catholic chapel in the townland of Eglish was erected in the year 1829. It is a plain commodious building, affording standing room for 800 persons.

There is a place for public worship in the townland of Derrylee, originally built for a Methodist meeting house but now was allowed to get very much out of repair. Colonel Verner put it into good order about 10 years ago and will not permit any but clergymen of the Established Church to preach in it. Service is performed there every Sunday afternoon.

Gentlemen's Seats

The principal residences are Crowhill, belonging to J. Atkinson Esquire, situated in the townland of Magarity; Clantilew, the residence of E. Obree Esquire and Cranygill, the residence of Captain Johnson.

Mills

There are 2 corn mills, one belonging to Colonel Verner in Derrylee townland supplied by Annagariff lake, and another belonging to E. Obree Esquire at Milltown is supplied by the lake in Derrylileagh townland. There is a windmill, called Cockhill windmill, situated in the townland of Drumanfy.

Communications

The principal roads passing through the parish are those leading from Verner's bridge to Portadown, from Maghery <Magery> ferry to Loughgall and to Lurgan by the Bannsfoot ferry. They are prepared with gravel and are kept in tolerably good order at the expense of the county. The by-roads and lanes are numerous. The latter are for the most part very bad, particularly in the townland of Drummannon. There is a canal about a quarter of a mile long across the neck of land between Maghery and Derrywarragh townland, which very much shortens the passage between the Bann and the Blackwater and enables barges to get at once from Lough Neagh to deep water in the Blackwater without crossing the bar. The ferries across the Blackwater and the Bann facilitate the communication between the county of Tyrone and Lurgan and Portadown. The charges at Maghery ferry are for loaded carts 8d, carriage and horses 1s 8d, gig or car 8d, cow or horse 1d, a pig a ha'penny, foot passengers 1d.

Ancient Topography

Ancient Graveyards

There is a very old graveyard in the townland of Eglish near the Glebe House, which is still made use of. It is generally believed that there was formerly an abbey near it, but there is no vestige of it remaining. There is another graveyard of the same description at Maghery and close to the shore of Lough Neagh which is also still made use of, and almost exclusively by Roman Catholics. Campbell is the prevailing name of persons buried there. The ruins of a small chapel in a very dilapidated state are standing within the burial ground. The townlands of Eglish and Maghery are both abbeylands and tithe free. The townland of Crankill is also tithe free, probably from the same cause.

Ancient Ruins

On Derrywarragh Island stands a ruin called "the Chimneys", which appears to be the remains of a large house, and on Coney Island there is a low tower of ancient date but not remarkable.

Ancient Road

There is a tradition amongst the inhabitants that there was formerly a road leading from Lough Neagh to Armagh passing through this parish. It is called "Saint Patrick's road". Unquestionably there are evidences of a road having once existed and of a very late date. It may be traced in a straight line through the bog, on the eastern side of the townland of Derrycorr. The formation of it is curious: much care and labour appears to have been bestowed upon it. It consists of rows of sleepers lying in a northerly direction upon what was at time the top of the bog, and upon it are laid in a direction perpendicular to the sleepers (as in flooring) strong oak planks of hewn timber about 15 feet long and 4 inches thick, with their edges lapped over to prevent the earth running down between them; the whole kept in its proper position by a row of stakes driven along each side. Then upon the bottom thus formed is placed a coat of gravel from 1 foot to 18 inches thick which completed the road. Turf bog has through the course of time accumulated over it to a depth of 4 or 5 feet. Inhabitants say that the continuation of the same road runs through the lake in Derrylileagh townland and very near the eastern side of it, that the timber flooring is only a few feet under the water and that they are in the habit of walking along it when bathing.

Modern Topography

General Appearance and Scenery

The southern extremity of the parish is all under cultivation, well wooded and contains 4 or 5 gentlemen's seats and several houses of respectability. The northern part of the parish consists chiefly of low flat bogs with insulated hills under cultivation, with here and there a few trees, no hedges and very little wood to improve the scenery. It has a cold bleak appearance. The shores of Lough Neagh as well as the county in the neighbourhood of the Bann and Blackwater rivers are very flat and far from picturesque. Annagarriff lake with the wood forms rather a pretty object in the country. The other lakes are insulated in the midst of bog. Mr Obree has built a pretty rustic cottage on the shore of Lough Neagh and close to Milltown, for the accommodation of water parties on the lake.

Social Economy

Local Government

The only magistrate residing in the parish is John Atkinson of Crowhill, Esquire.

Schools

[Table gives name of townland, when established, number of Protestants, Roman Catholics, males, females, how supported].

Breagh, nearly all Protestants, 40 males, 40 females, total 80; the male school is under the Association for Discountenancing Vice and the London Hibernian Society, assisted by private subscription; scholars pay 1d ha'penny per week. The female school is under the London Hibernian Society and Ladies' London Hibernian Society, assisted by private subscription; scholars pay on average 1d per week each.

Derryadd, 59 Protestants, 1 Roman Catholic, 30 males, 30 females, 60 total; under the London Hibernian Society, Colonel Verner gives 5 pounds per annum towards its support, scholars pay on average 1d ha'penny per week.

Derrylard, established in 1826, 34 Protestants, 6 Roman Catholics, 40 in total; under Kildare Place Society, supported by subscriptions, scholars pay 1d per week.

Derrylee, established 1812, 55 Protestants, 5 Roman Catholics, 60 total; supported by Colonel Verner, scholars pay 1d each per week.

Derrycorr, no information.

Teaguy, 40 males, 13 females, total 53; supported by subscription, formerly under Kildare Place Society, now about to be placed under the London Hibernian Society.

Drumraw, the National Board have just taken a house as a temporary schoolhouse.

Religion

There are 6300 inhabitants in the parish, of which 4020 are of the Established Church, 1880 Roman Catholics and 300 Presbyterians.

Habits of the People

The cottages are in general of mud, thatched, 1-storey high and divided into 2 or 3 rooms. There is a great want of comfort and cleanliness about them, particularly in the eastern side of the parish in the townlands of Derrykeevan and Derrykeeran, where they frequently consist of one very small apartment, the walls of which are built with sods placed upon the bare bog without any flooring and propped up by fir blocks, the roof covered with straw in a very loose manner without any egress for the smoke beyond a small opening in the roof. In fact, it is scarcely possible to conceive anything more miserable. Potatoes form nearly the only article of food amongst the lower order of people. Those of the better class use oatmeal or milk and butter and occasionally meat.

Emigration

Emigration does not much prevail. There are generally a few persons leave this part of the country every spring for Canada and but seldom return. A good many labourers go to Scotland every year for harvest work, only a few go to England.

Productive Economy

Weaving

A good deal of handspinning and weaving is carried on in the cottages. A very coarse kind of linen is in general manufactured. Mr Crone of Derryene employs between 600 and 700 looms in different parts of the country. He weaves all the sets from 300 to 1200. A tolerably good weaver can only earn from 3s to 4s and a spinner from 1s to 1s 3d per week.

Fairs and Markets

The fairs and marts usually attended are Portadown, Dungannon and Armagh. There are none held in the parish.

Rural Productive Economy

Farm Size and Rents

The farms vary in size from 4 to 40 statute acres, held from the head landlords under leases of 3 lives or 31 years, or more generally for 1 life or 21 years. The principal proprietors are J. Atkinson of Crowhill, E. Obree of Clantilew, Esquire and Colonel Verner M.P. The rent per acre of the best land is 1 pound 10s, of the middling from 1 pound to 1 pound 5s and of the worst about 16s, paid wholly in money. Cotters in many cases pay as high as 2 pounds 2s per statute acre. There is no land let in conacre. The fields are small, badly shaped and enclosed with banks of earth. Quickset hedges are more common in the southern extremity of the parish.

Soil and Manure

The nature of the soil generally is clay or gravel. The manure employed is stable dung, or bog mixed with a little lime. Lime is the manure best suited to the land. The nearest place at which it can be procured is in the neighbourhood of Loughgall, 4 or 5 miles distant. It cost 10d per barrel at the kiln and can be put upon that land for 1s per barrel. From 30 to 40 barrels should be put upon the statute acre.

Machinery

Carts and wheel carts are in general use. Oxen are not employed in agriculture. One horse is used in a cart or car and 2 in a plough.

Produce

The average produce by statute acre is of wheat 12 cwts, oats 40 bushels, potatoes from 200 to 300 bushels. Flax is 4 stone to a peck of seed. The average price of wheat last season was about 7s 6d per cwt. Oats from 6d to 9d per stone. Farm servants are paid 10d a day without board or lodgings.

Livestock

The common breed of cattle, horses and pigs are kept. Green feeding is not much practised. A few cattle are fed every year at some of the principal houses, either upon mangel wurzels, turnips (the Aberdeen yellow) or potatoes.

Uses Made of the Bogs

The bogs are used wholly as fuel, a great deal of turf is conveyed to the neighbouring towns. (The embedded timber is used for building, the roots and stumps are cut up for fuel). The process of cutting and drying turf provides employment for a great many poor people, particularly in the townlands of Derrinraw, Derrykeevan and Derrykeeran, where a great deal is cut and carried away in boats up the River Bann.

Planting

There is very little planting in the parish. The description of trees which appear to thrive the best are the larch, the Scotch fir and the birch.

Fishing

A great quantity of fish are taken in Lough Neagh. The most common are pike, eels, perch, trout, bream and large black trout called dologan. The other lakes are well stocked with pike, eels and perch. Some of the pike grow to 20 or 30 pounds weight. The fish in Lough Neagh are usually taken in nets, but owing to the quantity of stumps of trees in the other lakes nets cannot be used.

General Remarks

Cultivation is extended over all the hills or rising grounds. The general height above the sea of the cultivated land is about 200 feet. It would be useless to attempt entirely to drain the largest tracts of bog, but as soon as turf is removed within about 18 inches of the clay it is reclaimed, and when dug deep so as to bring up some of the clay, it produces excellent crops of oats for 2 or 3 years, after which it requires a great deal of forcing with manure. The northern extremity of the parish is greatly exposed to injurious winds. From its low situation and from the quantity of bog it contains, it is considered rather unhealthy. The prevailing soil is diluvial, consisting of clay or sharp gravel and sand. Lime is the manure best suited to the soil. There is no limestone within the parish, and owing to the distance from it and the inhabitants in general being too poor to purchase lime, very little is used. The land is best adapted to tillage. Copied from the original rough report by Corporal Peter Gibson, Royal Sappers and Miners. A true copy, [signed] C. Bailey, Lieutenant, Royal Engineers, 4th May 1835.

Parish of Tynan, County Armagh

Copy of Statistical Report by Lieut C. Bailey, 4 May 1835

NATURAL STATE

Name

The usual way of spelling the name is Tynan, see old vestry book in possession of the rector of Tynan (in which it is mentioned as far back as 1716) and various other documents. Probably derived from the Irish words tygh-nion signifying "the ash tree house".

Locality

The parish of Tynan is situated in the south west corner of the county Armagh and in the baronies of Armagh and Tiranny <Tureny>, bounded in the north by the parish of Armagh, east by the parish of Derrynoose, south by the parishes of Derrynoose, Clontibret and Tehallan and on the west by the parishes of Donagh and Aghaloo. It is of an oblong form, its extreme length from the north of Turry townland to the south of Crossdall being 9 and a half miles and average breadth 3 and three-quarter miles. It contains 17,046 acres, of which 16,580 are cultivated, 346 uncultivated and 120 water. Valuation to the county cess from 1s to 1s 6d per acre, half yearly.

NATURAL FEATURES

Hills

There are no remarkable features, but the surface presents great irregularities. The northern part consists of small round hills, chiefly of limestone formation. The southern part is rather more mountainous, consisting of a slatey rock frequently projecting through the surface and giving a more abrupt character to the hills. The heights of the principal hills above the level of the sea are Raws 615 feet, Rathcumber 576 feet, Carricklane 577 feet, Mullinary 426 feet, Cavanagarven 446 feet, Drummond 441 feet, Crievekieran 443 feet, Skerries 436 feet, Run 418 feet, Derryhay 335 feet, Cosey 306 feet, Palnagh 293 feet, Clinticarty 188 feet, thus decreasing in altitude from south to north.

Lakes

There are 9 or 10 small lakes (or loughs) within the parish, the largest of which is Portnelligate lake containing about 42 acres, 235 feet above the sea. There is a small island in the centre of it. None of the others exceed 16 acres in extent.

Rivers

The Blackwater river separates the counties of Tyrone and Armagh and forms the boundary between the parishes of Tynan and Aghaloo from the junction of the counties of Tyrone, Armagh and Monaghan (at the east of Caledon demesne) as far as the northern extremity of Turry townland, passing under Caledon bridge and close to the town of Caledon. It flows north and empties itself into Lough Neagh, breadth from 80 to 100 feet, depth from 4 to 8 feet. It is not navigable, nor very usefully situated for water power. It is very subject to floods during the winter season, owing to a natural barrier of rocks at Benburb which backs up the water. It has been found to rise at Caledon mill as much as 8 feet in a few hours of the heavy rain, but from 4 to 6 feet is the general rise. It, however, soon subsides and leaves a deposit of sand which is injurious to the land.

The River Cur meets the parish at the north west corner of the townland of Ardgonnell, flows north and forms the boundary between the parish of Tynan and Donagh for the distance of about 4 miles, when it becomes the eastern boundary of the townland of Cortynan and empties itself into the Blackwater river. Breadth 60 feet and depth from 2 to 6 feet. It is also very subject to floods.

The Tynan river forms the south east boundary of the parish of Tynan, separating it from Derrynoose parish from Cavandoogan to Belteagh when it takes its course through the parish, passes near the village of Tynan and empties itself into the Blackwater river near Caledon bridge. It is rather a rapid stream and usefully situated for water power. Its average breadth is about 20 feet and depth 2 feet.

There are several smaller streams: the principal one is that which passes under Ardgonnell bridge and falls into the Cur river at the junction of Tynan, Donagh and Tehallan <Tehollin> parishes. The parish is well supplied with springs, some of them in a certain degree chalybeate, indicating the existence of minerals, particularly one in the grounds at Ashfort, the residence of Hugh Harris Esquire.

Bogs

There are no extensive tracts of bog in the parish: Killylea bog contains about 80 acres, used wholly as fuel, is not more than 4 or 5 feet deep. The substratum is limestone or a whitish sand.

Cor Tynan bog (about 48 acres of which are in Tynan parish): it is used wholly as fuel, is very deep in the centre, the substratum is a blue clay.

Knockban bog contains about 50 acres, used for fuel or manure, is very deep indeed in the centre. The upper turf are very light and spongy, but there are good black turf at the bottom. The substratum is a slatey gravel. Most of the bogs contain a few blocks or stumps of trees, but very little timber.

Woods

There are no natural woods in the parish, but there are evidences of some having formerly existed.

NATURAL HISTORY

Zoology

The rivers contain a few pike, eels, perch and trout but they are by no means abundant.

Geology

The northern part of the parish is of a limestone formation. The centre consists of slatey gravel and loose boulders of limestone and greywacke slate mixed through the clay. The southern extremity is entirely composed of rock [and] greywacke slate. Most of the hills have a direction from north north west to south south east.

NATURAL STATE

Killylea: Name

It is spelt Killylea by the Reverend Dean Jackson, late rector of Tynan parish, in Armstrong's *Survey of the county Armagh* and by the inhabitants generally; Killilea by M. Cross Esquire and Killyleagh in Sir Thomas Coote's *Statistical survey of Armagh*.

Locality

Situated in the county and barony of Armagh, in the northern extremities of the parish of Tynan and in the townland of Killylea; it consists of only 1 street, built on the slope of a rather a high hill on the road from Caledon to Armagh, 2 miles distant from the former place and 5 from the latter.

Buildings

There is a very neat church standing on the summit of the hill, built in the year 1830 at an expense of about 1600 pounds. It will accommodate about 400 persons. The houses are either 1 or 2-storeys high and generally thatched.

SOCIAL AND PRODUCTIVE ECONOMY

Court

There is a court held monthly in the village of Killylea for the manors of Belteagh and Toaghey. The jurisdiction extends to the recovery of debts under 5 pounds Irish.

Trades and Occupations

The people are for the most part either small shopkeepers or labourers: [Table] shoemakers 4, stonemasons 3, smiths 1, tailors 3, carpenters 2, painters and glaziers 1, sawyers 2, weavers 4, chandlers 1, bakers 1, spirit sellers 7, grocers 6.

Fairs, Land, Building Materials and Post

A cattle fair (custom free) is held on the last Friday of every month. It is pretty well supplied as to numbers, but the description of cattle is generally of an inferior quality. The land about the village lets at about 1 pound 5s per statute acre. Timber and slates for building are bought from Blackwatertown. Stone, bricks and lime are easily procured in the neighbourhood. A post car from Armagh to Aughnacloy passes through Killylea every morning at about 7.30 o'clock and returns in the evening at about 4.30 o'clock.

Schools and Poor

There is a parish school within the village, supported principally by subscription (see table of schools). There is no permanent provision for the poor, aged or infirm. The village is not at all improving in appearance.

NATURAL STATE

Village of Tynan: Name and Locality

The name is usually spelt Tynan, for authority see as stated for the parish. About 76 statute miles from Dublin, situated in the diocese and county of Armagh, on the western side of the parish of Tynan. It is a small village standing upon the top of a hill, commanding an extensive view and forming a prominent feature in the country.

MODERN TOPOGRAPHY

Buildings

The parish church is situated within the village. It is capable of accommodating about 500 persons, is very neat and kept in excellent order. There is a Roman Catholic chapel about a quarter of a mile from the town, capable of containing about 500 or 600 persons. There is a court house, a small and neat police barracks, a school house, a dispensary for the use of the poor of the parish and a post office. The houses are built with limestone and are tolerably clean and comfortable.

SOCIAL AND PRODUCTIVE ECONOMY

Justice, Land and Building Materials

Petty sessions are held on every second Wednesday: 2 or 3 magistrates are generally in attendance. The police force consists of 1 constable and 2 subconstables. The land about the village lets at about 1 pound 10s per statute acre. Timber and slates for building are brought from Blackwatertown or Newry. Stones, brick, lime are easily procured in the neighbourhood.

ANCIENT TOPOGRAPHY

Tynan Cross

In the village of Tynan and in the centre of the street on the western side of the church, there is a remnant of antiquity consisting of an oblong stone standing on a large black stone. The characters on the oblong stone are nearly effaced. There have been 3 compartments and something like figures may still be traced in the centre one. At the foot of the black stone lies another stone which appears to have been part of a cross much mutilated. This stone formerly stood on the top of the oblong stone mentioned before, but was maliciously thrown down a few years ago.

NATURAL STATE

Middletown: Name and Locality

It is usually spelt Middletown. It is about 52 Irish miles from Dublin, situated in the diocese and county of Armagh, in the south west corner of the parish of Tynan, partly in the townland of Middletown and partly in the townland of Tullybrick Hamilton and on the high road from Armagh to Monaghan, 8 miles from the former place and 5 miles from the latter. The Cur river runs close to the town.

MODERN TOPOGRAPHY

Buildings and Streets

There is a neat church situated close to the town, built in the year 1796, to which a gallery was added in the year 1833 from the funds of the trustees of the late Bishop Sterne's charities. It is capable of accommodating upwards of 400 persons. There is a Seceding meeting house built in the year 1829, which will also accommodate about 400 persons. There is a large public building erected in the year 1829 by the trustees of the above charity, the upper part of which is used as a court and session house and the lower part as a market house. There is also a fever hospital built by the trustees of the above charity in the year 1832 at an expense of 500 pounds. It will accommodate 12 or 14 patients. A dispensary with surgeon's house attached is nearly completed, built also by the above trustees at a cost of 700 pounds.

The streets are wide and the houses from 1 to 2-storeys high, generally built with stone and thatched. There are some rather respectable houses in the body of the town, but at the entrance from Caledon the houses are very poor and dirty.

SOCIAL AND PRODUCTIVE ECONOMY

Justice and Occupations

There is a police force consisting of 1 constable and 3 subconstables. Petty sessions are held every second Wednesday, 2 magistrates are generally in attendance. [Table of] trades and occupations: smiths 3, nailors 2, carpenters 5, shoemakers 7, stonemasons 6, grocers 12, spirit dealers 10, tailors 6, wheelwrights 3, bakers 2, reed makers 1, saddlers 1, distiller 1.

Distillery, Market and Fairs

There is an extensive distillery belonging to Mr Johnson, which does a great deal of business and has been the means of greatly improving the corn market. It gives employment to a great number of people. A weekly market is held every Thursday for provisions, yarn and 2 grain markets on Wednesday and Saturday of each week. A cattle fair is held on the first Thursday of each month. Both fairs and markets are custom free.

Rent, Building Materials, Conveyances and Schools

The land about the town lets upon an average at about 21s per statute acre. Timber and slates for building are brought either from Blackwatertown or Newry. Stone, bricks, lime are easily procured in this neighbourhood.

The Belfast and Enniskillen mail coach passes through the town at 12 o'clock every night and the day coach from Dublin to Omagh every Monday, Wednesday and Friday at about 3 o'clock in the afternoon and returns to Dublin on the alternate days at a little after 10 o'clock a.m.

There is a boys' and girls' school close to the town in the townland of Shantally (see Table of Schools).

Bishop Sterne's Charities

The town is much improving from the exertions made by the trustees of Bishop Sterne's <Stern's> charities. Dr Sterne, formerly Bishop of Clogher, did by will dated 13th May 1741, give and bequeath certain lands in the counties of Armagh and Monaghan in trust to divers persons herein mentioned for carrying the charitable intentions and purposes of the said will into execution, blind children being particularly recommended to their care and consideration. The trustees at first appointed were empowered to fill all vacancies in the trust that occur from deaths or resignations, but, however, they all died without having appointed any successors and some years passed away without any persons to direct or manage the funds of the charity, in consequence of which an act of parliament was passed in the year 1772 appointing the following persons (holding the offices for the time being) as trustees for ever viz. His Grace the Lord Primate, the Bishop of Clogher, the Lord Chancellor, the Lord Chief Justice of the King's Bench, the Lord Chief Justice of Common Pleas, the Lord Chief Baron of the Exchequer, the Provost of Trinity College Dublin, the Rector of Tynan in the county Armagh, the Vicar of Donagh in county Monaghan. The property is worth more between 1,000 and 2,000 pounds a year.

The following is extracted from Bishop Sterne's will, in which he gives: "to a catechist within the city and suburbs of Dublin 80 pounds per annum, to be chosen every 3 years by the beneficed clergy of Dublin; a gratuity of 300 pounds to the Blue Coat Hospital, Dublin. A sum of 40 pounds per annum was settled on a resident clergyman of the Established Church at St Stephen's Hospital (which sum is reported to have been increased); 100 pounds per annum towards the binding apprentices to some trades 5 [? 55] children of deceased clergymen; a donation of 600 pounds towards the support of Swifts' Hospital; 1000 pounds towards building a spire to St Patrick's Cathedral, providing that the dean and chapter go seriously to work about it by assistance from the economy fund or by contribution within 6 years after his decease; 50 pounds per annum for 10 exhibitions at the choice of the Provost and Senior Fellows of the University of Dublin; 30 pounds per annum towards Mr Chetwood's charity in addition to that fund." The trustees were authorised to apply any surplus fund arising out of the estate to any other charitable purpose that they think proper. The present trustees have appointed some of the surplus funds in the following manner viz. at 126 pounds per annum towards the support of 21 blind persons at 6 pounds a year each; 50 pounds a year to other poor; 60 pounds a year and house to the surgeon of the dispensary and 30 pounds a year for fuel and medicines; 20 pounds a year for a housekeeper for the fever hospital, with many other occasional charitable donations which sickness, scarcity or any other necessity may require them to administer to.

MODERN TOPOGRAPHY

Public Buildings

The only public buildings within the parish are places of public worship which consist of 3 churches, Tynan, Middletown, Killylea, each of which is capable of accommodating about 400 persons; 3 meeting houses, viz. the Presbyterian meeting house in Lislooney which will accommodate about 600 persons and 2 Seceding meeting houses, one at Middletown and another in Drumhillery, each capable of accommodating about 400 persons.

Gentlemen's Seats

Tynan Abbey, the seat of Sir James M. Stronge, Bart, is situated about half a mile south west of the village of Tynan. The house, a remarkable handsome building, stands on an eminence 177 feet above the level of the sea. The demesne is extensive and well planted. Above a quarter of a mile east of the village of Tynan is the rectory, a plain neat building. The Reverend Mr Mauleverer is the present rector. About a mile and a quarter south of the village of Killylea is Fellow's Hall, the residence of J.T. Armstrong Esquire and nearly half a mile south of the same village is Darton House, the residence of M. Cross Esquire, and half a mile south of Fellow's Hall is Wood Park, the seat of Acheson StGeorge Esquire. On the west side of the road leading from Tynan to Middletown is Bondville, the residence of H.C. Bond Esquire and three-quarters of a mile south east of Middletown is Ashfort, the residence of Hugh Harris Esquire.

Mills

There is a corn and flax mill in the townland of Tynan. The wheel of the flax mill is 15 feet in diameter and 3 feet in breadth. The wheel of the corn mill is 14 and half feet in diameter and 3 feet broad, both breast wheels and standing close together. There is a flax mill in the northern extremity of Derryhaw, with a breast wheel whose diameter is 14 feet and breadth 4 feet; also a large corn mill 4-storeys high and well built in the townland of Belteagh, with a breast wheel 14 feet in diameter and 4 feet 2 inches in breadth. A flax mill in the townland of Tullyglush Kane and close to the parish mearing, with a breast wheel some 16 feet in diameter and 3 feet 2 inches in breadth. A flax mill on the east side of the townland of Drummond, with a breast wheel 14 feet in diameter and 3 and a half feet broad. A corn mill in the townland of Unshog, with an overshot wheel, 14 feet in diameter and 1 foot 9 inches broad. A corn mill in the townland of Doogary, with a breast wheel 14 feet in diameter and 2 feet broad, and a small malt mill attached to the distillery at Middletown. There is an old corn mill in Knockban, which has not been worked for several years and is entirely out of repair.

Communications

The principal roads are the one leading from Caledon to Armagh which passes through the northern extremity of the parish for a distance of about 3 and a half miles; the new line of road from Caledon to Castleblayney which passes through the centre of the parish for a distance of 7 miles; the road from Armagh to Monaghan through Middletown which runs across the parish for a distance of 4 and a quarter miles. The line of road from Caledon to Armagh might be greatly improved. The others are well laid out. These, as well as the principal cross-roads, are repaired with broken stone and are kept in tolerable good order at the expense of the county. The by-roads and the lanes are repaired generally with broken stone or gravel at the expense of the proprietor or the inhabitants. The line of the Ulster Canal (which is now forming) runs along the western side of the parish for a distance of 7 and a half miles, taking the eastern side of the Blackwater and Cur rivers and passing close to the town of Middletown, enters the parish of Tehallan at Ardgonnel bridge. It will be 19 and a half feet broad at the bottom and the depth of water 5 and a half feet and breadth at surface 36 feet, breadth at top banks 42 feet. It belongs to an incorporated company holding 3,200 shares at 50 pounds each. The contract entered into for the execution of the whole work is for the sum of 154,000 pounds. The cost of the work, including the purchase of land and management, is reckoned at 192,000 pounds.

Bridges

The principal bridges in the parish are Caledon bridge, Annagola bridge, Ardgonnell bridge and 2 or 3 smaller bridges over the Tynan river, which are all in good repair.

ANCIENT TOPOGRAPHY

Ancient Castles

In the southern part of the parish there are the ruins of 2 old castles, one in the townland of Crievekeeran, of which only part of the western gable is remaining. It is a perfect ruin, standing on the edge of a small lake. The walls are very thick with passages in the centre. The second is in Ardgonnell townland on the southern side of the Cur river and is more perfect than the other. The square tower over the porch, as well as the western gable and wall joining it to the tower, are still standing. There appears to have been 3-storeys and an apartment sunk below the surface of the ground. The fireplaces and some of the windows are still in good preservation. There is a curious projecting round tower at the flank of the western gable. It is generally stated and believed that there were originally 8 of these towers, which were probably used as places of defence. The square tower over the porch is loopholed. It must have been a strong and extensive place. Part of the walls are now detached from the body of the ruin, but its connection with the body of the building may be traced upon the ground. It is much to be regretted that the cut stones forming the doorway and those at the several corners have been wantonly taken away for a height as far as could be conveniently reached.

Ancient Crosses and Forts

There are 2 ancient stone crosses in Tynan Abbey demesne, one placed over a well near the northern entrance and the other in a small flower garden near the lake. They were brought by Sir James Stronge from the townland of Glenarb in the parish of Aghaloo and placed in their present situation as ornaments. There are several raths or forts in the parish but none that are entitled to a particular description. The largest and most perfect are those in Lislooney and Rathtrillick near Middletown, both of which are now planted. For stone cross in Tynan, see Tynan village.

MODERN TOPOGRAPHY

General Appearance and Scenery

The parish of Tynan consists of an almost uninterrupted series of small hills increasing in altitude towards the south, the valleys frequently containing bog or marshy ground. The northern part is rich and well cultivated, with several gentlemen's seats containing a good deal of wood and ornamental plantation. The southern portion of the parish consists of a poorer and less productive soil, with very few trees or hedgerows to improve the scenery. It has a bleak and cold appearance.

SOCIAL ECONOMY

Local Government

The resident magistrates are Sir James M. Stronge of Tynan Abbey, Bart, Acheson St.George of Wood Park, Esquire, Mr Irwin of Mount Irwin, Esquire and H.L. Prentice of Caledon, Esquire. The usual force of police consists of 1 constable and 2 subconstables stationed in the village of Tynan and 1 constable and 3 subconstables stationed in Middletown. There is a manor court held in Killylea (see Killylea). Petty sessions are held alternately in Tynan and Middletown every second Wednesday: generally 2 and sometimes 3 magistrates are in attendance.

Dispensaries

It is very hard to determine whether the health of the people generally has been much improved by the establishment of dispensaries. The smallpox and measles have been prevalent during the last year. The town of Middletown suffered much during the rage of cholera. There were 81 cases, of which 35 proved fatal and 46 cured. [Dispensary table blank, except for the following remark: no satisfactory information could be obtained].

Schools

The introduction of schools has certainly improved the moral habits of the people, who are anxious for information and knowledge. The schools are during the greater part of the year well attended by the children of both sexes, but during the time of gathering the potatoes there are comparatively few in attendance. [Table of schools contains the following headings: name of townland in which situated, number of pupils subdivided by religion ànd sex, remarks as to how supported, when established].

Shantally male school; number of pupils: 15 Protestants, 55 Catholics, a total of 70; supported by the charities of the late Bishop Sterne, the master is paid 30 pounds per annum, 6 acres of land with house and fuel free, books found by the trustees; established 1802.

Shantally female school; number of pupils: 19 Protestants, 26 Catholics, a total of 45; supported by the charities of the late Bishop Sterne, the mistress receives 30 pounds per year with house and fuel free, books found by trustees; established 1802.

Killylea; number of pupils: 74 Protestants, 15 Catholics, 56 males, 33 females, a total of 89; supported principally by annual subscription, from the Association for Discountenancing Vice 8 pounds, from Trinity College Dublin 5 pounds, from Colonel Viner 5 pounds, from the Reverend James Mauleverer 1 pound 1s, the scholars pay from 1s 8d to 4s 6d per quarter; there are at present about 40 free scholars in attendance.

Tynan; number of pupils: 147 Protestants, 28 Catholics, 113 males, 62 females, a total of 175; supported from the trustees of the Erasmus Smith's charity, 30 pounds per annum, from Reverend William Mauleverer 2 pounds 2s per annum, scholars pay from 1s 8d to 10s 6d each per quarter; established 1815.

Palnagh; number of pupils: 39 Protestants, 21 Catholics, 30 males, 30 females, a total of 60; supported by subscription; NB the Earl of Caledon annually [gives] 5 pounds 2s, Mrs Dobbin annually gives 2 pounds 2s, Lady Hazzard annually gives 6 pounds; not known when established.

Fayduff; number of pupils: 29 Protestants, 46 Catholics, 43 males, 32 females, a total of 75; [supported] by the charities of the late Bishop Sterne; established 1835.

Crossdall; number of pupils: 35 Protestants, 34 Catholics, 41 males, 38 females, a total of 69; supported by the Society for Discountenancing Vice; established 1823.

[Crossed out Shantally] Middletown (private school); number of pupils: 19 Protestants, no Roman Catholics, 10 males, 9 females, a total of 19; supported entirely by the scholars who pay 10s each per quarter; established 1833.

Poor

There is no permanent provision for the poor, aged or infirm with the exception of that afforded by the late Bishop Sterne's charities (see Middletown).

Habits of the People

Most of the cottages are built with stone, 1-storey high, thatched and divided into 2 or 3 apartments. There is great want of comfort and cleanliness about them. There are several mud cabins belonging to the poorer class of the people, which are wretched habitations and very dirty. The principal articles of food are potatoes, milk, butter, eggs and meal prepared in various ways.

Emigration

Emigration does not prevail to any considerable extent. There are, however, some families every year who leave this country (generally from the southern part of the parish) for America and but seldom return.

Productive Economy

Weaving

Handspinning and weaving is carried on in most of the cottages but not to any great extent. Linen webs of from 800 to 1,200 are generally manufactured, but few persons are constantly employed at it. They weave a web or two during the winter and at other times continue to have a web on the loom which they go to when they have no other employment. It is not at all profitable except to those who manufacture their own flax.

Fairs and Markets

There is a cattle fair held at Killylea on the last Friday and another at Middletown on the first Thursday of every month. The greater part of the produce of the loom is consumed on the spot, the rest taken to Armagh market.

Rural Productive Economy

Proprietors

The freehold proprietors in this parish are the Earl of Caledon, the Earl of Gosford, Sir James M. Stronge, Bart, Henry Coote Bond Esquire, Acheson StGeorge Esquire, Hugh Harris Esquire, John Cross Esquire, Colonel Verner, Major Edgeworth, the Reverend Beresford Johnstone, Major Campbell, Henry Pringle Esquire, the trustees of Bishop Sterne's charities. The lessees of churchlands are the Earl of Caledon, Sir James M. Stronge, Bart, Richard Blackistone Esquire and Lady Hazzard, and of college lands the heirs of Henry Maxwell, Maxwell Close Esquire and Councillor Lynne.

Farms and Soil

The usual size of the holdings is from 5 to 30 acres, generally held by leases of 1 life or 21 years direct from the head landlords, at the average rent per acre of the best lands from 30s to 2 pounds, of the middling 25s and of the worst land about 15s. The farmers in general cultivate the land for subsistence only. The fields are small and enclosed with quicks or banks of earth. Those of the large farms are more extensive and well fenced. The farm buildings are kept in order by the tenants. The landlords frequently give rough timber for roofing. Most of the resident landlords have large farms in their own hands, which serve as examples in their neighbourhood. The soil in the north part is a strong clay resting upon limestone. The southern part is a light soil and very stony.

Agricultural Practices

The manure used is stable dung or lime. Marl is in some cases found in the bottom of bogs, but is not used as manure. The limestone, which is so abundant in the north of the parish, is burned with coals and sold at 10d and can be put upon the ground for 1s or 1s 2d per barrel. The practice of burning the ground for manure prevails to a considerable extent. The improved iron plough is in general use on the best farms. Mr Armstrong of Fellow's Hall has erected a large threshing machine. Carts and wheel cars are employed in agriculture. Oxen are not much used. One horse is used in a cart and 2 in a plough. The usual rotation of crops is to take potatoes off the lea <lay> ground, then to sow oats and afterwards wheat and barley or a second crop of oats and to lay it down with clover and grass seed. The average crops per statue acre are wheat 12 to 16 cwt, oats 40 to 50 bushels, potatoes 250 to 300 bushels, flax about 4 stones to the peck when dressed. The average prices last year of wheat was 7s 6d per cwt, oats from 6d to 10d ha'penny per stone, potatoes from 6d to 10d per bushel, flax 10s per stone. The markets attended for the sale of wheat are Caledon and Armagh, for other agricultural produce the markets in the neighbouring towns. Farm servants if hired by the half year are paid from 2 pounds to 3 pounds with their diet. If hired by the day 10d to 1s without diet.

Cattle

The common breeds of cattle are generally kept. Some of the gentry and principal farmers are beginning to introduce improved breeds of cattle and sheep and also to introduce the practice of green feeding with turnips, mangel wurzels or potatoes.

Uses Made of the Bogs: Fuel

The bogs are used wholly as fuel with the exception of a small quantity which is drawn away and mixed with lime or dung for manure. The fir and oak blocks were cut up for fuel which, with the turf, is consumed in the neighbourhood.

Planting

Plantations are chiefly confined to the demesnes. Several of the forts on the top of the hills are planted with fir which add to the beauty of the country. There are 2 nurseries, one (very extensive) in the townland of Coolkill [Cockhill] and the other in Tullybrick Hamilton. Orchards are not at present much cultivated. They are, however, numerous in the townlands of Cur and Tynan and are becoming more general in other parts of the parish.

General Remarks

The parish may be considered all under cultivation with the exception of the bogs and here and there a small piece of rocky ground in the southern portion. As soon as any parts of the bogs are exhausted they are immediately brought under cultivation. The ground thus reclaimed produces excellent crops of rye or oats for 3 years. After that the land becomes poor and requires a great deal of manure to produce even a tolerable crop. The general height above the sea is from 200 to 400 feet. The highest ground in the parish is 615 feet above the sea. The west and south west are the most prevailing and injurious winds. Soil in general is a strong clay. Lime is the manure best suited to it and is easily procured in the parish or at a convenient distance. The land in general is best adapted for tillage. Trees of all kinds thrive well, except in very exposed situations.

SOCIAL ECONOMY AND HISTORY

Ecclesiastical Divisions and Rebellion of 1641

The parish of Tynan, being rather extensive and thickly inhabited, has been divided into 3 ecclesiastical districts viz. Killylea, which also confirms part of the adjoining parishes of Armagh and Derrynoose, Tynan and Middletown. The parish of Tynan is both a rectory and a vicarage, the right of presentation being vested in His Grace the Lord Primate. The parish is under composition for 800 pounds sterling per annum, independent of 217 acres of glebe land. The tythes are appropriate [impropriate]. The rector of Tynan in right of his office holds a prebendal state in the cathedral church of St Patrick's, Armagh. The rector has to pay the salary of 2 curates and the greater part of the salary of a third. PS In Sir John Temple's *History of the Irish rebellion, 1641*, p114, Robert Maxwell, Archdeacon of Down, in his examination states that "near unto the deponent's house 38 persons were carried to the Cure bridge at one time and drowned. At another time 6 and 50 men, women and children, all of them being taken out of the deponent's house, and at several other times, several other numbers besides those that were drowned in the Blackwater at Kinnard, in which town and the parish of Tynan <Tinon> (where the deponent was rector) there were drowned, slaughtered and died of famine and for want of clothes about 600." (Copied from the original rough report by Corporal Peter Gibson, Royal Sappers and Miners). A true copy, [signed] C. Bailey, 4 May 1835.

Fair Sheets on Modern Topography by E.A. Williamson, 22 January 1838

MODERN TOPOGRAPHY

Church

Tynan church, built 1780, is a roughcast building rather out of repair, will contain 300 persons, average attendance 200, William Mauleveror, rector. Rectorial tythes amount to 800 pounds per annum.

Glebe

Is a substantial 4-storey stone house in good repair, surrounded with planting and rather prettily situated on the declivity of a hill, quarter of a mile east of the village.

Dispensary

Established 1820, has been of the greatest use and is well supported. Fever very prevalent this year, December 1837. Mr W. Huston, surgeon.

Roman Catholic Chapel

A plain rectangular building, 66 feet long and 22 feet broad, is in good repair, whitewashed and contains 300 persons. Priest, Reverend John Hughes. Chapel built in 1818. A schoolhouse is in course of erection in the chapel yard.

Male and Female School

Established [blank], built by parish assessment. Is a square building situated in the village, surrounded by evergreens and sufficiently capacious. Number on the books, 1 November 1837, 160; of these 68 were girls. Instruction comprises reading, writing, mathematics, English grammar, spelling, drawing, arithmetic and needlework. Miles Magrath, schoolmaster, a member of the Established Church. He receives 30 pounds per annum from the Board of Education.

Village of Tynan

Tynan contains few inhabitants and has a gloomy wretched appearance. It has no regular street. The houses are in bad repair, chiefly whitewashed and slated. The remains of an old stone cross formerly used as a market cross are still visible. The inscription is defaced but 2 hideous little figures resembling idols may still be discerned. Height of the cross 6 feet, breadth 2 feet. 2-storey [houses] 19, 1-storey 24, cabins 6.

PRODUCTIVE ECONOMY AND MODERN TOPOGRAPHY

Trades

Bakers 1, blacksmiths 1, publicans 4, reedmaker 1, watchmaker 1, general store 1.

Public Buildings and Gentlemen's Houses

Public buildings none. Gentlemen's houses: Sir James Stronge's, a modern building built in the Gothic style, situated on a gently rising hill immediately overhanging a small lake, enclosed on all sides by a planting of Scotch fir. Mount Irwin, a plain substantial building.

Middletown: Houses and Trades

A cold dreary village, 2 miles south west of Tynan, contains houses 1-storey 40, 2-storey 52, 3-storey 3, cabins 46. Grocers 4, public houses 14, bakers 3, tailors 1, shoemakers 1, houses of entertainment 6, reedmakers 2, blacksmiths 2, nailors 4, delph <delf> shops 1, brewery 1, distillery 1.

Distillery and Brewery

Distillery built in 1831, Matthew Johnston, proprietor. 30 persons in constant employment at it. Brewery in course of erection, Mr Johnston, proprietor.

Market House

Erected by trustees of Bishop Sterne's charities, 60 feet long, 20 feet broad. Is in good order, has a clock and a cupola.

Church

A plain oblong whitewashed building, 60 feet by 20, situated on a hill south of and close to the village, William Mauleveror, rector.

Roman Catholic Chapel

A large oblong building quarter of a mile east of the village, situated in a hollow, surrounded with planting, whitewashed, in good repair and 98 feet by 40 feet, the Reverend John Hughes, P.P.

Seceding Meeting House

A small whitewashed building, 30 feet by 20 feet, situated near the school.

Gentlemen's Houses

Mr W. Irwin's, Angola House, close to the village, is a neat building having an air of comfort and is partly enveloped in planting.

Ashford, Mr Harris, proprietor, is a large substantial house, situated on a hill immediately above a chapel close to the Armagh road and a quarter of a mile from the village.

Fever Hospital

A large handsome building, stone finished and well situated on the slope of the hill close to the western end of the village.

Main Street

Middletown main street averages [?] 66 feet wide.